Food Security and Social Protection for the Rural Poor in China

T0298750

Economic growth and its relevant subjects have been given first priority in the research agenda since China initiated economic reforms in 1978, while the topics of social protection and gender equality have been largely left at the periphery for a long period.

This book is a collection of evidence-based studies conducted mainly in poor areas of rural China during the recent two decades. Based on individual interviews and sample data analyses, this book emphasizes the importance of cooperative organizations to poverty reduction and puts forward that gender equality is closely related with sustainable development. In addition, it addresses the issues of food security and elimination of social exclusion – the key to bridging the economic divide. It also studies social protection, including basic health protection systems, nutrition and healthcare for children, old age security for landless farmers and rural migrant workers. By providing first-hand accounts of different vulnerable groups, such as the poor, women, migrant workers, ethnic minorities and small farmers, this book offers valuable insights into studies of contemporary Chinese society and economy.

Zhu Ling is a research fellow in the Institute of Economics, Chinese Academy of Social Sciences (CASS). She has been engaged in the study of poverty reduction, social protection and rural development since the 1990s.

China Perspectives series

The *China Perspectives* series focuses on translating and publishing works by leading Chinese scholars, writing about both global topics and China-related themes. It covers Humanities and Social Sciences, Education, Media and Psychology, as well as many interdisciplinary themes.

This is the first time any of these books have been published in English for international readers. The series aims to put forward a Chinese perspective, give insights into cutting-edge academic thinking in China, and inspire researchers globally.

For more information, please visit https://www.routledge.com/series/CPH

Existing titles:

Internet Finance in China: Introduction and Practical Approaches
Ping Xie, Chuanwei Zou, Haier Liu

Regulating China's Shadow Banks
Qingmin Yan, Jianhua Li

Internationalization of the RMB: Establishment and Development of RMB Offshore Markets
International Monetary Institute of the RUC

The Road Leading to the Market
Weiying Zhang

Peer-to-Peer Lending with Chinese Characteristics: Development, Regulation and Outlook
P2P Research Group Shanghai Finance Institute

Forthcoming titles:

Government Foresighted Leading: Theory and Practice of the World's Regional Economic Development
Yunxian Chen, Jianwei Qiu

Free the Land: A Study on China's Land Trust
Jian Pu

Food Security and Social Protection for the Rural Poor in China

Zhu Ling

LONDON AND NEW YORK

CHINA SOCIAL SCIENCES PRESS

This book is published with financial support from Innovation Project of CASS

First published 2017 by Routledge

2 Park Square, Milton Park, Abingdon, Oxfordshire OX14 4RN
52 Vanderbilt Avenue, New York, NY 10017

Routledge is an imprint of the Taylor & Francis Group, an informa business

First issued in paperback 2020

British Library Cataloguing-in-Publication Data
A catalogue record for this book is available from the British Library

Library of Congress Cataloging-in-Publication Data
A catalog record for this book has been requested

ISBN: 978-1-138-23601-1 (hbk)
ISBN: 978-0-367-52289-6 (pbk)

Typeset in Times New Roman
by Apex CoVantage, LLC

Contents

PART IV
Poverty reduction and social protection 153

Figures

Tables

Preface*

Since 1988 when I completed the overseas education and returned to China, I have focused my research interest on income distribution, poverty reduction, social protection and rural development by conducting field studies on the status of the rural poor, migrant workers, women and ethnic minorities. The Institute of Economics, Chinese Academy of Social Sciences has extensively provided the support necessary for the studies that have been carried out mostly in the form of teamwork. I have benefited a great deal from the discussion and collaboration among the team members over the years, including in editing this book. For their invaluable assistance I am always grateful.

The research papers included in this collection mainly expressed the following ideas:

1. The perception of equitable development

Since 1978 when the economic reforms initiated in China, the subjects relating to economic growth have been given the first priority in the research agenda, while the topics of income distribution and social protection have been largely left at the periphery for a long period. Inspired by my experience of being an agricultural worker in the People's Commune during the "Cultural Revolution" and the rural survey conducted with a purpose of formulating my PhD dissertation, I chose the "marginalized issues" to study ever since the 1980s. Such experiences deepened my understanding on the rural-urban divide, regional gaps, sectorial and occupational disparities, together with gender discrimination in China.

Furthermore, the literature studies on developmental economics and the evidence-based research instilled in me the following perceptions:

- First, economic growth is embodied in the increment of the "pie" of an economy. The way to allot the "pie" falls into the field of income distribution studies. According to the theories regarding the market economy, equal access to

The main part of this article appeared in *Excerpts of Theoretical Contributions by 100 Chinese Economists*, Zhang Zhuoyuan, Zhou Shulian, Lü Zheng and Wang Haibo eds. Beijing, China: Times Economics Press, 2012 (3): 222–231.

opportunities is far more important than the equal results of market participation. Nevertheless, given the differences in family background as well as other socioeconomic factors relevant to the development of individuals, the starting points of the market participants in the competition must also differ. Therefore, people have to face different opportunities and achieve different results. It is then anticipated that the government intervention and the provision of public services will give an institutional security to an equitable competition while helping the vulnerable groups to overcome their development barriers and enhance their access to opportunities. Furthermore, social protection should also be offered to the disabled groups and those who are yet to develop capabilities of market participation.

- Second, the poor, women, the elderly, the disabled and ethnic minorities usually rank at the bottom in terms of access to health, knowledge, information, income and dignified participation in social activities. If a person possesses more than one of the above-mentioned attributes, he or she will be more likely marginalized in a society. According to Amartya Sen, a Nobel Laureate in economics, due to the limitations of existing social, political, economic and cultural conditions, such groups are unable to enjoy equal rights with other social groups, i.e. they are deprived and excluded. To mitigate and eradicate such a state represents the commitment of a society based on the concept of equality and justice. The commitment means that anyone in the society will not be deprived of the necessary products, services and opportunities due to their race, gender, age, wealth, health and religious belief.

  This idea can be understood in the form of a "thought experiment": a poor man or woman does not have to become rich to have access to basic health services; a woman does not have to become a man to have access to basic education; a disabled person does not have to become the non-handicapped to take part in his or her desired social activities; and a man or woman of ethnic minorities does not have to become one of the ethnic majorities to be able to move and seek employment freely, etc. For most developing countries, this is apparently an ideal condition yet to be achieved. Therefore, the development programs, poverty reduction and social protection system must be implemented to promote the fulfillment of the social commitments stated above. Based on such an understanding, I have been trailing the development barriers facing the rural people and particularly the poor, women, the elderly, the handicapped and the ethnic minorities over the past three decades, trying to identify their most pressing needs through field studies, evaluating the effects of existing development programs, poverty alleviation and social protection systems on these groups, and proposing policy improvement options.

- Third, for each and every person receiving social assistance, as long as he or she meets the criteria for the assistance, it is his or her right rather than luck to be aided. Hence, in the design and implementation of development programs and policies, the targeted beneficiaries should be regarded as the main actors rather than those passively receiving and involved in the programs. In reality, however, most recipients have little voice and even no voice in social activities, which is not only one of the reasons why they have been marginalized but a result of such a state of life as well. In order to ensure that the marginalized groups and individuals develop an awareness and position of actors who proactively take part in the decision-making process, measures for improving social, economic, political and cultural systems must be included into development programs and policies. On the basis of such a consideration, I have always paid close attention to the behaviors of different stakeholders and different effects of the general policies on them.

2. Cooperative organizations are vital to poverty reduction

In my treatise entitled *Rural Reform and Peasant Income* (London: The Macmillan Press LTD, 1999), I have verified with first-hand data and statistical analyses that during the period of 1978–1985, most Chinese farmers saw their income rise but the regional income gap widened; income inequality was greater in less developed regions than that in developed regions. The different conditions of the infrastructure and social services led to significant disparities between agricultural income and non-agricultural income of farmers. Insecurity in the land usufruct rights had negative effects on the mid- and long-term investments of farmers. Therefore, China needs further institutional innovation to secure farmers' land rights and provide them incentives to promote agricultural and rural development through cooperation among themselves.

In my research papers (*Journal of Development Studies*, second issue of 1990 and *Cambridge Journal of Economics*, the fourth issue of 1993), I have emphasized while incentivizing farmers to improve the efficiency of resource allocation, the implementation of household contract system and the abolition of the People's Communes left an institutional vacuum of agricultural infrastructure construction and public service provision. At the same time, the individual farm households faced increasing risks and uncertainties. With reference to the experience of developed countries and the institutional innovation of Chinese farmers, the following key countermeasures must be taken: first, enhance government's role in public investment and its service functions; second, give play to the self-governance of villages: after the dissolution of the brigades under the system of the People's Communes, the village community organizations may partially supplement the role of grassroots governance in public affairs and, when market mechanisms remain underdeveloped, the village community organizations may partially supplement the role of the market in the allocation of production factors; and third, promote the development of farmers' cooperative organizations.

In my subsequent studies on grain production and food supply, I have repeatedly addressed that a way to enhance the bargaining power of farmers is to promote cooperation among them. Even in advanced market economies, cooperatives still provide organizational resources for farmers to develop economies of scale and compete with large corporations. The traditional mutual assistance forms of China's agrarian and herding society can become the foundation for the marketing and credit cooperatives in a modern market economy. An important measure to achieve China's food security is to create the space of self-organization for small farmers to ensure that they develop equal rights in their current and future socio-economic environment. The weak positions of small farmers in economic structure adjustment, product value chain and policy preferential treatments, together with the exclusion facing them in sharing the achievements of industrialization and urbanization, reflect their marginal position in society. As a matter of fact, the vulnerable economic situation and marginal social position of small farmers mutually reinforce one another. The opportunity to break such a vicious cycle lies in the self-organization of small farmers to enhance their influence in political, economic and social spheres. Although not entirely in the scope of agricultural policy, empowering small farmers can be an indispensable institutional condition for China's sustainable agricultural development.

3. Gender equality is closely related with sustainable development

Prior to the United Nations Fourth World Conference on Women held in Beijing in 1995, gender studies rarely entered into the horizon of Chinese economists. In the income distribution analyses, economists would consider gender as a variable decisive to the income inequality. In examining the human capital returns, they would take gender as a determinant of investment motives. Nevertheless, women's development was not yet regarded as a subject matter of economics. In fact, as a long-term social and cultural phenomenon, gender inequality had more or less deprived women of certain social, economic and legal rights since their childhood. Hence, in the same competitive environment, women and men actually stand at different historic starting points with unique development issues. Assuming multiple roles of raising children, taking care of family and engaging in a career, women are subject to various constraints of individual development. These barriers to women's potentials also restrict the human development of the next generation. In this sense, without women's development, sustainable socio-economic development cannot be achieved as well.

In addition to opening up more opportunities, market-oriented reform is also associated with growing risks and uncertainties. Compared with urban residents, rural people are more vulnerable due to the lack of social protection. In the rural villages, women are more vulnerable than men due to gender inequality that exists today. Among rural women, those in less developed regions are at the most disadvantaged position due to double pressures of poverty and gender inequality. In order to fundamentally reduce and eradicate gender inequality and poverty, the development issue of rural women must be further addressed.

Based on the above understanding, I have employed statistical modeling to analyze gender inequalities in agricultural land allocation, basic health care and pension insurance. For instance, according to the statistical analysis of rural sample survey data in Shanxi province in 1996, despite the legal and economic institutional arrangements made to ensure the gender equality, loopholes in the details of these systems have deprived women divorcees of land right protection. Women, who have married elsewhere and thus missed the opportunities of land distribution within the village communities that they moved into, have no land rights and neither do their children. Although such a situation does not yet have any substantial effect on the bargaining position of women in their families, it is sufficient to trap their families into poverty. Therefore, it is necessary to include a gender perspective into the regulations of existing land management law and relevant government regulations on rural land contract system.

With the research findings from the fieldwork undertaken in the rural Tibetan Plateau during the period of 2005–2011, I have briefly explained the health threats of communicable diseases, gynecological diseases and insufficient maternal care confronting young and middle-aged married women of the farming and herding households and analyzed the reasons for the under-utilization of relevant health services. In my articles published in the tenth issue of *Management World* in 2010 and in the third issue of *China Economist* in 2014, I have underlined that appropriate prenatal care has been medically proven to be essential to maintaining the health of pregnant women, their fetuses and even their newborn infants. Ensuring timely access of pregnant women from poor households to such services helps individuals born into these families to start a healthy life, which means that the public action in combating poverty will be moved ahead to the time of life formation. In today's era of economic globalization, children born into farming and herding households will compete in the same arena with their peers of cities in their home country and even peers of Europe and America. Reducing disparities of prenatal care among individuals will help reduce congenital health inequality and thus mitigate the disparities of starting lines of life for different individuals. In this sense, ensuring appropriate prenatal care for each and every person is consistent with the principle of social justice. For this reason, appropriate prenatal care can be regarded as a "merit good," and its benefits to the individuals are in line with social expectations. In other words, the social value contained in the consumption of such products and services will not change no matter how the desires and preferences of consumers appear. Therefore, it is necessary for the government to take actions to promote appropriate prenatal care as it did for the implementation of compulsory education.

4. Eradicating social exclusion is the key to bridging economic divide

In the process of the economic reforms, rural workers have transcended the institutional barriers between the countryside and cities with their initiative and creativity and gained their freedom of the labor mobility. By moving across different occupations, industries and regions, they have effectively improved their income status and built a bridge over the existing urban and rural economic divide. However, the institutional framework of the urban and rural divide is yet to be fundamentally changed. The process of the economic marketization and global-ization has highlighted the social exclusion against rural people arising in the era of the planned economy. This not only took a toll on the efficiency of resource allocation but also compromised social stability. By focusing on income distribu-tion and social protection, I attempt to explore the approaches to eradicate social exclusion.

In an article based on the sample surveys and interviews (published in the fourth issue of *Comparative Studies* in 2009), I pointed out that undifferenti-ated institutional arrangements on old-age insurance schemes for rural migrant workers and the employees with the urban permanent registered residence alike will lead to inequitable results under the existence of significant socioeconomic disparities between the two groups. Firstly, the characteristics of urban social old-age insurance anchored at a certain locality hinder the labor mobility and hurt the interests of the employers and employees that both make pension con-tributions. Secondly, the excessive old-age insurance premium rates weaken the incentive of the enterprises to create more jobs. The wage levels of most migrant workers are lower than the floor level of the contribution base, but they have actually paid higher premium rates. The contributions made to the old-age insurance have a more severe impact on the disposable income of female work-ers, as their earnings are even lower than those of the male workers. Thirdly, migrant workers quit formal employment at an age younger than the statutory retirement age but their pension entitlements are lower than the average level. As a result, they are more likely to fall into poverty as they enter the old age. Fourthly, female workers have shorter employment tenure and at the same con-tribution wage level, their pensions are simulated to be only 55%–57% of those for males. While formulating the national old-age insurance policy for migrant workers, the factors such as promotion of employment, alleviation of old-age poverty and reduction in gender inequality in pension income distribution shall therefore be taken into account.

It is also worth noting that in the past three decades, China has made significant progress in poverty reduction. However, as far as the objective of poverty eradi-cation is concerned, China still has a long and arduous way to go. Agricultural development in the inception of reform and subsequent rapid economic growth had been the key impetus for the successful achievement of mass poverty reduc-tion. Poverty alleviation programs that focus on fostering local development are essentially pro-growth policy measures as well. Nevertheless, economic growth alone is not enough. Even with pro-poor economic growth models, it is hard for each and every one of the poor people to benefit. For instance, those with limited or no work ability, including the elderly, the diseased and the handicapped, are hardly able to take part in the process of economic growth and thus share in the benefits of growth. For such groups, an effective measure for poverty alleviation is to provide social assistance, nutrition and health interventions and care services rather than investments in production projects.

The "Di Bao" (minimum livelihood guarantee system) is a program designed to target the extremely poor people. In developed regions, the "Di Bao" social assistance program, social insurance and public services have effectively mitigated the difficulties of the extremely poor. In poor areas, however, addressing extreme poverty and marginality remains a challenge. Increasing the effectiveness of poverty reduction efforts in poor areas is, and will continue to be, central to the eradication of extreme poverty in China.

Ling Zhu
(Translator: Mingfeng Li)

Acknowledgements

This book is a collection of evidence-based studies. The Institute of Economics, Chinese Academy of Social Sciences has extensively provided the support necessary for the studies that have been carried out mostly in the form of teamwork. I have benefited a great deal from the discussion and collaboration among the team members over the years, including coauthoring research reports and editing the manuscripts of this book. In all fieldwork conducted during the recent two decades, the team acquired funds from international development agencies, coordinative support by the functional ministries and local governments, and positive responses from the interviewed people. For their invaluable assistance I am always grateful.

My sincere thanks also go to the input of China Social Sciences Press and the CASS Innovation Translation Fund for having the book published.

Zhu Ling
June 2, 2016

Part I

Transformation of land tenure system

1   Agricultural reforms during the 1980s

At the end of 1978, the economic reform in agriculture in the People's Republic of China began. As the sector at that time involved 80 per cent of the population and provided more than one-third of net national income, the changes had a strong impact on the development of China as a whole. This article will, first, give an overview of the operating mechanisms in agriculture prior to the reform. Second, the effects of the reform in agriculture on production, resource allocation and income distribution will be briefly discussed. Third, present problems which substantially impair the further development of agriculture will be examined and finally possible countermeasures will also be referred to.

1.1 The operating mechanisms of agriculture during the period of the People's Communes

The People's Communes were set up during the 1950s with the aim of helping to establish a centrally planned economy in China through a forced collectivisation in rural areas where agriculture always played a predominant role in the economy.

The communes consisted of three levels in terms of ownership as well as economic and administrative management: communes, general production brigades and production brigades. The production brigade was a basic economic unit and each included approximately 24 peasant households (OECD, 1985). By means of the communes' organisational structure, a hierarchical pyramidal system was formed for implementing national agricultural plans. Plans were drawn up to determine the choice of products, the volume of production, the amount of area planted and the quota of Central government procurement and were administered through different levels down to the production brigades.

Purchasing and marketing of farm products were basically monopolized by the state. In accordance with the collectivisation process, the state monopoly tended to cover the whole agricultural trading sector. The monopoly at one time included as many as 180 kinds of farm products. Farmers were required to sell products

(Originally published in *Journal of Development Studies*, Vol. 26, 1990 with the title "The Transformation of the Operating Mechanisms in Chinese Agriculture".)

to the state commercial agencies and were paid prices fixed by the government. However, the purchasing prices of farm products were set so low that there was no incentive for farm people to produce more. Being restricted by such a planning and implementation framework, the brigades were not able to make their own management decisions in such a way as to use existing resources efficiently and to obtain maximum profits.

The low pricing policy for farm products was used as a means of transferring resources intersectorally from agriculture to industry. Consistent with this strategy, a system of food subsidies was introduced to cover only the urban population, who were to participate directly in industrialisation. The strategy of developing industry at the expense of agriculture has been adopted by most developing countries. However, only the Chinese government virtually ruled the rural population out of the industrialisation and urbanisation process by prohibiting labour migration from the rural areas to the cities. In connection with a system of registration of people and their places of residence, the government directly controlled a rationing system for daily necessities with subsidies exclusively for urban residents. The hierarchical commune organisations were also used to prevent the rural–urban labour migration since farmers had to ask brigade leaders for permission whenever they wanted to travel. The government not only distributed national income between agriculture and other sectors but also directly allocated labour resources between them.

Furthermore, the government has always been the major investor in agricultural capital construction. Prior to the reform, investment in large and medium-sized projects for land infrastructure (irrigation, drainage and land improvement) was composed of public funds derived from the state budget and unpaid farm labour input while small projects were mainly financed by communes and brigades. Private investment was restricted to small farm implements for the farmers' personal use and small amounts of supplementary family production. During the period 1953 to 1978, the central government investment in agriculture amounted to 66,548 million yuan (Statistical Yearbook of China, 1986). (N.B. The current exchange rate in 1986 for yuan is 3.71 yuan: 1 US$; the 1978 rate being approximately 1.66 yuan: 1 US$.) This investment played a significant part in the formation and improvement of land infrastructure which basically determined the physical capacity of Chinese agriculture. Nevertheless, it was a far from adequate basis on which to modernise agriculture. Moreover, because of the extremely limited output of agriculture and the undervaluation of farm products, most communes and brigades were too poor to undertake investment. Chinese farm production thus retained a traditional character – despite the fact that under the commune system farm units were large. Personal income distribution within brigades was carried out in a way which was also stipulated by the government. The essence of the stipulations was egalitarianism which resulted in a vicious circle: the working incentive of brigade members diminished steadily, thus lowering average work efficiency, lessening the return to the brigades as well as personal income, and reducing incentives still further. In 1976 the nationwide average per capita income of the communes amounted to 62.8 yuan, which was lower than that of 1956 at constant prices. At that time, more than one-third of peasant households were in debt and about 100 million farming people suffered from a shortage of food (Lu, 1986). By 1978 China was no longer self-sufficient in grain and had to import grain to supply about 40 per cent of the total urban population (The World Bank, 1986).

Within the framework of the centrally planned economy, the government directly administered agriculture and took an entrepreneurial role in almost all links in the agricultural production chain during the period of the People's Communes. However, it was inefficient, as was indicated by the stagnation of farm production and the chronic poverty of the farm population.

1.2 The impact of the policy changes on agricultural development

The beginning of economic reform arose from the farmers' attempts to change the egalitarian income distribution system. The attempts finally led to the establishment of the 'Household Responsibility System'. It can be considered as a kind of tenant-farming system in which public ownership of land is combined with private ownership of capital. Individual peasant households as independent producers have freedom to manage their allocated plots of land and make their own decisions regarding economic activities. In this sense, family farms are now the basic agricultural production units.

In comparison with those in West European and North American countries, family farms in China have two marked characteristics: first, they generally use simple equipment and techniques, as well as continuing to use traditional methods of farm management; second, the farms are small in size (average: 0.5 ha of farmland) and they operate a mainly subsistence economy. With the emergence of family farms, the system of People's Communes was inevitably abolished. Those political and social functions which the communes had undertaken were then taken over by the local government in a community ('Xiang' in Chinese). Instead of the former general production brigade, a village management committee was put in charge of social affairs within an administrative village. Production brigades were replaced by village groups which formed mainly administrative management units at a grass-roots level in rural regions.

These institutional and organisational changes made it possible for market mechanisms to gradually be introduced and the instruments of state management of agriculture at the macro level to be partly modified. The tendency of the modifications seems to be that instead of undertaking entrepreneurial functions, the state conducts agricultural development mainly by means of making public policies to influence farmers' behaviour. During the reform the following significant measures were taken:

Price and marketing policies were changed by abolishing the state monopoly on purchasing and marketing of farm products, opening up a free market, introducing the state contract purchase system and raising prices. A comparison of the general state purchasing price index of farm and sideline products for 1986 and 1978 shows an increase of 77.5 per cent;

Structural policies were introduced for stimulating diversification of agriculture whereas, prior to the reform, only grain production had been promoted. A structural readjustment can be seen from changes in the composition of gross agricultural output value (in per cent):

Year	Crop production	Forestry	Animal husbandry	Fisheries	Total
1978	79.3	3.6	15.5	1.6	100.0
1986	70.4	5.1	21.5	3.0	100.0

Rural non-agricultural economic development policies were designed in favour of shifting the surplus labour from agriculture to other sectors where there was a labour demand within the rural areas. In 1987 more than 80 million surplus farm labourers, which constitutes 20 per cent of the total rural labour force, were either employed by village or township-owned industrial enterprises or worked as specialists in businesses outside the realms of traditional farming. The output value of rural industry amounted to 450 billion yuan constituting 50.8 per cent of total gross value of output of the rural economy.

An unprecedented growth in agricultural production and an increase in the income of farmers' families in recent years indicates that these policies have been successful. The gross value of output of agriculture, which increased at an average rate of three per cent yearly during 1957–78, rose to eight per cent in 1979–84.[1] Grain output grew from 305 million tons in 1978 to 402 million tons in 1987. The output of cotton, oilseeds, tobacco, tea and sugar-cane etc., doubled or tripled in the same period. The growing dependence on imported grains and cotton was reversed. Production of pork, beef and mutton exceeded 19 million tons in 1987, showing an increase of about 124 per cent over that of 1978. In the same period the output of aquatic production reached 9.4 million tons, an increase of 102 per cent.

The accelerated growth of agriculture and the development of the rural non-agricultural economy have greatly benefited the farmers. Per capita net income of peasant households increased at an average rate of 13.1 per cent a year between 1979 and 1987, compared only to three per cent in the period 1954–78, at constant prices. Although income inequality has grown, it is not very pronounced. This is shown by the changes in value of the Gini coefficients for peasant households in China as a whole (State Statistical Bureau, 1986):

Year	1978	1980	1981	1982	1983	1984	1985
Values of Gini Coefficient	0.2124	0.2366	0.2388	0.2318	0.2459	0.2577	0.2636

These achievements have basically resulted from an improvement in this economic system. As the government has gradually withdrawn from entrepreneurial activities with a view to transforming the centrally planned economy to a market oriented economy, initiative and entrepreneurship of farmers have been released. Since farmers won the right to manage the family farms – the prosperity of which increases their family income – they are strongly motivated to allocate both human and physical resources efficiently. Furthermore, the introduction of market mechanisms has enabled farmers to make the most use of their local advantages to adapt to the changes in demand. This has apparently improved the utilisation efficiency of local resources. Moreover, the rapid growth of agricultural production has been achieved under a relative and absolute decline in state investment in agriculture. Thus, the growth could be regarded as an outcome of a considerable improvement in efficiency.

1.3 Current problems

In addition to the unprecedented agricultural development which occurred during the economic reform, various problems have also emerged. These have been frequently criticized as being the outcome of the failures of the reform programmes. In fact, they arose mostly from the contradictions between:

- the existing ideological framework of Marxist orthodoxy and changing practices in the real world;
- the mandatory planning and market mechanisms;
- government interference and individual initiative;
- sectors which have experienced reform programmes to a varying extent; enterprises which are doing business within the same sectors but have different ownership and operating patterns;
- the interest groups which have gained benefits from the reform and those groups which have lost some advantages;
- introduction of a competitive environment and people's behaviour patterns based on egalitarianism, dependency on the state, etc.

Nevertheless, these contradictions indicate a dynamic development. The new problems may have just provided a motivating force for the Chinese people to find a new way out. Based on this understanding, the following discussion will focus on current problems which have substantially retarded the growth of agriculture and impeded the increase in income of peasant households.

In comparison with the period 1979–84, the growth rate of agriculture has apparently slowed down since 1985: the gross value of output of agriculture increased by 3.4, 3.5, 4.7 and 3.2 per cent in 1985, 1986, 1987 and 1988 respectively. The output of several key products such as grain, cotton, oilseed, pork, etc. has fallen from a record peak in 1984, although the decrease was reversed for some key products in 1987. The rise in prices of farm products, adjustment of the agricultural structure and rapid development of non-agricultural activities may have partly offset the negative influences of the stagnation in agriculture on farm income of farmers' families. As a result, the average total net household income of peasant households in China as a whole has still increased. After adjustment for price rises, the growth rate of average per capita net income of peasant households was calculated to be 2.1, 9.8 and 7.1 per cent in 1985, 1986 and 1987, respectively.

However, from a long-term view, the agricultural stagnation will seriously impair rural non-agricultural development as well as impede the increase in farmers' family income. An intensive discussion has therefore arisen regarding the causes of the new problems. Some authors believe that these phenomena indicate a transition in agriculture from super-conventional growth to conventional growth (Chen, 1987). Others regard this as a sign of a possible stagnation which resulted mainly from faults in the designing and implementation of some policies such as a reduction in public investment, limiting the volume of state purchased grain and depressing the state purchase prices, etc. (Gao, Li and Zhou, 1987). In fact, this fluctuation in growth of agriculture during 1979–87 may be evidence that agriculture in China has reached an equilibrium in a traditional economy. In order to break this equilibrium and so further the development of agriculture, China must establish an appropriate institutional and physical infrastructure for transforming traditional agriculture to modern agriculture. However, there is a lack of incentive for farmers to actively participate in constructing such an infrastructure. This can be seen from the present situation in the areas of agricultural production, marketing and investment.

As was pointed out earlier, rural economic reform involved a radical change in production organisations, but it has not affected the nature of traditional agriculture. Thus, the establishment of family farms, which were shown as an appropriate organisational pattern for Chinese agriculture, enabled farmers to use existing resources more efficiently than under the commune system. For this reason, although no significant technological breakthrough had taken place, a rapid growth in agriculture occurred in the period 1978–84. Nevertheless, the gains from organisational changes may have been exhausted and the inherent limitations of traditional agriculture have started to limit further growth. This is actually a reason directly determining the sluggish growth of agriculture since 1985.

The fundamental solution necessary for Chinese agriculture to emerge from this stagnation is modernisation. Agricultural modernisation means a manifold increase in output of farm products through employing high quality of physical capital which embodies new technical knowledge and less labour, which is capable of using modern inputs. From this viewpoint, the existing system of land utilisation substantially impairs the envisaged modernisation process.

According to the national sample survey, the farmland in a Chinese farm, on average, is dispersed in 9.7 plots. The extremely small farm size and the splitting up of farmland, which resulted from allocation through the introduction of the responsibility system, have become a barrier to obtaining the best from today's technology. However, there are neither effective land taxation nor rent systems nor does there exist a cadastral system for regulating land mobility so that it is inconceivable that farm size can be expanded and the allocative efficiency of farmland be achieved.

On the one hand, a significant level of land taxation may have an effect of preventing farmland from misuse, while on the other hand, it will give an impetus to farmers to increase output by using land more efficiently. This was already shown by the Japanese experiences in modernising agriculture: high levels of land taxation were effective in stimulating agricultural output and transferring resources to the government for financing general socio-economic development (Hallet, 1981).

The economic effects of rent on the allocation of farmland are shown by the economic reality as well having been anticipated by classical economics. Under a market system, land is transferred to alternative producers who are willing to pay a higher rent because they can find a more productive use for it, so that agricultural output will increase due to an improvement in efficiency of land utilisation.

In contrast to the successful experiences in many countries, Chinese agriculture is still hampered by the low level of land taxation (around two yuan/per mu) and the absence of rent payment for land utilisation. Although the transfer of the right of land use was written in an amendment to the constitution, the price (rent) system for such a transition seems to be difficult to envisage since a land evaluation system has not been set up as yet. Furthermore, there is lack of concrete legislation concerning leasing and subleasing of farmland which would serve to monitor and control this kind of deal.

Moreover, the envisaged expansion of farm size (concerned with transferring farmland to more capable farmers) has also been constrained by lack of a social insurance system and security of food supply for the rural population other than subsistence farming. Due to the limited industrial development and urbanisation at the present stage, neither the rural non- agricultural sectors nor the urban economy can create enough employment opportunities for absorbing the surplus labour from agriculture. Farms are actually viewed as security against unemployment, so that even the farmers who have already had a job in non-agricultural sectors will not give up their right to contracted land. This can be supported by a sample survey in seven counties of Henan Province of 600 farmers who already have nonfarm jobs (Hou et al., 1988). Only four per cent of these farmers transferred contracted land to other families. The rest let their own family members till the land and only helped with farm work in busy seasons. Furthermore, according to official regulations, farmers involved in non-farm sectors still have to supply themselves with their own grain rations. It is important to note that they are able to produce enough foodstuff for home consumption cheaply enough by spending a small amount of labour and time rather than purchasing food from the market. This is because land is freely available for use while food supplies in the market are unstable and market prices comparatively high.

In short, under the existing land utilisation system, the shift of surplus labour to non-agricultural sectors may lower the overall agricultural productivity, since farmers who actually left the agricultural sector may not have put enough effort into the development of farm production, while farmers who are willing to engage in agriculture are prevented from expanding their farm size and therefore from obtaining the potential returns to scale to farm size. Based on this understanding, a point must be made about the shift of labour to nonfarm sectors in present day China: it has actually resulted from the huge pressure of agricultural underemployment at a virtually constant productivity level and from farmers' requirements for supplementing low farm income by additional earnings, rather than from a substantial improvement in agricultural productivity.

Related to the problems involved in land utilization, undervaluation of farm products, in particular of foodstuff through government intervention, has brought about the distortion of incentives for farmers to increase output. Although the state purchase prices have risen substantially since 1979, they are still kept artificially low. This is reflected in the fact that market prices of farm products have been above that of government purchase prices. In this case, the nature of government policies regarding pricing and marketing of farm products has become apparent: the disparity between the two price levels is actually an implicit tax imposed by the state procurement system (Lardy, 1983) on farmers. Though such an implicit tax has the same effect as obtaining resources from agriculture as an explicit tax (for example, land tax in Japan), it has strongly discouraged farmers from producing more, since they are aware that they have to produce a certain quantity of products paid at the state purchase prices which are below marginal costs. If the purchase price were above the marginal cost, the state purchase price would not need to be compulsory (Chow, 1987).

At the state selling price, which has been even lower than the purchase price paid to farmers, there has always been an unsatisfied demand which has only partly been met by the market. Following the rapid increase in the income of urban residents during the urban economic reform, a continual growth in demand has strongly forced up the market price.

Furthermore, as a direct result of the influence of continual price rises for purchased inputs (such as chemical fertilisers, pesticides, diesel oil) and the unfavourable weather since 1985, a fall and fluctuation in output of some key products, especially grain, occurred. Because of this the farmers needed to sell a smaller quantity at the same market price as before. This has apparently pushed the market price further up.

The disparity between the rising market price and the fixed state purchase price has become wider, thus increasing the dissatisfaction of both farmers and urban consumers. Since the government still undertakes entrepreneurial activities in purchasing and marketing of a few key products – of which grain is a major item – it has been in a dilemma in terms of raising the purchase price of foodstuff for producers and keeping down the selling price for urban consumers. Nevertheless, the state has not completely abandoned the subsidy system for consumers mostly because of the possible social disturbances which might arise within the urban population. As farmers are not willing to sign delivery contracts with the government commercial agencies at the unfavourable prices, in 1985 state purchase orders were divided into quotas at different levels, each farm then receiving a quota to fulfill which specified volume and type of trade. Thus the contract purchase system, which was designed for trade between farmers and state commercial agencies in anticipation of introducing market mechanisms, actually reverted to the compulsory purchase system through administrative powers.

In addition to this, a kind of producer subsidisation was introduced. It has also been executed by the 'administrative pyramid' which is similar to the one operating during the period of the communes. In exchange for the contracted delivery volume of grain, farmers are entitled to obtain a certain amount of purchased inputs, at prices lower than the normal listed prices. What was not anticipated, however, was that the subsidy would be intercepted in part at different administrative levels, so that there are not many benefits left for the farmers. The worst case of this misuse occurred in the implementation of the two-tier price system with reference to inputs, as some speculators took advantage of the price disparity between the two tiers.

Clearly the whole state machine has been accustomed to conducting economic affairs by means of mandatory plans and administrative control. This has led to an acute contradiction between the administrative mechanisms and the market mechanisms and it has also resulted in a conflict between the farmers and the government institutions.

Apart from the restrictions of the partly existing mandatory planning system, there are also some other decisive factors which impair the development of the market mechanisms: (1) shortage of physical infrastructure such as roads, means of transport, packaging, processing, ware-house and market buildings (An, 1987); (2) lack of a service and supporting system and regulations; (3) growing protectionism and interference by local governments have become one of the main barriers to the formation of a unified nationwide market.

The problems in pricing and marketing of farm products were reflected in the shortage of supply. National statistics show that the commercialisation rate of grain has always fluctuated around 20 per cent although grain output has increased. Shortage in pork supply has become so serious that since 1987 the rationing system was reverted to in several large cities. One way of alleviating such pressure is to increase supply. The fundamental solution for increasing supply is to modernise agriculture through introducing technological progress. A prerequisite for achieving this is adequate investment in human and physical resources of agriculture.

However, capital investment in agriculture was depressed during the reform. The government still plays a major predominant part in investment but the public financial resources available for agricultural capital investment, which are derived principally from land taxation, are extremely limited. By contrast, industrial and service sectors have continued to be the priority in development programmes. Under these circumstances, as considerable growth in agriculture was achieved in the early stage of reform, the government has drastically reduced investment in this sector. The agricultural investment of the state amounted to 5,792 million yuan in 1979, constituting 11.1 per cent of total government investment, while investment decreased to 3,506 million yuan (3.0 per cent of total government investment) in 1986.

As a result of the depression in agricultural investment, the effectively irrigated area in China decreased by 3.4 million hectares between the years 1983–87, leading to a loss of grain totalling ten million tons. Moreover, the capacity of the existing capital stock for protecting agriculture from natural disasters has been weakened. It can partly be seen from a comparison between influences of natural disasters on crop production in different years during the reform period:

(Unit: 10,000 ha)	*1978*	*1980*	*1984*	*1985*
Total natural disaster covered areas	5,079	4,453	3,189	4,437
Disaster affected area	2,180	2,232	1,526	2,271
Area without yields because of disaster	354	389	373	523

Although natural disasters occurring in different years may not be comparable with each other in type and intensity, it can be ascertained, according to historical observations, that the damages would not have been so serious in the 1980s if adequate investment had been made for maintaining the existing irrigation and drainage systems. In other words, possible losses caused by natural disasters can be partly alleviated and even averted by adequate preventive measures, for example, irrigation agriculture in Israel (Schultz, 1964). On the other hand, faults in policies often aggravate damage from natural disasters, for instance, the agricultural crisis which has occurred in Ethiopia in recent years. Therefore, the depression in agricultural investment may have mostly resulted from deficiencies in the political and economic framework.

Family farms usually play an important role as investors in a market oriented economy. However, there is a lack of incentive for Chinese farmers to undertake intermediate or long-term investment in their farms due to low and uncertain returns. The uncertainties that farmers particularly feel are concerned with possessing secure leases of land and a secure ownership of capital stock, since ownership patterns regarding land and capital have always been a controversial area in ideology, theory and politics. Farmers' views were apparent in the response to a questionnaire administered by the Research Centre for Rural Development under the State Council early in 1988: around 58 per cent of 10,938 farmers interviewed in 300 villages in 28 provinces did not give a distinctly positive answer concerning political stability (People's Daily, Overseas edition, 12 April 1988).

It was calculated that the marginal savings rate of farmers' families (0.371) is much higher than that of urban residents (0.291), despite the fact that the former are at a considerably lower income level (The Institute for Rural Development Research, 1987). However, in a list outlining reasons for saving, 90 farmers interviewed in three counties of Henan province in a survey by the author, gave housing and children's marriage instead of capital investment in production as the most important reasons. The arguments supporting their choices can be seen in the fact that private ownership in housing in the rural sector has never been affected by the various political campaigns since the revolution, while private capital goods have always been in danger of expropriation. Moreover, marriage is, in the farmers' view, also a means of increasing labour, which can substitute for certain amounts of physical capital and it definitely belongs to their own family.

With regard to the three studied counties, farmers' spending on housing constituted 40.6, 62.2 and 33.1 per cent of the total investment in capital construction of each county in 1985.

The low profitability, viewed either in an absolute or in a relative sense, leads farmers' investment towards non-farm sectors. The profitability of key subdivisions of farm production may apparently be indicated by the following data referring to 1984 (Agricultural Statistical Yearbook of China, 1986):

	Grain	*Cotton*	*Oil-bearing seeds*	*Tobacco*
Average per Mu net receipts referring to one harvest (yuan):	62.61	187.55	72.39	223.66
Average net receipts per head of pigs (yuan):			15.75	

On the contrary, average per member net receipts of 'new economic Cooperatives'[2] amounted to 1,730 yuan in rural industry, 1,338 yuan in construction, 2,922 yuan in transportation, 1,949 yuan in commerce, catering and service trades. It is then not surprising that in accordance with the disparity in profitability between the sectors, the capital stock, in terms of value, increased by 56.5 per cent in transportation, 40.5 per cent in industry and 13.45 per cent in agriculture in 1985 compared with that of 1983.

Consistent with the decrease in investment in physical capital construction, the investment in human resources of agriculture is also depressed. Up to now about one-quarter of farm people are illiterate, and the school attendance rate in rural regions has tended to decline. A sample survey made in 1983 showed that around 30 per cent of children aged 13–14 dropped out of the education system and 6.2 per cent of them have never attended school. This is because a number of farmers let their children leave school in order to assist in farming. Such a choice is determined, first, by the existing traditional farming system which does not require an educated labour force. Second, this decision is actually a response to the deficiencies in the Chinese education system. It is overwhelmingly academically oriented. Farmers prefer to choose vocational schools which are in extremely short supply in the whole country.

With regard to other kinds of economic organisations, a possible cooperation between individual farms for making investment in agricultural service and supporting systems has virtually been neglected in China. This may derive from the fact that farmers have had a very strong aversion to over-collectivisation such that they cannot distinguish the co-operative pattern from collectives. In fact, farmers' experiences in many developed countries, such as Denmark, Federal Republic of Germany, Sweden, Canada and the US, etc. have shown that co-operatives based on voluntary participation can operate as efficient economic organisations to compensate for the disadvantages of family farms, for instance, shortage of capital and lack of economies of scale in processing, marketing, and the supply of credit, fertilisers, etc.

The part that collective production units once played in agricultural investment has not been successfully transferred to some other institutions. Although community councils and village committees substituted for administrative organisations of communes and brigades respectively, it is difficult for them to make investment as the former collectives did. Generally, these institutions experience a lack of a steady source of revenue, that is, financial resources, since there are, as yet, no legal regulations designed for them to levy taxes. Moreover, a subordinate relationship of farmers to the collectives does not exist between them and administrative institutions of villages and communities. Thus, some new management methods have to be found for involving intensive labour inputs in capital formation.

1.4 Some tentative conclusions and possible countermeasures

The previously described problems show that China has not yet succeeded in creating a political and economic framework which can continuously provide incentives to farm people to modernise agriculture using their own initiative. In order to achieve such a framework, an envisaged economic operating model was designed at the 13th National Congress of the Chinese Communist Party in October 1987. Under this the state regulates the market and the market then regulates the economy. According to this design, the essential role of the state in agriculture is understood here as being to provide legislation for a changing socio-economic environment and conducting agricultural development at the macro-level by means of policy-making and the use of economic instruments.

However, the government still concentrates on the kind of activity that enterprises should undertake, while the necessary operating rules for a changing socio-economic environment have not yet been completed, despite the fact that only the state is in a position to devise these rules. Clearly a starting point for achieving the envisaged model should be that the government must continue to withdraw from entrepreneurial activities. At the same time, in order to solve the problems which substantially retard current agricultural development, it is suggested that the following measures should be taken as part of a reform programme:

- Prices of agricultural products should basically be regulated by market mechanisms. A package combining higher farm output prices with reduced consumer subsidies, increased land taxation and added support to low income groups will benefit both producers and consumers as well as the state.
- The administrative distribution system for agricultural inputs should be replaced by a market allocation system.
- Neither structural adjustments in farm size nor increases in the shift of surplus labour from agriculture can be expected unless factor markets, including farmland, are introduced and a social insurance system is gradually established.
- The agricultural structural adjustment may not be realised unless a steady growth in non-agricultural sectors and decentralised urbanisation in rural regions can be achieved. Otherwise social disturbances possibly arising from unemployment pressure will make reform programmes fail before any goals

have been achieved. Therefore it is necessary to abolish the existing privileges of urban enterprises in procuring inputs, in order at least to create an equal opportunity for rural enterprises to be competitive through development of the market allocation system.

- Apart from measures to attract private investment in agriculture, a political framework in favour of manifold co-operatives in the service sector should be established for the purpose of improving the investment potential of farms. With regard to public investment, effective checks and balances mechanisms should be set up for monitoring and controlling public resource allocation, so that agriculture may be assured of receiving adequate investment to achieve the desired growth.

From the above statement it can be seen that a continual development of agriculture requires further changes in the existing operating mechanisms which are concerned with all other aspects of the national economy as well as the political system. Therefore, it cannot be expected that the current problems which emerged during reform will be resolved in the short term. At present, these measures will weaken, to a certain extent, the existing power of the administrative machine and reduce the privilege of those administrators, but they have to be implemented by means of an organisational network of the existing administrative system. Thus, there is already a contradiction arising at the starting point so that it can be predicted that China has still a long way to go to achieve the goal of reform.

Notes

1 Since 1985 the growth has become slower.
2 The new economic co-operatives are joint ventures set up by different groups of farmers in recent years. The enterprises are run in the form of joint operations and management by members on the basis of their own private investment and work performance.

References

An, 1987, 'The Development and Improvement of Agricultural Marketing in China'. Paper presented in the International Symposium for Rural Development Strategies, 25–31 Oct. Beijing.

Chen, 1987, 'The Rural Economy in China Is Transferring from Supra-Conventional Growth to Conventional Growth'. *Economic Research*, No. 12, 1987, Beijing.

Chow, 1987, *The Chinese Economy*. Singapore.

Gao, Li and Zhou, 1987, 'A Moderate Growth or a Sluggish Development'. *Economic Research*, No. 9, 1987, Beijing.

Hallet, 1981, *The Economics of Agricultural Policy*, Oxford.

Hou et al., 1988, 'Character of Behaviour of the Surplus Rural Labour Force at Present'. *Economic Research*, No. 2, 1988, Beijing.

The Institute for Rural Development Research, 1987, *A New Growth Stage of National Economy and Rural Development*, Hangzhou.

Lardy, 1983, Agricultural Prices in China (Staff Working Papers No. 606), World Bank, Washington, DC.

Lu, 1986, *Research on Systems of Responsibility*, Shanghai.

OECD, 1985, *Agriculture in China*, Paris.

Schultz, 1964, *Transforming Traditional Agriculture*, New Haven, CT.

State Statistical Bureau of the People's Republic of China, 1986, *Statistical Yearbook of China 1986*, Beijing.

State Statistical Bureau of the People's Republic of China, 1988, 'Statistical Bulletin Regarding National Socio-Economic Development in 1987'. *People's Daily* (overseas edition).

The World Bank, 1986, *World Development Report 1986*, Oxford.

2   Land tenure system in village communities

By abolishing the commune-brigade-team system and permitting much more market mediation in the rural economy, the current Chinese rural reform (1979–present) appears to constitute a major attack on collective principles. However, although the institutional changes created increasing opportunities for farmers to engage in individual economic activities, the reform provided a socioeconomic framework for a type of village community-based development. Owing to the abolition of the old institutions and the absence of a branch of the national bureaucratic system at the village level, the village community itself has sponsored essential public activities, such as providing social security for the aged, improving school facilities and maintaining basic health care. Many village communities close to cities promoted their villages' non-agricultural development in order to reduce underemployment and create an additional source of income for farm families. Reform of the centrally planned economy is far from complete and there are significant areas of non-market resource allocation, especially land tenure, in which the village community plays a decisive role.

Land allocation has become a major issue in resource allocation in the post-reform village community. The communities guarantee food supply for their members by regulating land tenure in response to changes in the size of farmers' families and to labour migration. Land allocation had also created extremely small farms and the fragmentation of farmland in the regions where rural industries are underdeveloped. This prevents the full use of modern technology. Similar problems have occurred in rural industry. The socioeconomic barriers created by each community have limited factor mobility, so that every village of a well-developed region has several small-sized enterprises in the same sectors. Inefficiency in using scarce capital seriously impedes macro-level progress. Other developing countries face similar policy options in development, and analysis of China's community-based development might be useful for them.

(Co-authored with Zhongyi JIANG, originally published in *Cambridge Journal of Economics*, Vol. 17, 1993 with the title "From Brigade to Village Community: the Land Tenure System and Rural Development in China".)

The form of land allocation is closely related to the development level of each village. Studies of the land tenure system in different regions may illuminate the Chinese experience as a whole. The land tenure and land-use system has always been controversial in both theoretical and practical discussions in China. One focus of discussion has been the possible changes in ownership of farmland (Liu, 1989), while another has concentrated on how to obtain economies of scale by expanding farm size (Dong and Chen, 1989). The comparison between the collective farm system and the family farm system is often related to these discussions (Zhou, 1989). Academic writing has paid more attention to future policy, while local research has focused on describing what has happened in each area [Bai (ed.), 1989]. Despite these limitations, these studies have provided valuable information about recent developments in different regions and ideas for policy options.

The Research Centre for Rural Development of the State Council of the People's Republic of China (RCRD) organised two research projects in 1988[1] in order to collect nationwide information about changes in the system of land tenure and use in the 1980s and to assist in designing an appropriate policy framework to regulate the changing system.[2] The village study includes a sample survey of 300 villages, implemented by sending a questionnaire through the Rural Survey System of the RCRD. The survey system was established in 1986. Except in Qinghai, Tibet, Taiwan and Hainan (which were not yet set up as a province at that time), each provincial RCRD of the remaining 27 provinces studied three village groups according to the average per capita net income of the peasant households of the village. Each group consisted of ten villages and three were chosen as representative for the high, middle and low income villages of their province, respectively. From those selected villages the RCRD of the State Council chose 300 sample villages, using national data collected by the State Statistical Bureau (SSB).

The average per capita net incomes of peasant households in the sample villages were higher than those in the national statistics of the SSB, as the provincial RCRDs actually selected above-average villages from each income group. Nevertheless, information about the farmers' response to central government policies was gathered effectively, which has helped national policy-makers understand the changing situation in different regions. The 300 sample villages are named the 'long-term survey point' (*guding guancha dian*). In each of the sample villages there is an investigator responsible for helping both village leaders and farmers to complete various socioeconomic questionnaires. The questions regarding land distribution and redistribution patterns of land-use taxation related to land, changes in land operation and the ways in which land disputes were settled were answered by chiefs and the book-keeper of each sample village.

For the farmland policy study conducted at the farm level, a questionnaire was circulated through the national statistical network of the SSB to 600 farmers in six counties (100 farms per county).[3] The national statistical network covers 66,642 farms, selected through a random sample conducted by the SSB. They keep records of farm and non-farm production as well as of home consumption. The 600 farms are part of this network. With the help of the rural investigation teams of the SSB, the 600 farmers who are the heads of their families filled in the questionnaire about their farm's resources, inputs and outputs of each branch of production, their qualifications and their household income and expenditure.

In addition to the two sample surveys, several field studies using interviews were conducted in 1988–1989. The field study in which the authors took part, covering 11 counties (*xian*), 18 townships (*xiang*), 32 villages (*cun*) and 63 farms from seven provinces was carried out mainly by means of interviews with government officials at county and district level, with staff members or rural supporting systems (research, extension, purchase and marketing, water management, etc.) with leading members of village communities and with farmers.[4] Based on the authors' field studies and results from data processing, this paper first gives a brief review of the transformation of the collective land tenure system and the resulting changes in rural institutions during the reform. Second, the patterns of the land tenure, which have become prevalent since the initial land distribution made at the beginning of the 1980s, are examined. Third, the main effects of the community-based land allocation are identified and policy options outlined.

2.1 The establishment of the family farm system and the changes in rural institutions

The current Chinese reform started with the distribution of collective land tenure to farmers' families. This policy was designed to stimulate agricultural growth by eliminating the egalitarian income distribution of collectives and establishing a closer link between farmers' work performance and remuneration. This contrasts with China's land reform of 1949–1952 and that of some Asian and South American countries around the same time, as those reforms were undertaken with the object of alleviating marked income inequalities caused by large inequalities in land ownership. The recent land distribution in China (basically according to family size) and the establishment of family farms enabled farmers to use existing resources. There was unprecedentedly rapid agricultural growth in 1979–1984, while inequality in farmers' agricultural income did not become pronounced (Zhu, 1991).

After the transition from collective land tenure, production teams, which had been the basic units under the communes, were replaced by family farms. This led to the abolition of the commune system, with the political, social and economic functions formerly under-taken by the commune now taken over by the township government. The management body of the production brigade (*shengchan dadui*) was turned to administrative villages while farmers of production teams were organised in villager groups (*cenmin xiaozu*) which formed the basic administrative units in rural regions.

The organisational and institutional changes apparently transformed the agricultural operating mechanism from the centrally planned economy to one in which the State regulates the market and then the market regulates the economy. However, the separation of functions between administration and public economic enterprises is still incomplete. As a result, the mechanisms of the centrally planned economy remain in operation along-side rudimentary market mechanisms. The coexistence of these two types of economic mechanism makes the functions of the village communities special.

The term 'village' is used in China to indicate both a settlement of several farm home-steads and a given rural territory where a formal institution is located and administers its political and socioeconomic affairs. These two meanings have given rise to two words: 'natural village' (*zirancun*) and 'administrative village' (*xingzheng cun*). An administrative village may consist of only one natural village or it may comprise several natural villages. We use the term village community here to indicate the administrative village. The law concerning the organisation of village (24 November 1987) stated that a village committee consisting of three to seven persons should be elected by villagers and that the committee should operate as an autonomous self-governing institution. The village committees have to find the money to support their operation from their own village, as they have no access to national financial resources.

However, since the system of centralised political and administrative control has not yet completely changed, the village committees still function as an extension to the national bureaucratic system in carrying out the most essential public activities of rural society. The leading body of a village community consists of two institutions: a branch of the Chinese Communist Party and the village committee. It is commonly the case that important members of the two leading groups within a village community are the same person, because the functions of the Party and those of the government at higher levels are still not separated.

The policies decided at the top levels of the Party and the government are pushed down to village committees for implementation. The committees turn the principles of the policies, such as those on rural education, social welfare, family planning and protection of the natural environment, into concrete feasible measures according to the situation of their own villages, and then execute them. Thus, the implementation of a policy differs slightly even between village communities in the same township.

Village committees do represent local farmers to some extent. In terms of their interests and behaviour, the members of a village committee are closer to farmers than are government officials, as they themselves are farmers. Moreover, they are paid for their organisational activities not by the government but by the villagers. Furthermore, there are checks and balances involved in village-level decision-making, because the village community actually has unwritten rules which limit people's behaviour, and farmers participate directly in community decision-making.

The organisational characteristics of the village communities outlined above do not differ greatly from those of the former brigades. It is always necessary for a village to have an organisation to conduct social and public affairs, although its form may vary.

The most important feature of the village community is its role in resource allocation. In some areas of resource allocation, where neither the government nor the market mechanisms operate effectively, the village community serves as both supplement and substitute.

The allocative function of the villages was initially brought about by the change in collective ownership. Owing to the institutional changes outlined above, some property which formerly was owned by production teams (e.g. farmland) or production brigades (e.g. non-agricultural enterprises) was transferred to community ownership. Though the Constitution declared that there still is collective ownership of farmland, confusion has arisen from the fact that the agricultural production collectives no longer exist.

In a former production team, in theory only a labourer could obtain membership and share in the collective property rights, since the team was an economic entity. Now, however, all the inhabitants of a village community naturally have membership in and rights of access to community-owned properties, as the village community is considered a social entity. In most instances, an individual gains his new share of communal property rights through a household in which he/she lives, since households are the basic social units in a village community.

With the emergence of communal property rights, village communities have assumed responsibility for community-based resource management. First, given that a land market is prohibited, the committees are in charge of the distribution and redistribution of farm-land among family farms within each village for specified periods. This will be discussed in detail in the following sections.

Second, village communities have organised non-agricultural development in the light of policy adjusting the rural economic structure in the 1980s. Some villages inherited the non-agricultural enterprises of the former production brigades and took over their management. In most cases, village committees established industrial enterprises by obtaining loans from the official financial institutions, by using the accumulated funds of the former collectives and by collecting money from villagers.

This pattern of rural industrialisation mainly resulted from the absence of a capital market. At the time of writing, formal finance institutions are still state-owned and under government control. Village committees as quasi-governmental authorities have priority over individuals in obtaining bank credit. Moreover, it is difficult for individual farmers to invest in industrial enterprises. The minimum capital necessary for setting up an industrial enterprise is usually far beyond that available to a farmer, since the subsistence economy of generally small-sized family farms provides limited opportunities for farmers to save.

Private loans are often short term and go to the trading sector or for consumption, which are viewed as being less risky. Apart from the capital shortage, there is a lack of legislation to protect the lender against bad debts. High risk leads to high interest rates. The monthly interest rates for private loans fluctuates at around 3–5%, which is about twice the official interest rate. High interest rates deter individual farmers from setting up enterprises using private loans.

Private ownership of the means of production continues to be a controversial area in ideology and politics. In view of the continuing political uncertainty, most entrepreneurs from among the farmers prefer to run collective or cooperative enterprises rather than run them individually. Thus, most rural industrial enterprises (the so-called Township-Village-Enterprises) belong to village communities and township governments. In the 1980s the village-owned enterprises created about 24 million jobs for rural surplus labour, which accounts for 30% of the labourers who shifted to the non-agricultural sectors in that period.

The rural labour surplus places great pressure on the Chinese national economy, as in most developing countries. In pre-reform China, sectoral and regional labour migration was rigorously controlled by administrative means. Rural surplus labour was tied to farming, being strictly monitored by the leading groups of the former collectives. This was associated with intensifying rural underemployment.

Re-introduction of the family farm system in the 1980s caused the elimination of administrative control on inter-sectoral labour migration, but restraints on rural-urban migration remain. Farmers are encouraged to search for non-agricultural employment while remaining in the villages. Thus, the reduction in rural surplus labour depends mainly upon the absorptive capacity of the rural non-agricultural sectors. Township-Village-Enterprises are usually able to mobilise more resources than small self-employed non-agricultural enterprises and provide relatively stable incomes for their employees who formerly were unskilled surplus labour. Furthermore, they may prove a way in which China can shift the economy away from its dualistic structure. A new institutional environment has emerged with community-based resource allocation and altered public sector activity. In order to draw a clearer picture of the functions of village communities, the influences of the government at different levels on village decision-making is now analysed briefly.

The policies and instruments of the central government still form a socioeconomic framework for rural society. Owing to the decentralisation which accompanied the reform, local government, at the level of provinces, cities, counties and townships, had greatly increased autonomy. Within the overall government hierarchy, both the township governments and the county governments are part of rural society, as they are located in rural areas and deal with rural affairs, but township governments have closer socioeconomic ties with the subordinate village communities. They are the grassroots government and must cooperate with village communities in fulfilling all the tasks undertaken by county authorities, and they have direct economic relations with the village communities. They often own capital assets to which farmers contributed, such as township-owned industrial enterprises which often were constructed with farmers' unpaid labour. Some township governments also collect money from peasant households to support specific local policies, such as the maintenance of an old people's home or improvements to school facilities. Generally speaking, both the unpaid labour and the cash payments provided by farmers are obtained via the village committees. Moreover, township governments run the agricultural support system which was set up during the commune period and still continue to provide services to farmers such as the supply of credit and purchased input goods (e.g. seeds, mineral fertiliser, herbicide, pesticide, etc.), tractor-ploughing, and the management of irrigation.

It appeared as if the re-emergence of the family farm system and the associated institutional changes led to a shift from the centrally planned to a market-oriented rural economy. In fact, the reform was incomplete. Neither of the two partly operational economic mechanisms was entirely effective in regulating resource allocation and the village communities stepped in to help overcome this failure.

2.2 Land redistribution and community-based rural development

Using the authors' own field studies and sample surveys conducted by the RCRD, this section first provides an overview of the general pattern of agricultural land tenure and the allocation of land between different crops. Next, a few specific, distinct regional patterns are examined. The analysis focuses on the determination of each pattern and the role of village communities in the allocation of farmland. ('Farmland' in the context of China means land used for crop production, which has always dominated agriculture. The sown area has been used overwhelmingly for growing grain crops since food grain forms a major part of the Chinese diet.)

According to the rules that the central government gradually laid down (1984–1986) with respect to land tenure, farmers have only usufruct rights. The duration of such rights was stipulated to be 15 years and during this period a right could be inherited by a farmer's descendants and be transferred to others with the approval of the village committee, but a land market is still strictly prohibited.

Usufruct rights are greatly restricted since there is little room for farmers to make decisions on land use. Under the state compulsory purchase system which remained in operation, state purchase orders are divided into quotas at different administrative levels and each farm receives a quota for a specified amount and type of product. Farmers are allowed to sell the surplus produce in the free market only when they have completed the quota delivery. Since Chinese family farms are very small-scale and are still run on traditional lines, a farm's output is small. Food needed for the subsistence of farmers' families plus the delivery of the grain quota force farmers to use over 70% of their land for growing grain, while only the remaining small portion can be employed for cash crop production. In the few well-developed regions where both population density and the quantity of quota delivery exceed the national average, more than 80% of the arable area is used for growing grain (SSB, 1989a, pp. 192–3).

Though the state has always regulated land tenure and land use, it does not own the land. The state cannot directly dispose of village farmland because it is in collective ownership. In order to construct roads, railway and state-owned enterprises, the state has to compensate village communities for taking over the plots of their land. Furthermore, most cases of land dispute in relation to the land tenure and land use systems are settled by village committees. The RCRD sample survey about land disputes occurring in 1988 shows that 11% of the cases were decided by the court and 16% were patched up by township governments, while the rest were all resolved by the village committees.

However, community ownership of land is incomplete, since communities do not have the right either to sell or to lease land. While every member of a village community does have a share of the property rights to the land of his/her community, this share is not embodied in any concrete form such as a title-deed stock, so that no one in the community is a real owner of land. This vagueness in the land ownership means that there is neither a market for transferring the usufruct right nor a real tenant-farming system. Thus the farmland allocation became virtually a socio-political process rather than an economic one. The initial land redistribution was not coordinated through the market but took place through negotiations between the farmers of a former production team. This was more likely to produce dramatic organisational changes than would have been the case if the re-allocation had taken place in normal economic circumstances. Under the new distribution, each household in a given village community received a few plots of land, the land area being allotted basically according to household size. The individual plots were each classified by soil fertility, location and availability of irrigation and also were equally divided between the households. Drawing lots was a commonly used procedure for allocating plots. This means that the farmland allocation mainly stressed equality of opportunity rather than allocative efficiency. Moreover, drawing lots is a simple procedure, and suitable for village communities where there is no market mechanism to regulate farmland allocation and where most farmers are poorly educated.

Since the person-to-land ratio is high this method of land distribution generally resulted in small, fragmented farms: farms in China today have an average of 0.56 hectares of land dispersed over 9.7 plots. The transition to the family farm system provided incentives for farmers to use existing resources more efficiently, but this method of land distribution makes it impossible to obtain allocative efficiency.

It is remarkable that this kind of distribution is frequent and has become the pattern of community-based land allocation, which amounts virtually to regular land redistribution. The sample survey of the RCRD shows that 65% of the 250 sample villages have redistributed land every 2 years since 1983. The redistribution in 91% of those villages was caused by demographic changes. Only 5% of the villages reallocated land in order to enable farm size to grow and less than 2% did it for plot consolidation (about 3% of those questioned gave no reason). Such frequent land redistribution might not take place if there were an effective rental system, or if there were a cadastral system for regulating land mobility. Without these preconditions, only changes in the person-to-land ratio in different households within a given village can cause land redistribution.

Land redistribution is also powerfully affected by the food security function involved in the land tenure system. Since the early 1950s, food supply for the urban population has been guaranteed by the government compulsory purchase system, while the food requirements of the rural population (which makes up 80% of the mainland Chinese) had to be met directly by the collective farms. The collectives provided land produce (food, grain, vegetables, oil-seeds, straw fuel, etc.) to farmers and their families at every harvest, which also constituted a part of the personal income distribution of the collective's members. This framework for supplying food remains in place, so that the rural food distribution system has turned into the land distribution system.

Closely related to the food security system is the fact that, although the farmers do not pay rent for the tilled plots, they have several obligations relating to this allotted land: (1) quota deliveries; (2) agricultural tax; and (3) village community charges. The exact amount of these three items that farmers must pay varies from place to place.

The quota delivery involves an implicit tax, as market prices are often above quota prices. In order to estimate the implicit tax paid by grain producers, sample survey data from the RCRD regarding grain production and sales in 155 villages in 1984 and 1988 are used.[5]

In Table 2.1, the 155 sample villages are classified according to the share of the non- agricultural sector in the villages' total gross output value, in order to show the differences between villages at different stages of development. The SSB does not provide data on the characteristics of villages. The data in the rows (6), (10), (11) and (12) of Table 2.1 do not yet appear in the national *Statistical Yearbook*. However, national data can be used as a reference point for certain items. The per unit area grain yield of the sample villages is generally higher than the national average, reported to be 239 kg/*mu* in 1988 (SSB, 1989b, p. 205). Nevertheless, there are no significant differences in rates of grain between sales in the sample villages and an average Chinese peasant farm. The grain commercialisation rate in the village groups of the sample varied in a range of 18.8–30.5%, while the rate for the average peasant farm is 28.4% (SSB, 1989c, p. 228). The share of quota sales in total grain sales for a national average family farm cannot exceed the following estimated range. The amount of the state 'basic purchase' (*Dinggou Renwu*) varies between provinces, counties, townships as well as villages. It is determined by the central planners and in 1988 it accounted for 12.7% of China's grain output and 41.7% of its commodity grain (The Editorial Board of the Ministry of Commerce, 1989).

Row (6) of Table 2.1 shows the actual amount of grain sold at the state quota price. It is not equivalent to the amount of the purchase 'task' (since farms do not all complete the purchase 'task'). Moreover, row (6) includes the agricultural tax,[6] which is usually paid in kind, calculated according to the quota price and delivered together with the quota products to the state commercial agency.

The 'market prices' mentioned in row (10) include both the local free market price and the 'negotiated price' offered by the state commercial agencies, which in most cases is identical to average local market price. 'Total grain sales' [row (8)] is the sum of rows (6) and (10). Grain sold at the quota price accounts for around 13.5–21.6% of the total grain output. The highest commercialisation rate reported in Table 2.1 is only 30.5%, which shows that surplus grain production is still low compared to that of family farms in developed countries. However, the quota accounts for a major share of the grain surplus, while the volume of grain sold at market prices formed at most 24.1% of total grain sales in 122 sample villages (78.7% of the sample villages). The quota price of grain is often 50–100% below the market price, so the implicit tax constitutes at least 6.8–10.6% of the total grain output of the sample villages. Owing to the implicit tax burden, farmers are not always willing to deliver the quota. Some farmers who earned sufficient cash in the non-agricultural sectors paid the state commercial agency the difference between the quota price and the negotiated price. In this way, these farmers could

Table 2.1 Grain production and sales of 155 sample villages in 1988

Items referring to a sample village on average	Village groups classified by the proportion of non-agricultural gross receipts in the total gross output value				
	Up to 20%	20–40%	40–60%	60–80%	Over 80%
	n = 53	n = 50	n = 22	n = 19	n = 11
(1) Number of households	306	358	319	373	646
(2) Population (persons)	1341	1553	1387	1432	2510
(3) Farmland (mu) of which:	2809	2570	1873	1487	1746
grain sown area	2172	2015	1487	1200	1388
(4) Total grain yield (tons)	758	1096	659	518	1071
(5) Per *mu* yield (kg)	349	544	443	432	772
(6) Volume of grain sold at quota price (tons)	164	192	121	105	145
(7) Percentage (6)/(4): (%)	21.6	17.5	18.4	20.3	13.5
(8) Total grain sales (tons)	216	206	201	138	317
(9) Commercialisation rate (8)/(4): (%)	28.5	18.8	30.5	26.6	29.6
(10) Percentage of grain sold at market prices (8) (%)	24.1	8.0	39.8	24.1	54.3
(11) Volume of purchased grain for fulfilling the quota (ton)	4.7	4.3	2.6	6.0	0.0
(12) Monetary payment for fulfilling the quota (1000 yuan)	8.9	6.0	1.2	12.9	5.3

Source: A national sample survey on the state compulsory purchase system, made by the RCRD, 1989.

Note: n = number of the sample villages.

at least save on transport costs and their own time. A number of farmers who used a major part of their land to grow cash crops chose to fulfil the quota with grain that they bought from the market, since the price of cash crop is often much more favourable than that of grain. Rows (11) and (12) in Table 2.1 mainly reflect such cases.

The community charges have generally been used to build a land-tax-revenue base to support the operations of the village committees. The community charges varied from 10 to 50 yuan/*mu* of farmland among the 300 villages in the RCRD sample survey of the land tenure system. These amounts constituted up to 10% of the per *mu* net receipts for the sample villages in 1988. Of the sample villages, 10.4% had successful non-farm enterprises and met their public financial obligations out of their industrial profits, so that village households were exempted from any such payment.

During the commune period, the three types of tax were also levied but the direct tax-payer was the production team. The quota products and the agricultural tax were delivered and the community charges deducted from the net receipts of the teams before any personal income distribution took place, so that individual farmers paid much more attention to distribution between themselves than to those tax payments.

With the rural reforms, the organisation and institutional changes caused a power shift in terms of the distribution of agricultural products. Now farmers hold the initiative in the distribution of their products and have become direct tax-payers. Where the market mechanism and the family farm system have gradually been introduced, the previous implicit tax burdens (quota and community charges) have been highlighted. Farmers have no objections to paying the agricultural tax but are unwilling to deliver the quota because of the unfavourable prices. They are also reluctant to pay community charges, mainly owing to lack of concrete legislation concerning the form of taxation. Thus, local governments and village committees have to bargain with farmers so as to meet the state purchase 'task' and in order to collect the community charges. They possess an important bargaining weapon in the shape of the possibility of changing the pattern of land tenure. In this situation the methods of distribution of products determine the method of land allocation.

A slight variation in the basic pattern of land tenure has led to a system called 'two-block tenure' (*liangtianzhi*). The farmland of a village community is divided into two blocks corresponding to the two purposes for which land is used: one block, which is in fact dispersed among several plots, is tilled to meet the needs of all the family farms for food and fodder, while the other is used to supply commodity products. The state purchase 'task' (quota) for the community as a whole will be undertaken by the second block, so that the first block is free of the implicit tax burden and linked only with the agricultural tax and community charges, while all three items of taxation are levied on the second block. Every household in the community is entitled to get a plot from the first block according to household size and number of pigs raised. The food ration per person and the fodder ration per pig, as well as the area of land needed to produce those rations, are calculated using communally agreed empirical estimates. Thus, the ratio between the two blocks is different between village communities.

Apart from the two distributed blocks of land, some village communities have reserved another relatively small block for additional allocation relating to demographic changes. The village committee organises bids for the reserved block in order to obtain considerably higher community charges. For instance, the reserved block made up approximately 5% of the total area of each village community in Jingyang County, Shaanxi Province. The community charges linked with this block amounted to 70 yuan/mu, which is about five times the value of the agricultural tax in that region.

Some village committees in Qinggang County of Heilongjiang Province have a system based on the two-block tenures, which has openly been called a tenancy system. An obvious difference between this tenancy system and the usual two-block tenures lies in the allocation process for the farmland. The village committees in this county require farmers to pay community charges in Spring before they can use the land, whereas it is more usual for village committees to collect the charges after the Autumn harvest. Moreover, the tenancy system introduced in Qinggang County has led to the introduction of some market mechanisms in farmland allocation, such as absolute rents and relative rent rankings. This goes beyond the intention of those who designed the system, who had only wanted to find an easy way of collecting community charges.

In order to identify the impact of this institutional innovation, a representative sample survey of 20 village communities was made within four townships where the tenant system had been put into effect comparatively early. The chief member of each sample village committee completed a questionnaire, designed by the authors, while ten farmers interviewed in each sample village community were chosen (in proportion) from three groups in the community (with special reference to the changes in farm size under the new institutional arrangements): farmers who had expanded their farms, those who had kept to the former size, and those who had reduced their land. The chiefs and farmers were asked to describe the resources and socioeconomic characteristics of their village or farm, as appropriate, and both gave information and opinions about the introduction of the tenant system.

In the course of introducing the tenant system, the majority of the sample farmers (74% of 200) had participated actively in classifying land by soil fertility, topography and location, as well as in ranking the rent linked with the different land classes. This is an important reason why the county government was later able to promote this land tenure pattern throughout the county, since making differentiated payments by farmers according to the quality of land fits into the farmers' views on equality and justice.

In 1988, the rent ranged between 2–60 yuan/*mu* in Qinggang County. Many of the chief members of village committees who were interviewed emphasised that farmers would give up tilling the poorest land if the lowest rental rank were set too high, although the threat is an overall excess demand for land. The rent is fixed at a proper level as a result of the farmers' own cost-benefit calculations. Furthermore, every year village committees adjust the total rent within their community in response to the rise in quota prices and weather-related harvest predictions. The committees try to keep a stable relationship between rent and output.

Along with the establishing of the tenant system there went a partial separation of the functions of land in respect to social security and resource allocation. Of the sample farmers, 5.6% had given their land over to village committees and specialised in non-farm businesses. In exchange, they were exempt from all three taxation payments, which is almost one-third of the per *mu* of the gross margin (output less variable inputs) derived from the maize output of the per *mu* best land in the county under normal weather conditions. Among the 200 sample farmers, 9–2% gave up a part of land belonging to the second block because they were only able to pay a part of the rent. Another group, constituting 2% of the sample farmers, did the same because they lacked farming ability. Village committees have helped these two groups to look for non-farm jobs and by providing social relief out of the communities' revenues (i.e. rent).

This reduction in land caused the emergence of a certain amount of land mobility. In the 20 sample villages, 4% of the total area of farmland was transferred and 7.7% of farmers expanded their farm size. In this case land was transferred to other farmers willing to pay a higher rent because they could use it more productively, so that the agricultural output of these villages may increase as a result of improved efficiency of land use.

Such a system has not yet become a completely market-oriented tenant system, since the necessary institutions and legislation for market-regulated factor mobility are not yet in place. In Qinggang County, village committees have virtually become landlords backed by the county and township governments, so it is impossible for the lessors and lessees to carry out free transactions from equal bargaining positions. Moreover, the use of rent is not clearly regulated and the functions of rent and tax are entwined. A key problem which has arisen is that a lease lasts only one year, since tenancy is used here to guarantee the village committees' annual revenue. The tenant system is also used as an instrument for village committees to implement their own policies, which may change frequently. It is obvious that land tenure is not secure under such a system. Additionally, the transfer of land tenure is carried out only between the farmers of the same community, so that the advantages of land mobility are limited.

Land mobility is limited not only by community boundaries but also by the slowness in labour migration resulting from the pace of non-agricultural development. In Qinggang County the overwhelming majority of the inhabitants still rely on agriculture. In such regions, the changes in land tenure have resulted in further fragmentation of farmland and reduction in farm size. For instance, the average farm size in Wugong County, a research region in Shaanxi Province in north-west China, fell by 28.6% (from 7 *mu* to 5 *mu*) during 1982–1989. The land cultivated by a single farm will be dispersed in at least four to five plots, and perhaps as many as eight to nine. The smallest plot may be less than 0.1 *mu*. In such regions, two-block tenures have not become widespread. This is because either the annual grain yield per capita of the average area of farmland approximates to the amount necessary for the subsistence of farmers' families, or the leading groups at the county, township and village levels have not yet become aware of the differences, in relation to farmland, between the functions of food security and commodity supply. Therefore, Qinggang County can be considered as an exception to the institutional arrangements in less-developed regions. The prevalent method of land distribution in those less-developed regions where two-block tenures were introduced appears to be that the second block has been allotted equally between the labourers of a village community owing to the strong demand for farmland as a result of rapid population growth and the lack of opportunities in non-agricultural employment.

This suggests that the pattern of the land distribution has still been essentially determined by the principle of equalising income distribution within a village community, as income disparities between farmers in present-day China are

Table 2.2 Changes in the employment structure of 155 sample villages between 1984 and 1988[a]

Items referring to a sample village on average	Year	Village groups classified by the proportion of non-agricultural gross receipts in total gross output value					The rural labour of China as a whole[b]
		Up to 20%	20-40%	40-60%	60-80%	Over 80%	(million)
		n = 53	n = 50	n = 22	n = 19	n = 11	
Labour force	1984	596	721	654	689	1153	353.7
(no. of persons)	1988	639	788	711	743	1390	400.7
Share of non-	1984	9.0	16.4	17.7	41.9	64.0	10.4
agricultural employment (%)	1988	11.0	23.9	28.8	52.8	75.1	21.5

Source: [a] As Table 2.1.

[b] State Statistical Bureau, 1989a, Statistical Yearbook of China, p. 162.

fundamentally affected by differences in employment opportunities. Where the underemployment caused by a labour surplus in agriculture has not yet been solved, non-agricultural development has become a decisive factor in alternative patterns of land tenure and in the tendency towards land mobility. This is even more clearly shown by the land concentration occurring in the well-developed regions, such as the suburbs of the large cities (e.g. Beijing, Shanghai and Tianjin) and the southeast coastal areas (e.g. Jiangsu, Zhejiang and Guangdong). Rapid growth in the non-agricultural economy and large scale inter-sectoral labour migration both took place in those well-off regions in the 1980s (see Table 2.2). Village communities where over 50% of the labour force are employed in non-agricultural sectors make up less than 20% of the total sample of villages. It is in such villages that some relatively large farms have emerged, because the economic structure changed and some land was transferred from non-agricultural employees to those remaining in agriculture.

Land concentration also occurs in other ways, determined by the regional socioeconomic framework. In a few areas where direct administrative control of the economy has been largely given up and the market left to coordinate major economic activities, large farms have emerged through the free transfer between farmers of rights to the usufruct from land. A typical example of this pattern can be found in Leqing County (in the Wenzhou region of Zhejiang Province), which has a relatively liberal economy. In this county, the average area of farmland per capita was 0.41 *mu* in 1988. A number of farmers already had stable sources of off-farm income and labour opportunity costs had increased to the point where they wished to re-allocate their labour into non-agricultural activities as far as possible. Through individual negotiations they sub-let land to those who wished to expand their farms. In general, the sub-lessees must fulfill all the obligations for tax payments linked with the land and supply the lessors with around 120–150 kg rice/*mu* as rent (i.e. about 20% of the per *mu* annual yield). Up to the end of 1988, farms over 10 *mu* in size (five times the average size) constituted 1% of total farms and their cultivated 8.1% of total farmland in the county. This small group of farmers provided yields per *mu* about 10% higher than the average, mostly owing to stronger motivation, above-average farming skills, and priority in receiving the services provided by the agricultural support system.

The difficulties encountered by the large farms mainly arise from the fragmentation of cultivated land and the short duration of the lease. The lease is usually for 1–3 years, as the sub-lessors are heavily affected by the fact that the Chinese rural population does not have a social insurance system or security of food supply such as the urban residents possess. They may lose their jobs when their Township-Village-Enterprise goes bankrupt, or when government policies swing from expansion to retrenchment, with a reduction in non-agricultural jobs. The sub-lessors regard land as a security against unemployment and this is an impediment to land concentration, despite the fact that larger farms have higher productivity.

In contrast to this case, land concentration occurred through recollectivisation in Shun Yi, a county belonging to the municipality of Beijing, where a relatively successful economy already existed during the commune period and strong administrative control remains. The present collective farms are distinguishable from the former production teams by their land-labour ratios which have been affected by inter-sectoral labour migration. The ratio now is 1 hectare of land: 0.9–1.0 labour units (persons), while formerly it was around 1 hectare of land: 4.5 labour units during the commune period, which suggests that labour now is being used more efficiently.

Furthermore, a collective farm is a kind of village community-owned enterprise. Managers plan land use, the production process and distribution of the product, while members each work on their assigned plots and are responsible for the costs incurred by the plots and the yields harvested from those fields. The costs and the yields are used as two indicators of the members' work performances, which is reflected in their remuneration. Under the arrangements of village committees, they can earn a similar amount as the non-farm workers in the same village.

Also, according to the regulations of village committees, besides the grain delivery quota to the state commercial agencies, the collective farms must supply their non-agricultural households with a food ration, as well as a fodder ration if the non-farm household raises pigs. Such internal trade has been carried out at prices set by village committees, which are lower than local market prices. Apparently, these village committees have been in a similar dilemma to that of the state in terms of keeping down consumers' prices and guaranteeing producers' incomes. A producer subsidy system has been introduced which covers part of the costs incurred in purchasing machines and other input goods as well as in using machinery and providing irrigation. The subsidies have been provided by the local government at different levels and by part of the profits of Township-Village-Enterprises.

Collective land tenure provides the easiest way for rural officials and heads of village committees to fulfill their grain delivery quotas. The collective farm system is a more appropriate institution than the family farm for the state compulsory purchase system, which still exists as a component of the partially reformed mandatory planning mechanism. Moreover, if those officials and village heads tried to tackle new problems by using new instruments it would involve some risk to their careers. Consequently, they often use only familiar measures.

Nevertheless, family tenure is still the most popular pattern in present-day China. Farmers generally are very averse to recollectivisation and an overwhelming majority of local governments and village communities are not in a position to subsidise agriculture in the way outlined above. In those well-developed regions where village committees have operated effectively with a successful community-owned non-agricultural economy, such as Shanghai and Jiangsu, land concentration has been organised by the committees and only concerns the second block of farmland. Intra-village grain trade is unnecessary in this case since every household retains the tenure to a plot of land from the first block. The criteria on which the second block was distributed were: first, land concentration should be promoted in order to increase commodity grain sales and easily fulfill the quota delivery by relying on full-time farmers; and second, the area of land that full-time farmers cultivate should be large enough to provide them each with about the same amount of net income as the average wage of a non-agricultural employee in the village.

Thus, in the regions under consideration a group of comparatively large farms (10–20 *mu*) emerged, while the few farms over 20 *mu* in size in most cases makes up around 5% of the large farms.[7] Along with land concentration, some village committees have also transferred part of the profits from non-agricultural enterprises to farmers in the form of direct payments (in addition to input subsidies) related either to the cultivated area of the second block or to the quota delivery. In the well-organised villages of Shanghai, Jiangsu and Zhejiang Provinces, a further measure has been adopted in parallel with subsidies: farmers who do not cultivate their second block of land, or fail to deliver the quota, are fined.

A key point which emerges from these case studies is that a village committee, in organising the community-based resource allocation, usually depends on the development of village-owned non-agricultural enterprises. Many villages have none of these and even members of the village committees are poorly paid. These committees have great difficulty in organising community-based public activities, including land redistribution.

The determinants of the present land tenure and land use system can be summarised as follows:

1   Given that the ownership of farmland has not yet clearly been defined and that farmland cannot officially be bought and sold, land transfers have occurred mainly through redistribution within a village community, involving agreement between the village committee and the farmers of a given village. The institutional arrangements which are described for this are central to the formation of a pattern of land tenure.

2   The method of land distribution is determined fundamentally by the distribution of its produce between the state, the village committees and farmers, and further affected by the principle of guaranteeing food supply for each member of a village community and of equalising income between its members.
3   The level of non-agricultural development of a given village and its surrounding region is a decisive factor affecting land mobility. In less-developed regions, average farm size is generally similar, while land concentration increases gradually in the well-developed regions.
4   The pattern of land mobility has been shaped by the balance between administrative power and market forces in different regions and the organisation of each individual village community.

2.3   Possible policy changes affecting the land tenure system

Alongside the establishment of the family farm system, Chinese agriculture grew rapidly in 1979–1984. However, after 1985 the rate of growth slowed down and the output of some key products (especially grain) fell below the 1984 peak. However, population continued to grow by around 10 million people per year, which caused increasingly heavy pressure owing to the shortage of farm products.

Sustained growth in Chinese agriculture requires the establishment of an appropriate institutional and physical infrastructure for farm modernisation. A key component of the institutional infrastructure is an agricultural land tenure system, which can automatically regulate land mobility in step with changing economic conditions in order to reap allocative efficiencies.

Some elements of the current land tenure system, and of the various tentative institutional arrangements established in the reform period, hinder agricultural growth and overall rural development. Outstanding among these is the lack of specific legislation concerning the land tenure system. This has meant that local governments, village committees and farmers negotiate with each other on the basis of their own interests, and decisions emerge from bargains struck between them. These are common weaknesses among the different patterns of allocation that emerged. Without specific legislation to clarify the rights and obligations of both owners and users of land, it is impossible to protect farmland from misuse, despite the fact that land is extremely scarce. Official data show that China's farmland fell by 490 thousand hectares per annum after 1981 (State Land Administration Bureau, 1 June 1987), while a general decline in soil fertility has been reported (*People's Daily*, 28 January 1988).

Owing to the frequency of land redistribution, farmers do not possess secure tenure and the term of their tenure is too short. They are uncertain about how land will be allotted in the future. This has resulted in them pursuing short-term profits from land to the neglect of long-run investment. They had to invest in home-building and non-farm businesses rather than in agricultural capital constructions. This is reflected in the booming rural building construction in the 1980s coincident with a decline in the capital stock in agriculture.[8] The irrigation system has gradually been run down, owing to lack of maintenance, so that the effectively irrigated area fell from 90 to 70% of China's total farmland during this period, while the effectively irrigated area over China as a whole fell by 3.4 million hectares from 1983 to 1987, causing a loss of 10 million tons of grain (Gao and Zhou, 1987).

Rent relationships are constrained within the existing socioeconomic framework, and village committees virtually substitute for these in regulating the allocation of farmland. Although re-allocations by the committees are frequent, they do not occur sufficiently often to meet the requirements of individual farmers, since factor allocation within each farm changes continuously as economic conditions alter. The contradiction between instantaneous demand for land and intermittent supply has markedly hindered the optimisation of factor allocation.

The allocation of farmland according to household size seems to be equitable but it is unfair from the standpoint of each individual farmer, as households can be of different sizes. Competition among farmers to obtain more plots of land resulted in competition to have more children. For instance, during the allocation in Wugong County in 1989 in order to obtain more land, some farmers adopted an extra child besides their own. Thus, the principle implemented in the redistribution of farmland encourages rural population growth, thereby intensifying underemployment caused by excess labour relative to farmland.

Without rent as the coordinating mechanism, the village committees find it difficult to obtain objective criteria with which to improve allocative efficiency even when it is, indeed, possible to increase land concentration. It is mostly those farmers who are innovative and capable in both farm and non-farm activities who are the first to enter non-agricultural production, while farmers who are not especially enterprising usually remain in agriculture and receive more plots of land as a result of the village committees' policy for equalising income distribution in well-off communities. This explains the absence of a significant correlation between farm size and grain yield per *mu* (i.e. relatively large full-time farmers have not achieved a significantly higher per unit area yield than average and small part-time farmers). This implies that optimal resource allocation has not yet been achieved in individual villages through community-based land distribution.[9]

The lack of clarity in community property rights means that factor returns, such as farm rents and wages, profits and wages of village-owned non-agricultural enterprises, are not differentiated from each other, so that each village is reluctant to employ outside labour. The community barrier, built for protecting the returns to community property, has hindered factors of production from moving among different villages and prevented the optimisation of resource allocation at the macro level. Well-developed villages tend to adopt capital-intensive technology in both agricultural and non-agricultural sectors because of labour shortages, despite the fact that the regions in which they are located as a whole have a large labour surplus.

Viewed as the cost of running a socioeconomic system (Arrow, 1987), the transaction costs of community-based land redistribution are particularly high. A market-coordinated land transfer involves only a few participants, whereas community land redistribution involves all members of the community. Apart from the time spent by each family head in meetings, informal discussions and bargaining, the family has to pay specific fees to fund the administration of the entire process. For example, during the land redistribution in Wugong County after the Summer harvest of 1989, 10,000 labour units (persons) per day went on measuring and dividing farmland, which lasted one month, and the cost was around 800,000 *yuan*. Moreover, sowing for Autumn crops was delayed by the redistribution, which obviously affected the harvest. This can be considered an additional cost beyond the explicit costs of land redistribution.

Although there are manifold problems in the current land tenure and land use systems, family tenure has been a better organisational form for utilising farmland that was collective tenure. Community-based allocation is an important element in a transitional economic operating mechanism and it may merely be a temporary phenomenon. Market coordination can only be introduced gradually into the process of land allocation by further reform of the existing socioeconomic framework along the following lines.

First, the state compulsory purchase system, which has seriously impeded the introduction of the market mechanism, should be eliminated. This suggestion is also consistent with the stated government objective of reducing urban-rural income disparities. The compulsory purchase system has a strong 'urban bias' as it has in most instances under-priced farm products in order to maintain low prices for urban consumers. Through the subsidies provided by transferring profits from rural non-agricultural enterprises to farms, rural industries indirectly have subsidised urban ones. When such an inequitable system is abolished, farmers will be relieved of the implicit tax burden and may be able to obtain a reasonable price for their products.

Second, if administrative influence on resource allocation is gradually going to be reduced, then tax and rent must be differentiated. Village committees could then shed the role of landlord and instead could levy either an enterprise tax, a property tax or a poll tax to finance their expenditures. It is necessary to pass specific laws about the financial management of villages in order to guarantee sources of revenue for the village committees and encourage community-based development through improving public facilities and social welfare institutions at the village level.

Third, detailed legislation to establish a cadastral system and the free transfer of usufruct rights to land should be prepared in order to introduce the market mechanism in the allocation of farmland. Such a process is very unlikely to start in the near future, but one thing could be done now: a specific regulation should be enacted to prohibit the further reduction of farm size and the continual fragmentation of land. This would be the basis for providing farmers with long-term secure leases and could become an effective factor in slowing rural population growth. Furthermore, such a regulation might give an impetus to labour migration and to changes in the rural employment structure as well as to the adjustment of the national economic structure.

Finally, the rights and obligations of land owners and users should be clarified by law. This would at least facilitate the current land transfer and might protect farmland from misuse. In any case, the currently envisaged legal and institutional arrangements concerning the land tenure system may not lead directly to increased agricultural output, which is the most important target of current Chinese agricultural policies. Steady growth depends on long-term, integrated rural development.

Notes

1 The RCRD was abolished at the end of 1989. However, its Rural Survey System remains and is now administered by the Research Center for Agricultural Policies, The Ministry of Agriculture, Animal Husbandry and Fishery.
2 One project conducted at the village level is supported by the World Bank. Another is being carried out at the peasant farm level in cooperation with the University of Hohenheim, Germany.
3 Songjiang County in Shanghai Municipality, Yuyao County in Zhejiang Province, Changshu County in Jiangsu Province, Shunyi County in Beijing Municipality, Lingui County in Guangxi Province and Wugong County in Shaanxi Province.
4 Some selected economic indicators of those counties including the six sample counties are included in the appendix.
5 The 155 villages are a subsample taken from the 300 sample villages of the RCRD Rural Survey System and those selected for the survey were villages where growing grain is the main agricultural activity. Then, five to six sample villages were chosen from each of the 27 provinces included in the RCRD Rural Survey System.
6 The state agricultural tax, which averaged 3.7 yuan/*mu* in China as a whole in 1988 (SSB, 1989, pp. 174, 663). (1 *mu*=0.0667 hectares.)
7 For example, in Songjing County near Shanghai, larger farms now cultivate about 30% of the area of the second block, i.e. 15% of the total farmland.
8 For example, investments in capital construction on farmland and in irrigation works almost stopped in Wugong County of Shaanxi Province in the 1980s.
9 From a sample survey of RCRD on the management of 600 farms.

References

Arrow, K. J. 1987. The potentials and limits of the market in resource allocation, in *Issues in Contemporary Microeconomics and Welfare*, Bloomington.

Bai, Y. (ed.). 1989. *Studies on Economy of Farm Scales*, Beijing.

Dong, J. and Chen, X. 1989. On economy of farm scales, in Bai, Y. (ed.). *Studies on Economy of Farm Scales*, Beijing.

Editorial Board of the Ministry of Commerce. 1989. *The Commercial Yearbook of China*, Beijing, Ministry of Commerce.

Gao, L. and Zhou, X. 1987. A moderate growth or a sluggish development. *Economic Research*, No. 9.

Liu, F. 1989. Inquiry to privatisation of farmland, in Bai, Y. (ed.). *Studies on Economy of Farm Scales*, Beijing.

State Statistical Bureau, 1985, Statistical Yearbook of China, p. 214.

State Statistical Bureau. 1989a. *The Statistical Yearbook of China*, Beijing, Chinese Statistical Publishing House.

State Statistical Bureau. 1989b. *The Agricultural Statistical Yearbook of China*, Beijing, Chinese Statistical Publishing House.

State Statistical Bureau. 1989c. *The Abstract of Agroeconomic Statistics of Counties of China 1980–1987*, Beijing, Chinese Statistical Publishing House.

The Statistical Bureau of Qinggang County. 1988. *A Statistical Yearbook of Qinggang County*, Qinggang.

Zhou, X. 1989. Investigation and analysis of the family farm system, in Bai, Y. (ed.). *Studies on Economy of Farm Scales*, Beijing.

Zhu, L. 1991. *Rural Reform and Peasant Income in China*, London, Macmillan.

Appendix Table 2.A Selected economic characteristics of the studied counties (1987)

Items	Unit	Shunyi (Beijing)*	Songjiang (Shanghai)*	Wufm (Jiangsu)*	Changshu (Jiangsu)*	Kunshan (Jiangsu)*
Rural population	10 thou. person	43.9	39.3	116.4	90.9	46.2
Farmland	10 thou. mu	86.6	54.2	134.9	104.9	86.0
Sown area	10 thou. mu	147.6	99.2	238.7	183.9	158.5
of which: grain	10 thou. mu	132.8	74.9	207.9	132.5	118.6
Cotton	10 thou. mu	0.1	3.1	0.5	19.3	
oilseed crops	10 thou. mu		10.9	10.6	16.9	29.1
Grain output	ton	469,123.5	285,174.0	752,821.0	474,703.3	427,203.0
Cotton output	ton	55.0	2053.0	252.0	12,424.3	6.0
Oilseed output	ton	3458.0	15,191.0	10,667.0	18,491.5	30,259.0
Pork, beef, mutton	ton	29,648.1	19,062.0	35,746.0	15,672.0	15,343.0
Total power of agr. Machinery	10 thou. watt	45,041.8	19.4	66,587.5	57,150.0	29.6
Tractor-ploughed area	10 thou. mu	79.2	49.2	115.1	73.4	72.0
Effectively irrigated area.	10 thou. mu	82.1	52.1	116.7	102.5	82.4
The use of chemical fertiliser	ton	25,296.0	14,307.0	34,190.0	25,567.0	27,162.0
Electricity consumption	10 thou. KWh	12,970.0	26,770.0	35,918.3	39,632.0	18,118.0
Total product of rural society	10 thou. yuan	189,231.2	194,679.0	503,600.7	563,359.3	224,327.6
Gross agricultural output value (1987 prices)	10 thou. yuan	60,439.6	46,893.0	91,609.7	63,743.7	51,427.2
Net agricultural output value (1987 prices)	10 thou. yuan	36,738.3	24,155.0	51,480.3	43,382.6	34,767.8
Gross output value of agriculture (1980 prices)	10 thou. yuan	34,233.9	30,336.0	59,693.3	43,605.0	35,125.4
Volume of purchased agr. & sideline products	10 thou. yuan	8961.6	13,930.0	22,440.0	36,542.0	26,643.0

Items	Unit	Leging (Zhejiang)*	Yuyao (Zhejiang)*	Qinggang (Heilongjiang)*	Lingui (Guangxi)*
Rural population	10 thou. person	90.3	67.0	38.9	38.9
Farmland	10 thou. Mu	41.3	64.6	213.3	52.0
Sown area	10 thou. mu	99.5	161.7	213.3	91.0
of which: grain	10 thou. mu	75.5	99.4	171.6	76.1
cotton	10 thou. mu		11.6		
oilseed crops	10 thou. mu	0.5	15.5	3.8	0.5
Grain output	ton	256,999.0	343,805.0	281,288.0	160,342.0
Cotton output	ton		6477.0		
Oilseed output	ton	339.0	16,636.0	2979.0	341.9
Pork, beef, mutton	ton	10,216.0	10,008.0	4465.0	5824.0
Total power of agr. Machinery	10 thou. watt	10,476.4	18,967.1	7500.0	3827.2
Tractor-ploughed area	10 thou. mu	23.9	35.2	85.5	6.4
Effectively irrigated area	10 thou. mu	31.4	60.5	14.9	35.9
The use of chemical fertilizer	Ton	7847.0	20,207.0	8522.0	7370.0
Electricity consumption	10 thou. KWh	4100.0	17,268.0	1495.0	1527.8
Total product of rural society	10 thou. yuan	114,522.0	198,807.0	25,336.0	17,807.0
Gross agricultural output value (1987 prices)	10 thou. yuan	37,013.0	50,886.0	19,466.0	14,913.0
Net agricultural output value (1987 prices)	10 thou. yuan	26,658.0	38,770.0	11,896.0	9867.0
Gross output value of agriculture (1980 prices)	10 thou. yuan	23,276.0	32,167.0	15,862.0	10,003.0
Volume of purchased agr. & sideline products	10 thou. yuan	6421.0	20,587.0	6480.1	4104.0

(Continued)

Appendix Table 2.A (Continued)

Items	Unit	Jingyang (Shaanxi)*	Wugong (Shaanxi)*
Rural population	10 thou. person	39.7	31.6
Farmland	10 thou. *mu*	71,843.0	
Sown area	10 thou. *mu*	107.2	65.2
of which: grain	10 thou. *mu*	90.5	58.8
cotton	10 thou. *mu*	7.5	0.1
oilseed crops	10 thou. *mu*	2.2	4.2
Grain output	ton	221,065.0	157,498.0
Cotton output	ton	5063.0	15.0
Oilseed output	ton	2388.0	5065.0
Pork, beef, mutton	ton	3410.0	79,276.0
Total power of agr, machinery	10 thou. watt	12,838.0	9501.5
Tractor-ploughed area	10 thou. *mu*	25.5	32.3
Effectively irrigated area	10 thou. *mu*	61.8	39.4
The use of chemical fertilizer	ton	13,430.0	8246.0
Electricity consumption	10 thou. KWh	5232.3	5234.1
Total product of rural society	10 thou. *yuan*	34,405.0	24,957.0
Gross agricultural output value (1987 prices)	10 thou. *yuan*	23,429.0	14,154.0
Net agricultural output value (1987 prices)	10 thou. *yuan*	14,988.0	8857.0
Gross output value of agriculture (1980 prices)	10 thou. *yuan*	16,048.0	9485.0
Volume of purchased agr. & sideline product	10 thou. *yuan*	4601.0	4403.0

Source: The State Statistical Bureau (1989). The Abstract of Agroeconomic Statistics of Counties of China (Zhongguo, Tenxian, Nongcun, Jingii, Tongii,Gaiyao), 1980–1987.

*The name in parentheses is the province to which the county belongs.

3 Gender inequality in land tenure system

This paper will firstly review the current legal framework of securing equal land rights between women and men in China. Secondly, based on the sample survey undertaken in Shanxi Province in 1996,[1] the paper will examine the current state of land distribution, identify the causes of gender inequality in terms of security of land rights, and determine the impact of "insecure" land rights on the socioeconomic status of women. Finally, the policy implications will be examined. This paper proves that the legislative framework and economic institutions in general protect gender equality in land distribution. However, loopholes in the detailed institutional arrangements lead to the insecurity of women's land rights, especially for divorced women, women re-locating due to marriage, and for their children who miss out on land redistribution as undertaken in their village communities. Although these phenomena have not yet significantly affected the intra-household bargaining power of the agricultural women, they do tend to reduce the households of the landless women to poverty. It is therefore necessary to add a gender perspective to the current Land Administrative Law and to relevant government regulations regarding farmland tenure.

3.1 Women's land rights

In those countries where land can be freely traded, inherited and leased, inheritance acts, marriage laws, and contract laws define from different perspectives the ways and rights of individuals to obtain land (FAO, 2000). However, in a number of countries – western Ghana, for example – customary laws of the local communities as well as religious beliefs still affect the enforcement of the formal laws (Quisumbing et al., 1999). They even play a decisive role in determining an individual's entitlement to land (Subramanian, 1998). Inasmuch as in China, laws prohibit the free trade and presentation of land, farmers obtain land tenure mainly through land distribution by village communities, by renting from other households, by inheriting household contract entitlement, and so on. Therefore, in order to achieve a better understanding of the land rights that village women possess in China, it is not only necessary to review the related laws and policies, but also to examine how village communities distribute land among farmers in general.

(Originally published in *China and World Economy*, No. 2, 2001.)

During the period between 1979–83, China's land system was completely transformed from collective ownership and cultivation to the household contract system (also known as the household responsibility system). This change was based on the equalized distribution per household size of contracted land within production teams (The Research Team for the "Study of Farmland System in China", 1993). This change implied that every member of a household would receive an equal plot. In fact, however, land was distributed among households instead of individuals. This pattern may be explained firstly by the ideal blueprint that farmers, as the initiators of the reform, had in mind, i.e., the traditional ideal of Chinese agricultural society where the household, rather than the individual, was the unit of ownership and cultivation. Secondly, it could be explained by the actual per-capita land ratio. According to the annual socioeconomic survey of the Ministry of Agriculture, the average area of farmland per capita in rural China in the 1980s (Office for Rural Long-term Observation Points, 1992) was computed at less than 2 mu,[2] or per household 9 mu that was segmented into 9 plots. If the land were to be divided and allocated to each member of the village community by the same area and quality, it would not only lead to even more serious land fragmentation, but would also incur higher organizational costs.

Furthermore, the policy documents issued in the early 1980s by the top level decision-makers to permit the practice of land distribution – at that time a policy document had legal effect – determined the prevailing land system to be the household contract system. In these documents, there was neither clear definition of a natural person's individual rights, nor reference to the rights of women. This neglect or absence of individual rights may be due, firstly, to the tradition of esteem for household rights in China's agricultural society. Secondly, it may be due to the social preference toward collective rights (as a carry-over from the time of the planned economy); and to the pre-existent premise of gender equality held by the policy designers.

This premise is certainly true in law: Article 96 of the first Constitution of the People's Republic of China clearly stipulates that women and men enjoy equal rights in every aspect of political, economic, cultural, social, and family life (National People's Congress [NPC], 1954). The marriage law and inheritance act issued or amended in the 1980s highlighted gender equality in terms of economic relations among family members. Article 18 of the Marriage Law (1980) declares that husband and wife enjoy the right to inherit legacies from each other; Article 31 states that in the event of divorce the joint assets of husband and wife will be disposed of upon agreement of the two parties. If they fail to reach an agreement, the court will determine distribution on the principle of prioritizing women's and children's interests (NPC, 1980). Article 9 of the Inheritance Act (1985) confirms that women and men enjoy equal rights of inheritance. Article 10 names the spouse as the first person in the inheritance order. As farmland is not private property, the legislative committee of the NPC provided in a special statement that the inheritance of farmland contract rights could not be dealt with in the same way as legacy inheritances. The heir of the contractor would assume the responsibility of fulfilling the contract (NPC, 1985). Most land contractors within a village community are household heads, and, as village women usually join the households of their husbands, most household heads are men. Only those household heads are women where men married into the household, or where the male heads died.

Given this background, women may not have encountered problems in land distribution at the beginning of the economic reform. Problems occurred when the population of a village community changed. As land could not be transferred between village communities when villagers re-located, or migrated, or when they married into other villages, women lost their land tenure in their village of origin. Because of this, Article 30 of the Law for the Protection of Women's Rights (NPC, 1992) emphasized that women's entitlement to land should be protected in the case of marriage and divorce. However, this law does not specify the means of providing such protection. If this type of migrant wishes to obtain farmland, the only means (other than by leasing from other farmers) is to rely on the land redistribution among those households in the villages they moved into. According to the Land Administrative Law (NPC, 1998), during the duration of a given land distribution contract, land re-distribution among individual land contractors can be held only when it is agreed to by more than 2/3 of the overall villagers meeting or by 2/3 of the villagers' representatives. Moreover, the decisions of the village communities must be submitted to township government and agriculture admin-istrative authority of the county government for final approval.

Inasmuch as the village community is the unit that exercises the villagers' autonomy, the stipulations of the Land Administrative Law apparently comply with the principle of internal democracy in decision-making within the village communities. However, the decisions on farmland redistribution of the overall villagers' meeting are based mainly on the relevant policies of the central and local governments. As these policies are usually worked out with a lack of gender perspective, it seems that whether the land rights of the non-indigenous women are secured eventually depends on the extent to which most villagers accept the concept of gender equality rather than considering their own interests.

Based on our understanding of the existing legislative framework and opera-tional procedures of land distribution, we put forward the following hypotheses to be tested against the analytical statistics:

- There is no significant discrimination against women in land distribution in rural China.
- The insecurity of land entitlement for migrated women is directly related to the decisions made by village communities.
- In areas with less developed non-agricultural sectors, the possibility of falling into poverty is higher for those nuclear families with landless women.

3.2 Gender inequality in the security of land rights

Given the practices of the initial farmland distribution undertaken in the early 1980s, it can be reasoned that every member of the village communities is naturally entitled to share in the land ownership of the villages.[3] However, once the distribution was over, the tenure of a specific household on a certain plot during the valid period of the contract was exclusive. This resulted in the phenomenon that those community members joining the villages during the contract period could not instantly acquire plots from the community. However, the existence of landless members was often covered up by the mean values in the analysis on the land size of the sample households.

Table 3.1 revealed that 8.5% of the interviewed women did not have access to land in the villages where they are living. Linking the replies to question 2 and question 3, it could be deduced that the land rights of divorced women are insecure. If a woman did not receive a land plot in the village into which she moved by marriage, on what could she live after divorce if she were still obliged to reside in her ex-husband's village? It is a custom in rural Shanxi for a divorced woman to return to her parents' family. However, if her native village community had already rescinded her land tenure, she fell into the awkward situation of being obliged to live on the land of her parents or brothers. In reality, most divorced women re-marry very soon so as to solve the problem of losing their income sources. This might explain why we neither found nor met any divorced women in our sample villages.[4] More than half of the interviewed women were not even aware of the land rights of a divorced woman (Table 3.1). It was then presumed that the lowest transaction cost for the divorced women to gain a new source of income would be re-marriage as opposed to a lawsuit for land.

Though the case that women lost their land tenure due to divorce is not statistically proved by the sample data, the insecurity of the women's land right is manifested by the figures in Table 3.2. There are 70 interviewed women reporting landless and they are distributed in every village except villages 1 and 2. If a village community does adjust land holding between households by their size in an expected 3–5 years, then, the landless women are considered to have owned a predictable tenure on land. If such were not the case, the phenomena would

Table 3.1 Specific Issues of Women's Land Right

Questions	Responses of the Interviewed Women			
	"Yes"	*"No"*	*"I don't know"*	*Total*
(1) "Do you have your own plots among your family land?"	91.5% (763)	8.5% (70)	–	100% (833)
(2) "Did the village take back your girl's land when she married into another village?"	53.4% (126)	46.6% (110)	–	100% (236)
(3) "Can a woman keep her land tenure after divorce?"	4.3% (36)	45.5% (380)	50.2% (419)	100% (835)

Note: Figures in the brackets are the numbers of the interviewed women to have given valid answers to the question. "–" Indicates that there are no multiple choices to the question.

Table 3.2 Distribution of Landless Women by Sample Villages

Villages	Vil. 1	Vil. 2	Vil. 3	Vil. 4	Vil. 5	Vil. 6	Vil. 7	Vil. 8	Vil. 9	Vil.10	Total
Frequency	0	0	1	4	1	2	20	2	24	16	70
Percentage	0.0	0.0	1.4	5.7	1.4	2.9	28.6	2.9	34.3	22.9	100.0

Table 3.3 Estimation of Probabilities of Women's Possession of Land Tenure (Logistic Modal)

The variable to be explained: Women's possession of land tenure (with land tenure = 1, without = 0)	Modal 1 (Observations = 832)		Modal 2 (Observations = 832)	
Explanatory variables	Parameter estimate	Standard error	Parameter estimate	Standard error
Annual net income per capita of village (Mean = 1547 yuan)	1.9253*	0.3353	2.7159*	0.3994
Land area per capita of village (Mean = 1.9 mu)	0.5251*	0.1530	0.6265*	0.1806
Number of households perennially working off village (Mean = 5.1)			−0.0637*	0.0270
Number of non-agricultural enterprises of village (Mean = 9.8)			−0.0558*	0.0163
Constant	−1.0809*	0.4761	−1.5206*	0.5345
Cases correctly predicted	91.6%		91.6%	
−2 Log Likelihood	423.67		402.24	
Goodness of Fit	1459.54		1178.84	
Chi-Square	56.82*		78.24*	

* The parameters are significant at 99% confidential level.

become the norm: a part of women (with their children) would remain landless[5] in their rural society. Thus, it can be concluded that gender inequality dramatically emerges in the dynamic process after land distribution, but does not explicitly occur at the time when villages are performing the distribution procedure. This inequality does not imply that women have no access to land tenure, rather it is represented by the fact that women are less or even not secure in their land rights compared with their spouses.

It is also striking that nearly 86% of landless women are concentrated in villages 7, 9, and 10 (Table 3.2). Although the figures do not yet provide evidence to prove that these three villages do not redistribute land regularly, they do indicate that whether women hold land tenure or not is closely related to the decisions made by the village communities they currently belong to.

Both regression functions presented in Table 3.3 demonstrate that the larger the land area and the higher the per capita income in a village community, the more likely it is that women will obtain land. The difference of the two equations can be noticed from function 2, which contains additional information about the non-agricultural employment opportunities available in the sample village. The information is indicated by the variables of the number of non-agricultural enterprises and the number of the households that travel out of their home villages for business opportunities. The estimated coefficients of the two explanatory variables testify that the more non-agricultural employment opportunities there are in a village, the less probability there is that women will obtain land tenure.

This result is consistent neither with the reality in the more developed regions of China nor with our expectations. However, it indicates the facts in rural Shanxi Province and can be explained by a variety of economic theories. Urbanization and industrialization in Shanxi Province lag far behind those in the southeast coastal area, thereby making it difficult for most of the rural laborers to find long-term non-agricultural jobs and earn steady non-agricultural income. Therefore, the majority of those working off-farm have been unwilling to scotch their land tenure claims. Furthermore, a considerable number of the households actually have to seek non-agricultural earning sources to supplement their agricultural income, because the yields of land are so low that the households cannot survive on agricultural income alone. This further explains why the increase in non-agricultural employment opportunities here does not necessarily lead to greater possibilities for additional village members to obtain access to land tenure. These arguments can be confirmed by the descriptive statistics from the sample data from rural Shanxi. In 1996, a male laborer on average worked 48 days in non-agricultural business and earned 17.3 yuan/day, whereas a female laborer worked 12 days and earned 6.6 yuan/day. During the same period 85% of all the rural laborers were still engaged in agriculture.

It is noticeable that the proportions of the households with landless women to the total sample households are as high as respectively 20.8%, 16.2% and 22.5% in villages 7, 9 and 10. However, the demand of such households on additional land plots[6] might not be strong enough to push the village communities to take action. This confirms once again the hypothesis that *when* the landless group obtains plots allocated by village communities and *how large* those plots would actually be does not relate to the individual characteristics of the landless, but rather depends directly on the decisions of the communities.

At the heart of the problem lies the fact that a village community can always find support for their decision in the various laws and governmental documents regardless of what decision they have made. A community conducting land redistribution according to population changes might argue that their decision complies with the Law of Land Administration (NPC, 1998). A village that does not balance land size by household size might use as the grounds for their decision the various policy documents regarding stabilizing long-term contract of farmland (CPC Central Committee, 1984, 1996).[7]

3.3 Impact of land right insecurity on women's status

The studies conducted by Indian and Bangladesh scholars (Agarwal, 1997; Subramanian, 1998) demonstrate that in southern Asian countries the holding of property

Table 3.4 Estimation of Probabilities of Women's Participation in Agricultural Decision-making (Logistic Modal)

The variable to be explained: Women's participation (part. = 1, else = 0)		Modal (Observations = 802)	
Explanatory variables	Mean	Parameter estimate	Standard error
Land tenure of women (with = 1, without = 0)	0.92	–.8118**	.3304
Annual agricultural work-days of wife of household head	106.4	.0037**	.0011
Age of wife of household head	45.2	.0981**	.0314
Age of male household head	47.6	–.1035**	.0307
Years of education of male head (9 years and above = 1, else = 0)	0.04	.7657*	.3971
Household location (dummy variables)			
Village 1	0.11	–1.7883**	.4706
Village 2	0.08	.7407*	.3522
Village 3	0.09	1.1692**	.3169
Village 4	0.08	–.4182	.3435
Village 5	0.11	.9674**	.3126
Village 6	0.11	.6375*	.3231
Village 7	0.11	–.8719**	.3322
Village 8	0.16	–	–
Village 9	0.07	1.6772**	.3796
Village 10	0.08	.6480*	.3181
Constant		.0338	.5813
Cases correctly predicted = 70.07%			
–2 Log Likelihood = 920.848			
Goodness of Fit = 794.359			
Chi-Square = 159.628**			

Note: "–" Reference group.

* The parameters are significant at 95% confidence level.
** The parameters are significant at 99% confidence level.

rights, including land rights by women, could substantially strengthen their intra-household bargaining. This research result allows us to postulate that women who actually possess their land shares allocated by village communities are more likely to participate in making the agricultural management decisions of their households. In the logistic regression model (Table 3.4) the managerial decision is indicated by the decision on marketing agricultural products as the participation in this process is thought essential to reflect the status of a family member in the management of a household economy. Moreover, the participation of the interviewed women in making decisions on plan of crops-growing and procurement of input goods is highly correlated with their participation in marketing decision-making.

The information about woman's participation was derived from the answers of the interviewed women. A woman was regarded as having participated in making decisions if she thought that it was she herself who decided, or if she thought that she had jointly participated with her husband in having decided the disposal of the farm produce. Alternatively, if a woman reported that it was her husband or other family members who determined these matters, she was regarded as not having taken part in making these decisions. Nearly 40% of 821 interviewed women did participate in making decisions. As the purpose of this study was to examine gender relations, those female-headed households bereft of the spouse were excluded in the logistic regression analysis.

Counter to our hypothesis, the regression results ascertained that the women with land tenure were less involved in making management decisions than those without the tenure. This can be explained by the fact that landless women in rural China actually hold predictable land tenure, i.e. they will receive land plots earlier or later from their villages in a redistribution process. Thus, *de facto* land tenure was less important than women's involvement in agricultural production for their participation in the decision-making process. Furthermore, in the households with landless members, the male labor was more likely involved in non-agricultural activities while the female worked in agriculture, resulting in a state where women probably tended to share more opportunities in making agricultural management decisions. The results of the estimation illustrate also that the individual characteristics (age and education) of the farmers engendered less prominent effects on women's participation in comparison to their household location presented by village dummy variables. This was because the women's participation to a large extent depended on the social, economic, and cultural environment they were living in while the village communities embodied most the features of that environment.

It is widely believed that women in poor households have suffered more seriously from poverty than other members of the households in those rural societies where the male's power dominates. Based on this understanding, the impact of land rights insecurity on women's economic well-being is mainly illustrated by estimations of the probability that the sample households will fall into poverty. The sample households overwhelmingly derive their livelihood from agriculture, and on average nearly 54% of their net income was attained from agriculture. Farmland remains the most important income source for farmers, especially poor farmers. Hence, we assume that the households of the landless women are more likely to fall into poverty without supplementary income from non-agricultural activities.

Again, a logistic regression model was employed to test the above assumption. The explained variable of the modal was deprived in such a way that a cut-off point at 600 yuan (equivalent to 36% of the mean annual net income per capita of the sample households) was used to classify the poor and the non-poor.[8] It was calculated that poor households accounted for 13.6% of the total sample. The results of the logistic regression confirmed that the households with landless women, smaller assets, fewer laborers, and fewer non-agricultural workdays more likely fell into poverty (Table 3.5). Here, the effects of the age and education level of the main labor on the household economic well-being also appeared to

Table 3.5 Estimation of Probabilities of Sample Households Falling into Poverty (Logistic Modal)

The variable to be explained: Household's poverty (the poor = 1, the non-poor = 0)		Modal Observation = 830	
Explanatory variables	Mean	Parameter estimate	Standard error
Land tenure of women (with = 1, without = 0)	0.9	−1.4282*	.3180
Original value of fixed assets per capita at end of 1996[1] (1000 yuan)	3.0	−.4796*	.0920
Annual non-agricultural workdays of the household couple	86.4	−.0040*	.0013
Number of family laborers	2.1	−.3153*	.1301
Age of the main laborer in household	43.8	−.0950	.1038
Years of education of the main laborer in household	6.5	−.1474	.1530
Constant		1.8476*	.6551
Cases correctly predicted = 87.23%			
−2 Log Likelihood = 517.14			
Goodness of Fit = 888.42			
Chi-Square = 97.51*			

[1] Here "fixed assets" include non-production and production assets but do not include land.
* The parameters are significant at 99% confidence level.

be insignificant. This may reveal that the dominant economic activities in rural Shanxi have not yet become skill- and technology-demanding so that the educational background of the laborers are not strictly relevant or required.

As the above statistical analyses prove that poverty is the final outcome for landless people, we have to revise those perceptions formulated 10 years ago about the features of poverty in rural areas. At that time, the authors believed that both the land reform undertaken in the 1950s and the household contract system implemented in the 1980s had fundamentally eliminated the class-based poverty resulting from the unequal distribution of the land ownership (Zhu, 1990). In present rural China there will always exist a landless group if the problem of insecure land rights of agricultural women is not solved when the period of land contracts is further extended. Without sufficient non-agricultural income sources, this group will most likely plunge into an asset-poor situation. Such proletarian poverty will no doubt result in a profound negative impact on the society.

3.4 Conclusion

From the analytical results it can be concluded that women's land rights have not yet been effectively secured in rural China. Although gender equality in land distribution appears to be protected in terms of the legislative framework and economic institutions, sufficient ambiguities remain to create loopholes in the day-to-day functioning.

At present, the insecurity of women's land rights is most prominently displayed by the fact that divorced women are less protected from losing their land tenure. Frequently, both the women re-locating due to marriage and their children who miss out on land distribution temporarily cannot obtain land tenure from their new villages. Although such a phenomenon has not yet significantly affected the intra-household bargaining power of the agricultural women, it does tend to reduce the households of the landless women to poverty. Therefore, it is pressing indeed now to amend the Land Administrative Law and those government regulations relevant to farmland tenure.

The village communities determine the fact of both land distribution and redistribution, and the decisions of the community were made following the traditions of a male-oriented rural society. Therefore, for the purpose of protecting women's land rights, it is necessary to emphasize clearly in the legislation that village communities must take the relevant laws as their criterion. Moreover, individual rights urgently need to be defined and protected by laws and policies during this economic transition. The logical outcome of our suggested changes in the legal framework is the insertion of gender perspective into the legislative and policy-making process. The active participation of rural women in this process will certainly contribute to these changes. Meanwhile, the diffusion of legal knowledge and information should be further undertaken so as to help rural women use the laws consciously to safeguard their own land rights. If this is not done, the progress in promoting gender equality in China achieved since the 1950s might regress under the appearance of a democratic decision-making process of the village community.

Notes

1 This survey was undertaken through the Rural Social and Economic Survey Network of the Ministry of Agriculture. All of the 10 sample villages are places selected by the Network for long-term observation in Shanxi Province. All of the 960 sample households are the bookkeeping households from those observation places. The sample population totals 3,623, of which women account for 48%. The collected data refer to the state of the sample villages, households and individuals in 1996.
2 15MU = 1ha.
3 According to the current residential registration system, villagers' committees identify the membership of villagers based upon their permanent residential records. Those who registered as permanent residents in the village but were out of the villages for years (perhaps engaged in non-agricultural business) would nevertheless hold their plots allocated by the community, or would still maintain their right to share the land plots upon their return to the village. On the other hand, migrants working in the village, even if living in their 'new' village for long periods, may only obtain a permit of temporary residence, and are not be able to enjoy the same rights as community members.
4 The statistics derived from the national sample survey on 1% of the population in China in 1995 tell the same story: divorced men accounted for 1% of the rural sample while the divorce rate of the rural women was not reported in the same sample (SSB, 1999).
5 During the period between 1980–90, about 1/3 of villages across the country did not redistribute land. (The Research Team for the "Study of Farmland System in China", 1993, pp. 38–39.)

6 Since the households contract system was implemented, it has become the prevailing phenomenon that every household sends only one person to participate in community meetings. In our sample, 82% of the households usually had their male heads attend the villagers' meetings. Given this situation women's voices would not be well expressed in the decision-making process of the village communities. Nevertheless, in terms of claiming land tenure, the interests of the landless women were consistent with those of their husbands and clans.

7 The CPC Central Committee document no.1 (1984) stipulated that the contract period for farmland should generally last more than 15 years, implying that 1980 was the starting point for the household contract system spreading across the country: the contract period would therefore end in 1995. In early 1996, the policy document regarding the second round of land contracts emphasized that the contract period should be extended to 30 years (CPC Central Committee, 1996). The two regulations not only supplied farmers with incentives to invest more in farmland, but also affirmed to the farmers a commitment to the implementation of the household contract system for the long run. This was especially meaningful for those farmers who had experienced enforced collectivization in the 1950s, and plays a positive role in protecting the interests of farmers as a whole as well as maintaining social stability (Jiang and Bao, 2000). Unfortunately, due to the absence of a gender perspective, these policies have tended to exacerbate the insecurity of women's land rights in patriarchal rural societies. For example, it was reported that several villages in Hunan Province, when settling the second round of farmers' land contracts, practiced what we might term a predictable allocation. Girls younger than 23 years old who expected to marry someone outside the village in the near future received nothing or less than the average area of the land plot. Males around 25 expected to marry in the near future acquired double or triple the per capita plot area (The Editorial Board of *The Newspaper of Chinese Women*, 1999).

8 The officials of the Poverty Reduction Office under the State Council informed the authors that the poverty line for rural China was set by the office at 580 yuan of per capita annual net income of a household for 1996.

References

Agarwal, B., 1997. "Bargaining" and gender relations: Within and beyond the household, in *Feminist Economics, Vol. 3*, no. 1, pp. 1–51.

Central Committee of the CPC, 1984. *Zhonggong Zhongyang Guanyu 1984 nian Nongcun Gongzuo de Tongzhi (Notice about the Rural Work in 1984, January 1)*. Shierda Yilai Zhongyao Wenxian Xuanbian (Selections of Important Policy Documents Issued since the 12th CPC Conference). Beijing: People's Publishing House.

Central Committee of the CPC, 1996. *Jinnian He Jiuwu Qijian Nongcun Gongzuo De Zhongdian He Zhengce Cuoshi (Main Tasks and Policy Measures of the Rural Working in the Ninth Five-Year-Plan Period and This Year, January 21)*. Shisida Yilai Zhongyao Wenxian Xuanbian (Selections of Important Policy Documents Issued since the 14th CPC Conference). Beijing: People's Publishing House, pp. 424–439.

The Editorial Board of *The Newspaper of Chinese Women*, 1999. Tudi Chengbao Zhong Weihu Funue Hefa Quanyi Xilie Baodao (*A Series of Reports on Protection of Women's Legal Rights to Land Contract*), published by Zhongguo Funuebao (*The Newspaper of Chinese Women*), March 4–April 8, Beijing.

FAO Women and Population Division, 2000. Women and Land Tenure, FAO web site on Food Security, http://www.fao/sd/fsdirect/FSP002.htm, May 30.

Jiang Ailin and Bao Jixiang, 2000. Tudi Chengbaoqi Cong 15 Nian Yanchang Dao 30 Nian (To Extend the Contract Period of Land Tenure from 15 Years to 30 Years), in *Zhongguo*

Guoqing Guoli (in *Journal of National Conditions and Capacity of China*), *Vol. 5*, pp. 6–9, Beijing.

NPC, 1954. Zhonghua Renmingongheguo Xianfa (*The Constitution of the People's Republic of China*), in Chen Hefu ed., Zhongguo Xianfalaibian (*The Compilation of China's Constitutions*), Chinese Social Sciences Publishing House, printed in 1980, p. 233, Beijing.

NPC, 1980. Zhonghua Renmingongheguo Hunyinfa (*The Marriage Law of the People's Republic of China*), Chinese Law Publishing House, printed in 1996, pp. 2–3 and 6, Beijing.

NPC, 1985. Zhonghua Renmingongheguo Jichengfa (*The Inheritance Act of the People's Republic of China*), Chinese Law Publishing House, 1996, pp. 2 and 8, Beijing.

NPC, 1992. Zhonghua Renmingongheguo Funue Quanyi Baozhangfa (*The Law of Protection of Women's Rights of the People's Republic of China*), Chinese Law Publishing House, printed in 1996, p. 15, Beijing.

NPC, 1998. Zhonghua Renmingongheguo Tudi Guanlifa (*The Land Administrative Law of the People's Republic of China*), Chinese Law Publishing House, printed in 1999, pp. 5–7, Beijing.

The Office for Rural Observation Points of the Ministry of Agriculture, 1992. Quanguo Nongcun Shehui Jingji Dianxing Diaocha Shuju Huibian (*Data Collections of Sample Surveys on the Rural Society and Economy of China*), CPC Party's School Publishing House, pp. 4–6, Beijing.

Quisumbing, A.R., Payongayong, E., Aidoo, J.B., and Otsuka, K., 1999. Women's Land Rights in the Transition to Individualized Ownership: Implication for the Management of Tree Resources in Western Ghana, IFPRI, FCND Discussion Paper No. 58, February, Washington, DC.

The Research Team for the "Study of Farmland System in China", 1993. Zhongguo Nongcun Tudi Zhidu De Biange (*Changes of Land System in Rural China*), Beijing University Publishing House, pp. 16–18 and 39, Beijing.

State Statistics Bureau, 1999. Zhongguo Shehui Zhong De Nanren He Nueren, – Shishi He Shuju (*Women and Men in the Chinese Society, – Facts and Figures*), The Statistics Publishing House of China, Beijing.

Subramanian, J. 1998. Rural Women's Rights to Property: A Bangladesh Case Study. A report prepared for the International Food and Policy Research Institute (IFPRI), March, Washington, DC.

Zhu Ling, 1990. Gonggong Gongcheng Dui Xiangcun Pinkun Diqu Jingji Zengzhang, Jiuye He Shehui Fuwu De Yingxiang (*Effects of Public Works on the Economic Growth, Employment and Social Services in the Poor Rural Areas*), in Jingji Yanjiu (*Journal of Economic Research*), *Vol. 10*, Beijing.

Part II
Food security and the future of small farmers

4 Development in Tibetan agriculture

During the recent two decades, the weakening in accessibility to the basic public goods has become a common problem in the most inland provinces and it is in particular the case in less-developed regions. In contrast to this situation, the local government in Tibet has secured the normal operation of the agricultural supporting system, strengthened investment in primary education and basic health care, as well as guaranteed social assistance to the key vulnerable groups. The most important reason is considered that the large-sized regional aid enables the local government to perform its public function with adequate fiscal resources. Second, the supervision existing outside has driven the local government to maintain the sufficient political will to provide the low-income groups the basic public services at a low cost or free of charge. This is essentially a type of investment-oriented income redistribution. In both the short and long terms it will contribute to reduce the economic inequality that the operation of the market mechanism brought about. In another words, it will help to narrow the regional, sectorial and individual gaps.

Through observing the basic public services that the farmers and herdsmen obtained, this research report is devoted to evaluating the local governments' effort for poverty alleviation in rural Tibet. Firstly, the roles of the agricultural support system in realizing the food security will be identified. Secondly, the public services that could directly improve the household welfare of farmers and herdsmen will be examined. Finally, we will explore the possibilities for the poor to get rid of poverty by creating non-agricultural employment opportunities. The information in the report mainly stems from three respects: First, the published statistics and literature; Second, governmental documents, work reports, contracts between governments and enterprises, obligation statements concluded by the superior and the subordinate governments, and public bulletin of service providers; Third, the meetings between the research team and the government officials at different levels in studied areas, visits in the public service providers, discussions with the villagers' committees, interviews with farmers, herdsmen, entrepreneurs, workers and merchants.

(Originally published in *Population Science of China*, 2004 with the title "Labor Migration in Marketization Process in Tibet".)

4.1 Agricultural supporting system and food security

The output of agriculture[1] amounts to about one-third of the GDP and the agricultural sector contains nearly one million people that account for 80 per cent of the native laborers in Tibet. The agricultural laborers mainly gain their incomes from cropping production and pasturing husbandry even though sometimes they more or less engaged in non-agricultural works. Furthermore, their families directly consume the major part of the agricultural products while the amount of residual products that could be sold is very limited. By 2000, food consumption still made 80 per cent of the total consumption expenditure of the agricultural households.[2] These phenomena endow Tibetan agriculture with the characteristics of a subsistence economy. The significance of cropping production and pasturing husbandry not merely lies in the fact that most Tibetans live on the agricultural sector. It also means that agriculture is a kind of life style. Then, the agricultural development may not only help most Tibetans to achieve food security, but also it may raise their family income. From this point of the view, the public policies that promote agricultural development will contribute to the welfare improvement of the Tibetan people.

At present the agricultural villages still shape the Tibetan society at a grassroots level. It is also the realm that the seasonally migrated labor from other ethnic groups rarely get involved in. Since the 1950s, the factors that have significantly influenced the village life in Tibet consist of the changes in socioeconomic systems and the lasting investment that the government made in agriculture.[3] The radical changes that are worthwhile to pay close attention to include the abolition of the serf system during the period from the end of the 1950s to the beginning of the 1960s, the establishment of the People's Communes in the mid 1970s, and the replacement of the agricultural collectives with the household-based production system in the mid 1980s. A recent impact on rural life was brought about by the preferential policies that the central government formulated in the 1990s for accelerating the socioeconomic development of Tibet.

The agricultural development can be seen as a reflection of the effects of the institutional changes and the public investment in Tibet. Figures 4.1, 4.2, and 4.3 clearly depict the achievements in sectorial expansion and strengthening of intensity in the cropping production and pasturing husbandry in the recent 50 years. Since the later 1990s, either the output or the intensity has kept on a high level during the statistical period. This growth tendency is closely related to the constantly strengthened public investments and services in agriculture from the beginning of the 1990s as described below:

- First, the government disburses nearly 300 million yuan annually[4] to invest in agricultural infrastructure projects such as improving meadows and constructing irrigation works, etc.
- Second, with the public financial resources the systems of technological extension, plant protection and veterinarian services are still effectively running in the marketization process. The performance of the agricultural

supporting system in Naidong County can be taken as an example. The financial expenditure of the county government on agriculture amounted to 700,000 yuan in 2003. It implies nearly 45 yuan for each person assuming apportioning the money fairly to the total of 54,000 agricultural laborers.[5] The part-time technicians who are trained farmers responsible for technological extension, protection of crops, livestock and forests at village level are still working in the administrative villages. These farmer-technicians are received free technical trainings every year at the township and county levels respectively. Moreover, the financial bureaus at the TAR, the prefecture and the county levels share the expenses on disease prevention of crops, sheep and cattle. Commonly, the agricultural bureau at the county level provides pesticides and organizes the farmer-technicians to spray in a designated period. The animal epidemic prevention station organizes at least twice a year vaccine injections for livestock in the county. The animal epidemic prevention workers at village level who also work part-time are responsible for injecting the vaccines for the total of 50,000 cattle and 100,000 sheep. In the pure pasturing area, for example, Dangxiong County, located in the north plateau in Tibet, the husbandry bureau provides herdsmen animal remedies specifically free of charge for curing dysenteries of cattle and sheep. The livestock preventive system is especially important for ensuring the food and income security of the herdsmen living in the border areas because the yak, cattle and sheep come and go across the border often. According to the introduction of the villagers in Yadong County, the unified immunization system prevents the yak, cattle and sheep almost entirely from the infectious diseases at the Chinese side of the border, while in the adjacent Bhutan, the livestock there often die due to illness because of lacking such measures.

- Third, the local governments collaborate with village communities in maintaining the agricultural supporting system. The production services at village level are one of the most needed and used public services. It is an organizational prerequisite for farmers and herdsmen to enjoy convenient and reliable production services by keeping and developing the farmer-technician teams. Some of the county governments pay regular wages to the farmer-technicians in order to maintain the team. For example, the financial bureau in Dangxiong County pays 200–800 yuan per month to 212 folk veterinarians with different qualifications in the county.[6] Furthermore, some villagers' committees subsidize farmer-technicians a certain amount of working allowances with the financial resources of their villages. For instance, the villagers' committee in Kesong Village in Naidong County disposes the technicians 5 yuan a workday according to the time they spent on the public services when the village account is settled at the end of a year. Though such a payment is less than half of the daily wages of the unskilled workers in the locale, it contains the committee's expectation and villagers' respect and thus encourages the technicians to put their weight to serve the village.

- Fourth, the collaboration between the local governments and herdsmen in prevention and reduction of natural disasters has been going on. The climate of Tibetan Plateau is changeful while natural disasters frequently happen. According to historical records, snow disasters have averagely occurred every 3 years since 1816.[7] In addition hails take place occasionally and floods come about wherever the rivers are numerous. Therefore, the hail prevention outlay is budgeted into the agricultural supporting funds of the counties in the cropping production areas and it is mainly used on dissolving hails with cannons. In the pasturing husbandry areas, the fodder store funds are included in the local government budgets. For example, the government of Ningzhong Township in Dangxiong County spends annually about 20,000 yuan on purchasing, drying and storing grasses. The herdsmen in the same township are eligible to obtain the dried grasses just paying with the cost-cover prices whenever snow disaster occurs.[8] The herdsmen's households preserve not only the forage grasses but also food grain sufficient for their family consumption at least one year. In case a disaster takes place, the herdsmen in disaster-affected areas usually try to alleviate the possible damages in a way of grazing in the disaster-unaffected areas besides the government's relief measures. Such mutual assistances among herdsmen existed in the Tibetan history and they still function well at present. This might be related to the fact that both the ownership and utilization of the meadow remain collective from the period of the People's Commune up to now. An effective measure to resist floods is to build dams. It was estimated that a total of 300,000 yuan is needed for investing in construction of the riverbank in Ningzhong Township. However, the herdsmen are not able to afford the riverbank since the total number of the households is less than 800 and per capita net income of the households was only around 2000 yuan in 2002. In this case the pasturing husbandry bureau in Dangxiong County provided the necessary funds and machines while all the villages in the township shared the labor input according to their population size.

- Fifth, the central government has been adopting a preferential policy to Tibetan farmers and herdsmen all the time, for example agricultural tax-exemptions.

The public support stated above and the agricultural reform that provided farmers and herdsmen an incentive to produce more and sell more brought about a continuous agricultural growth over the past 15 years. This resulted in an increasing food supply in the farming and pasturing areas. In 2000, per capita agricultural products in 18 poor counties in the Tibetan Autonomous Region are reported to 415 kilograms of food grain, 19 kilograms of rapeseeds, 64 kilograms of meat and 73 kilograms of milk.[9] With regard to the poor households weak in the production capacity and payment for food, the local governments at different levels have rendered them food relief besides assisting them with capital inputs through anti-poverty programs.[10] Such supporting measures can be read from the case that the author studied in Jijiao Village in Lazi County. All households in Jijiao Village are purely engaging in pasturing husbandry. The village was moved to the highland 5000 meters above the sea level because of the warming-up climate and the rising snow line. All houses in the relocated village were built at the cost of the governments and the poor households also receive the relief in food grain every year. For example, the shepherd Wangda couple have 5 children and own 130 sheep. In 2003 they obtained about 1320 kilograms of the highland barley with 20 sheep (a sheep was changed for 66 kilograms of highland barley) that were not sufficient to meet the needs of their family. Therefore the couple received 450 kilograms of relief grain from the department of civil affairs in the township government.

In the valley areas where the natural conditions are relatively favorable to agriculture, the majority of the rural households already achieved food security. In the past 5 years, a total of 35–40 million kilograms of food grain have been put in the governmental storage every year such that the grain stock expanded to 250 million kilograms in 2003. Though the current situation is actually caused by the fact that the grain produced was in poor quality while the government had to purchase it at the supporting prices, the volume of the stock reflects the size of the surplus grain that the Tibetan farmers produced. In response to the problem of the grain surplus, the local governments have promoted structural adjustment in agricultural sector. A few commercialized production branches have gradually emerged, such as greenhouse vegetables, scaled chicken feeding and fast sheep breeding that directly meet the food demands of the increasing urban population. This is considered a result of the extension of the appropriate technologies and an apparent contribution of the public supporting system to the Tibetan agricultural development.

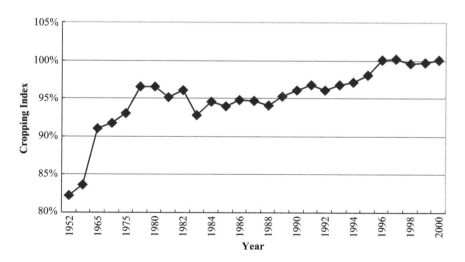

Figure 4.1 Changes in Multi-Cropping Indices of Cultivated Land in Tibetan Autonomous Region (1952~2000)

Source: *Tibet Statistical Yearbook 2001*, Table 9–15 and 9–17, www.tibetinfor.com.cn

Figure 4.2 Changes in the Size of Livestock (1952~2000)

Source: *Tibet Statistical Yearbook 2001*, Table 9–23, www.tibetinfor.com.cn

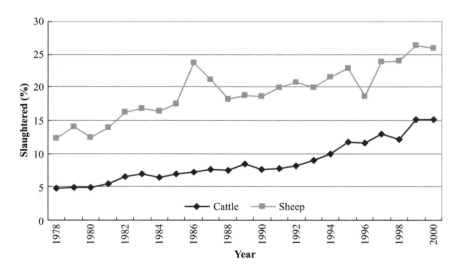

Figure 4.3 Change in Slaughtered Rate of Cattle and Sheep (1978–2000)

Source: *Tibet Statistical Yearbook 2001*, Table 9–24, www.tibetinfor.com.cn

Table 4.1 The Crops Yield of the Unit Area in Naidong County*

Crops	Wheat	Rapeseed	Highland barley	Potato	Fodder-maize
Reported yield (jin/1.6 mu)	1200	400	900	2500	500
Yield of unit area (jin /mu)	750	250	562	1563	312
National average** (jin /mu)	(720)	220	(1300)	2600	1600

*The figures referring to crops yield in Naidong were acquired from the meeting held in the agricultural bureau in Naidong County on August 25, 2003. The commonly used measure of the cultivated area in Naidong County is also called "mu" but it is actually equivalent to 1.5–1.6 mu. 1 hector =15 mu.

**The figures of the national average can be found from the Agricultural Information 2002–03, www. agri.gov.cn/xxlb. It must be noticed that the varieties of the wheat and barley growing in Naidong County are different from what have been planted in other regions in China.

Table 4.2 Production Activities of the Farmers in Muba Village in Gongbujiangda County*

Month	Jan-Feb	Feb-Mar	Mar-May	Jun-Jul	Aug	Sept-Oct	Nov-Dec
Activities	Fuel collection	Sowing barley and rapes; Fertilization	Gathering aweto	Gathering mushroom	Harvest: rapeseed, wheat, barley	Sowing wheat fertilization	Level off land, transport manure

* Table 4.2 was formulated with the information provided by three male farmers in Muba village on August 3, 2003. They told the author that women in all households engage in animal husbandry over an entire year, for example take care of draught cattle, cows and pigs, etc.

Table 4.3 Production of a Farming Household in Kanglai Village in Lazi County*

	Jan-Feb	Mar	April	May	Jun-Aug	Sept	Oct-Nov	Dec
Jiacan and his eldest son	Celebrating New Year; piecemeal-farming work	Fertili-zation	Sowing wheat	Sowing barley, rapes and peas	Field work Growing vegetables	Harvest	Thresh produce	Piece-meal farming work
Jiacan's brother	Ditto	Off-farm work far away from Lazi County					Turning back home	Ditto
Female HH head	Taking care of children and housework							

* The information listed in Table 4.3 was collected through the author's visit to Jiacan, a part-time health worker in Kanglai Village and the wife of Jiacan with his brother (the family is based on a multi-partners marriage) on 9 August 2003. The male head of the household is Jiacan. Besides the 4 members stated in the table, there are 3 other children aged below 14 years and Jiacan's aunt living together in the family. The household cultivates 25 mu of land, owns 2 cows and 3 horses. In addition, Jiacan trusted the village shepherd to take care of 22 sheep of his family.

Table 4.4 Labor Division of a Family with Pasturing Husbandry in Qucai Village, Ningzhong Township, Dangxiong County*

Family members	Jimei, two adult sons	Brother Zenguo	Brother Gongga	Daughter	Teenage Son	Female head of HH
Activities	Running own shop in Bange County for purchasing and marketing fur and cashmere	Housework and unskilled non-agricultural job	Caring grazing sheep	Caring grazing cattle	Schoolboy	Housework
Cash income	40000 yuan/ year	700 yuan (2003)	–	–	–	–

* Table 4.4 is formulated with the information mainly provided by Zengguo on 29 August 2003. The male head of the household is Jimei (the family is based on a multi-partners marriage). The household owns 53 yak, 20 sheep and 12 goats. At the time when the author made the interview, there was no produce to be sold yet in 2003.

4.2 Investing in human resources and social services

During the recent two decades, the financing responsibility of the government on public services has been partly shifted to the market under the decentralized fiscal reforms undertaken in the inland provinces. This brought about two-sided results: on the one hand the provision of the basic public services such as disease prevention has plunged at the lower level in both quantity and quality than what the society needs in the less developed regions; on the other hand, the services, for instance, basic education and medical care, have become so expensive that the low-income families even cannot afford them. One of the social consequences can be observed from the reducing accessibility and availability for the poor to these basic services. In contrast to this situation, the continuously increasing investment in public services in the TAR can be considered an exception. With the growing public transfers channeled by the central government, the local governments at the different levels in the TAR have persistently invested in the following fields:

• *Firstly, obligatory education:* a free accommodation system for the school-children has been implemented with a purpose of alleviating the transport difficulties for the students whose home locations are very scattered in the farming and pasturing areas. In addition, the children are also eligible to receive food and clothes for free in middle and primary schools. The effectiveness of these policies can be noticed from the educational backgrounds of the different age groups. Among the family members of the farmers and herdsmen whom our research team interviewed, the kids above 7 years old are all covered by school education.[11] A part of the adults below the age 30, especially the male labor in this group, experienced 3 years schooling. The illiterate apparently formed a large group of the interviewed over age 30.

• *Secondly, the subsidized cooperative medical system*: prior to the second half of 2003 when the new-type of the Rural Cooperative Medical System (RCMS) was put into a nation-wide experiment, the central government never financed any RCMS in the inland provinces. However, it has annually provided the rural Tibetan medical subsidies with its fiscal resources. The annual subsidy averaged 5 yuan for each rural Tibetan before 1992 while it increased up to 15 yuan by 2002 when the central required the local governments to appropriate matching funds with a ratio of 1:1 for supporting the RCMS. Under the governmental support the RCMS covered 80 per cent of the rural Tibetans by now. All the households that the author visited participated in the RCMS. Their family medical accounts showed that there were more or less family members to have seen doctors for the medical treatments on light diseases, although the reimbursement that they obtained from the RCMS funds was very limited.

• *Thirdly, subsistence guarantee measures:* besides the aid at emergencies and the regular relief described in the last section, the local government and the village communities have collaborated in guaranteeing the minimum living standard of the aged who live alone. Generally, the government provides the aged financial assistance while the villagers' committee organizes the households to take care of them in rotation.

• *Fourthly, energy and drinking water supply:* in terms of the varieties of the energy supply, Tibet can be rated as the number one among the different regions in China. Besides the energy derived from water, coal and diesel oil, the wind force, earth heat and solar power are also applied as energy sources.[12] However, the fuel that most rural families use for cooking is still faggot and cattle manure. The progress in the energy supply for the rural people mainly emerged as a way of acquiring the access to electricity that has significantly improved the quality of their life. A number of small sized hydroelectric stations have energized the power that the rural households consumed to a large extent for lightening and operation of the small electronic devices. In the counties of Lazi, Jiangzi and Naidong, which are rich in sunshine, a part of the households often employs solar cooker to boil water. With regard to the drinking water supply, those who have benefited from the tap water services are mostly inhabited in the large villages near water sources. The other beneficiaries, who acquired safe water through the construction projects on drinking water supply systems in the recent decade, account for about 20 per cent of the rural residents.[13] The utility of the installations for the safe drinking water supply lies in that it is not only decisive for maintaining the health security of the rural people, but also the safe water supply facilities can function well for preventing the women acquiring diseases brought about by the heavy task of carrying water every day.

- *Finally, telecommunication and satellite TV services*: it can be observed that the information technologies adopted in the TAR are as advanced as what applied in the developed provinces. For example, the mobile phone can be used everywhere for both the nation-wide and international communication. However, it must be pointed out that the digital divide between the urban and rural sectors is considerably wide. It is manifested by the fact that the use of computers and Internet has not yet extended to rural Tibet. Moreover, the urban-rural gap and the disparities between the rural income groups are evident in the possession of TV sets and telephones. Though the transmission of the broadcast and television covered 50 per cent of the population in the TAR, per 100 urban households possessed 120 TV sets while per 100 rural households only 14 sets. Moreover, the total telephone subscribers in the TAR amounted to 380 thousand, that implies every 7 residents a subscriber when the entire population is taken into account. In point of the rural population the ratio of the phone possession was estimated for 0.2 per 100 households only.[14] According to our observation in the fieldwork, the pay phone became a good business of the groceries in the non-poor villages while in the poor villages phone access was rarely found. Furthermore, a TV set not only made a sign of the well to do families but also it played a role in the groceries for attracting customers in the villages with access to electricity.

The provision of the services stated above is considered in favor of the rural people in various dimensions. Some services, for instance the social relief measures, play a key role in subsistence security, while the others, such as the improved facilities for energy and drinking water supply, directly enhance the quality of life. The basic education, basic health protection and information services could evidently promote the development. No matter what specific function the single service performs, all of them could fundamentally contribute to poverty reduction through improving the human resources of the poor and strengthening the capability of the vulnerable groups in resisting natural and market risks. It is then understood that to ensure the poor to obtain these services free of charge or for low prices by means of public investment and social assistance could also contribute to narrowing the economic disparities between different regions, industries and social groups.

Undoubtedly, the government is obligated to guarantee the provision of the basic public services since fulfillment of such responsibilities is related to the performance of the public power (Bukannan, 1992; World Bank, 2003). It implies to resign a part of the public power and lose the political resources founded on the general public support if the government shirks its responsibilities in financing the basic services. At present, the dissatisfaction among the general public has been aggravated because of the insufficient supply and extremely unequal distribution of the public services in most Midwestern provinces. This case explains the above arguments from a negative side whilst the Tibetan case proves the same logic from the positive side. The direct causes that made the Tibetan case special lie in the following facts. Firstly, the nation-wide intensive assistance enables the local governments at the different levels in the TAR to possess the amount of financial resources necessary for implementing their public functions. Secondly, both the central and the local governments maintain a strong political will to ensure the provision of the basic services.

What are the major motives backing such a political will? It is not difficult to observe that the Tibetan development is one of the subjects that the decision makers at the top level of the Chinese government have always paid close attention to if the frequencies of the publication of the White Paper on the Tibetan development issues are viewed as a measurement. The White Paper concerning the socioeconomic development in the TAR was most frequently announced in the recent decade in comparison with that specifically referring to the other autonomous regions and provinces.[15] This can be further considered as a response of the state to the interest existing in both the domestic and international communities about the Tibetan development. No matter why the interest is engendered and no matter where it comes from, it has already become a kind of effective supervision to gather the information openness together. This is exactly in deficiency in the most inland provinces. It is then assumed that the transparency of the governance can be enhanced through intensified information dissemination about the provinces that even cannot attract attention from the external world as the TAR. In this way both the central and provincial governments may more or less receive the external supervision that would promote the improvement in the provision of the public services.

4.3 Creation of the non-agricultural employment

The improved food safety and health care brought about a rapid growth in the size of the Tibetan population. During the period of 1980–2000, the number of the Tibetan who were inhabited in the TAR increased by more than 40 per cent (1980: 1,718,238 people, 2000: 2,421,856 people).[16] Meanwhile, though the agricultural productivity achieved an evident progress, the per capita agricultural land has been gradually reducing. This on one hand drives the farmers and herdsmen to make the best from the agricultural potential, while on the other hand it pushes them to try their best to attain higher incomes from the gainful non-agricultural employment opportunities.

However, the ecological limits on the agricultural growth are more strict in the Tibetan plateau than those in the other regions due to the peculiar geographical and climate environment. Regarding the pasture husbandry, the seriously over-loaded livestock on the existing meadows has led to a noticeable degradation of grassland. The theoretical carrying capacity of the meadows in the TAR was estimated for one sheep-unit per 30 mu of the grassland. The meadows in Dangxiong County are well known as one of the best in Tibet in terms of the grass quality, yet the over-loading rate reached to 170 per cent; the ecological burden is too heavy for the meadows to bear. On 10.37 million mu of the meadows in Dangxiong there are 200 thousand yaks, 230 thousand sheep, 120 thousand goats and more than 7700 horses that are converted into 942 thousand sheep unit, i.e. one sheep unit is carried on 11 mu of the meadows.[17] Under the consideration of solving the problems of the fodder shortage, the county Bureau of Animal Husbandry organized to cultivate 40 thousand mu of the artificial meadows during the recent years. It is realized that several new ecological problems have resulted from the fact that the strong wind blew away the fertile soil layer of the cultivated meadows in winter.

In the farming areas not only the arable land is scarce,[18] but also the existing cultivated land is reducing along with the urbanization and development of the infrastructure construction. Now the per capita cultivated land is calculated for less than 1.5 mu.[19] Moreover, the main crops (wheat, rapeseeds, highland barley and potatoes) can be harvested only once a year because of the climatic limitation. The annual yields of the unit area are inevitably lower than those in the farming land on plains and hills. Naidong County is located in an area with the most productive crops production in the TAR where the unit area yields of wheat and rapeseeds are approximately comparative to the national average when the differences in the varieties are not accounted for. However, the potato yields per unit area are apparently 30–40 per cent below the level of the national average (Table 4.1). In any case, the income increment that can be anticipated from the increase in the yields per unit area is still very limited, even if more advanced technologies are continuously applied and the input is more intensive. An alternative strategy is suggested for developing the cash crops with high added value through adjusting the cropping pattern.[20] In reality the strategy is only feasible for the suburbs and the locations where the traffic is relatively convenient and the market demands on those higher value-added produce have increasingly emerged at present.

The current commercialized agriculture cannot totally absorb the existing surplus labor, nor can it bring about a continuing income growth in a visible near future. This is similar to the situation in other rural provinces and regions. The way out of such a predicament is nothing different from the efforts made everywhere in rural China for creating non-agricultural employment opportunities. Especially it is essential for reducing income inequality in the TAR, as per capita rural net income is still ranked at the last position in the nation while the urban-rural income gap stands at the first. In 2002, per capita net income of an average household of the farmers and herdsmen was reported for 1570 yuan; that was equivalent to 63 per cent of the national average (2476 yuan). The ratio of the urban income to the rural was estimated for 3.1:1 in the entire China but nearly 5:1 in the TAR.

Both the government officials and scholars have viewed tourism as the most promising sector given that the manufacturing lacks comparative advantages in Tibet. At present the annual number of the tourists maintains at the level of one million visitors while the number of employees who have been directly or indirectly absorbed in the tourism sector totals around 40 thousand. In a foreseeable short term, tourism does not seem to become a backbone industry to contain the rural surplus labor. Aware of the current restraints, the farmers and herdsmen have made their rational choices to meet market demands based on their own resource endowments in seeking additional income sources. Tables 4.2–4.4 show the patterns of the labor division and working time arrangements within the households living at different altitudes. The farmers in Muba Village in Gongbujiangda County located at 3000 meters over the sea level earn their cash income through harvesting byproducts of forestry such as aweto and mushroom besides crop and livestock production. Kanglai village is located at altitude of 4000 meters in Lazi County, characterized as an agricultural area with both crops production and pasturing husbandry. Every household in the village has one or two members seasonally working in the infrastructure construction sites on the northern Tibetan plateau. Qucai village in Dangxiong County, located at 4300 meters above sea level, belongs to a pure pasturing area. The non-agricultural income sources of the villagers mainly consists of the trade and unskilled work in construction sites.

Currently the majority of the farmers and herdsmen obtain their non-agricultural income from the unskilled work while only a few of them run businesses or hold skilled job positions outside of their home villages (see: Goldstein et al., 2003). With a purpose of assisting the farmers and herdsmen to acquire more skilled jobs, the public services relating to human capital formation and assets creation need to be adjusted in the following aspects: first, it is necessary for the government to put more emphases on improving the qualities of the basic health care and primary education instead of laying overwhelmingly the weight on expansion of the hardware investment. Second, the non-agricultural employment oriented skill training and information services need to be addressed. Third, an incentive system shall be designed for the financial institutions in order to provide more convenient services for the farmers and herdsmen in engaging in non-agricultural activities. Fourth, more rural public works combined with job creation shall be set up specifically for the Tibetan villages.

4.4 Summary

The systems for public goods and service provision such as the agricultural supporting system, primary education, basic health care and information services have significantly contributed to the food security, poverty reduction, human capital formation and family welfare in the rural Tibetan Autonomous Region. It is evident that assisting the poor, the vulnerable groups and the less developed regions by means of providing public goods and services plays an important role in the income redistribution with an investment orientation. Such a way is practiced in the present TAR actually with several prerequisites. On one hand an enormous public transfer has been continuously derived from the central government and the provincial governments in the relatively developed regions; on the other hand the information announcement system of the central government has virtually left the local governments in the TAR under a nation-wide supervision in respect of fulfilling their public functions. It is also commonly realized that a sustainable rural income growth in the long run depends heavily on job creation in the non-agricultural sectors. This requires more from the provision of public services: namely the services oriented to human resource advancement and those targeted to the farmers and herdsmen for establishing undertakings. Under the market economy, it is a key factor for the rural people to participate in and to benefit from the nation-wide socioeconomic development by enhancing their capacity for job creation and assets accumulation.

Notes

 1 Herein and thereafter "agriculture" indicates farming and pasturing husbandry in the report.
 2 The calculation is based on the data issued by the China Tibet Information Center. See: *Tibet Statistical Yearbook 2001*, Table 8–15, http://www.tibetinfor.com.cn
 3 See: Duojiecaidan and Jiangcunluobu eds., 1995, *A Brief History of Tibetan Economy*, The Tibetology Publishing House of China, Beijing, pp. 200–209.
 4 Source: The interview with Mr. Ciwangduobujie, Deputy Director from the Office for Poverty Alleviation in TAR (Tibetan Autonomous Region), 31 of July 2003.
 5 Source: Discussion with Mr. Wang Jun and Mr. Huang Weijun, the officials of Agricultural Bureau in Naidong County, 25 of August 2003.
 6 Source: The interview with Mr. Guo Wanjun, a deputy director of the pasturing husbandry bureau in Dangxiong County, 29 of August 2003.
 7 See: Yang Qinye and Zheng Du, 2001, *Tibet Geography*, Five Continents Information Dissemination Publishing House, Beijing, pp. 34–36.
 8 See: Zhaluo, 2003, "Nip in the Bud" (a case story included in the monograph of *Marketization and Public Services*, to be published by Minzu Publishing House, Beijing).
 9 Source: The interview with Mr. Ciwangduobujie, Deputy Director from the Office for Poverty Alleviation in TAR, 31 of July 2003.
10 According to the introduction of Mr. Ciwangduobujie, the poverty line was set per capita annual net income 700 yuan for the households engaging in pasturing husbandry, 650 yuan for those engaging in crops production and pasturing husbandry part-time, 600 yuan for the pure crops growers' households in 1994. According to this criterion the rural poor amounted to 70,000 people in 2000 and accounted for 3.2 per cent of the rural population in the TAR. In fact, about 1.2 million rural people whose annual net income is below 1300 yuan are all classified as the targeted group eligible to receive special support from the current anti-poverty programs.
11 According to the White Paper "The Modernization Development of Tibet" issued by the information office of the State Council, the school enrollment rate in the TAR nearly reached 86 per cent in 2000. (http://www.people.com.cn / Chinese Government's White Paper, November 8, 2001)
12 See: *Tibetan Daily News* on August 16, 2002, Tibetan Energy Resource and Technology, http://www.chinatibetnews.com/GB/channel10/62/200208/16
13 Source: The interview with Mr. Ciwangduobujie, Deputy Director from the Office for Poverty Alleviation in TAR, 31 of July 2003, and the Statistics Center of the Ministry of Health, 2004, Digest of Health Statistics, pp. 82–83, http://www.moh.gov.cn/statistics/digest04/s82.htm
14 Source: Tibet Information Center, 2001, *Tibet Statistical Yearbook*, Table 8–5,8–6,8–18, http://www.tibetinfor.com.cn/zt/tongji; http://www.tibetinfor.com.cn/zt/newyear/news/1–09.htm; http://www.chinatibetnews.com/GB/channel5/38/200208/19/2138.html
15 See: The White Paper of the Chinese Government, http://www.people.com.cn/GB/shizheng/252/2229
16 Source: Tibet Information Center, 2001, *Tibet Statistical Yearbook*, Table 3–4, http://www.tibetinfor.com.cn/zt/tongji/03/3–4
17 According to the explanations of the State Statistics Bureau, a sheep unit is estimated based on the daily grass consumption of an adult sheep on average in a sample region during a season or a year. With this benchmark the following formulas are applied for estimating the carrying capacities of the meadows: 1 horse = 6 sheep unit, 1 yak= 4

sheep unit, 1goat = 0.8 sheep unit, a suckling animal = 1/3 grown animal, an ablactated animal in the birth year = 1/2 grown animal, a young animal = 3/4 grown animal. http://www.zhb.gov.cn/download/1055362444823.doc

18 Liu Huiqing, Xu Jiawei and Wu Xiuqin, 2003, An Appraisal on the Health of the Eco-logical System in Naidong County in the TAR, in *Geography Science*, No. 3, Volume 23, pp. 366–371.

19 It was reported that the area of the cultivated land in Tibet decreased by 130 thousands mu during the period of 1981–1990. See: Jiang Bin, 2002, The Migration of the Rural Surplus Labor into the Small Towns in the TAR, in *Journal of the Southwest College for the Minority Ethnic Groups*, philosophical and social scientific edition, No. 9, pp. 17–20.

20 See: Chinese Academy of Sciences, 2001, Suggestions for Achieving the Development in a Way of Striding over a Few Developing Stages in Tibet, http://www.cas.ac.cn/html/Dir/2001/12/10/5493.htm

References

Bukannan, 1992, (Chinese Version) *Finance in the Democracy Process*, translated by Shouning Tang, pp. 3–5, Shanghai Sanlian Bookstore, Shanghai.

Goldstein, Melvyn C., Ben Jiao, Cynthia M. Beall, and Phuntsog Tsering, 2003, Develop-ment and Change in Rural Tibet, in *Asian Survey*, Vol. 43, No. 5, pp. 758–779, University of California Press, Berkeley.

World Bank, 2003, *World Development Report 2004: Making Services Work for Poor People*, A Co-Publication of the World Bank and Oxford University Press.

5 Impacts of food and energy price hikes

Based on sample survey data for the years 2006 and 2007, we find that inflation of food and energy prices in China is moving at a slower pace than in the international market; however, the livelihood of low income groups has been significantly impacted. Urban sample households in low income groups have been shifting from consumption of high value food to lower value substitutes; and all of the rural sample households are reducing their total consumption expenditure in real terms. The Engel's coefficient of the rural household enlarged while their proportion of spending on clothing and energy declined. Farmers' households are moving toward more imbalanced diets, and the nutritional status of the poor is apparently deteriorating. The emergency-response measures that the government should implement include stopping subsidies to biofuel producers, who use foodstuffs as inputs, and providing food aid to the poor. The mid-term strategies should include anti-monopoly tactics, improving the market environment for the right competition, and eliminating price distortion. Mid-term and long-term socioeconomic policy reform must be undertaken to adjust the social structure, to correct the mechanism of factor price formation, and to transform the pattern of economic growth.

5.1 Introduction

Since 2007, global food prices have been on a steep rise, joining the preceding energy price hike. Global food prices are hitting the world economy with great force, like a "silent tsunami" (Earth Institute, 2008), and affecting in particular the economies that rely on energy and food imports. At the present time, social unrest is emerging in some 30 countries around the world that are affected by rising food prices. Food and energy security are more closely connected with political stability than ever before. The issue of how food security and energy needs can be balanced is becoming a hot topic in the international community. China has promptly responded to the global food and energy crisis with a number of measures, including export bans, price intervention and subsidies. However,

(Originally published in *China and World Economy*, No. 6, 2008.)

reducing inflationary pressure through export and price intervention is a short-run effect that does not change the drivers of the rising prices but will likely distort price signals and mislead resource allocation, which could be a potential cause for real crisis in the future. The present paper will use available statistics and sample survey data for China for the years 2006 and 2007 to show the impacts of price hikes on low-income groups and the poor in terms of food and energy consumption. In addition, we will consider the public actions that need to be undertaken to balance food security and energy requirements. The present paper is organized as follows. In Section II, the impacts of the food and energy crisis on the poor will be analyzed and the changes in the food and energy consumption of rural sample households in China will be considered. In Section III, strategies to cope with the crisis will be suggested based on the findings stated in Section II.

5.2 Impacts of the food and energy crises on the poor

With regard to "energy security," the International Energy Agency (IEA) has very much emphasized oil supply security. In the current globalized market, the concern of the IEA is focused on the balance of energy supply and demand, including the supply and demand of petroleum, natural gas and electricity (Houssin, 2007). There are very different opinions relating to this balance, because of the opposite standing points taken by the major importers and exporters. Albeit, there has long been a consensus on the notion of "food security"; according to the FAO: "Food security exists when all people, at all times, have access to sufficient, safe and nutritious food to meet their dietary needs and food preferences for an active and healthy life" (FAO, 2008). The rising food and energy prices significantly impact people of all countries; however, the social unrest occurring in some developing countries shows that the survival of the local poor is threatened. Therefore, the provision of aid to the poor for food and energy is urgently needed.

For the purpose of delivering sufficient and timely assistance to the poor, it is necessary to identify the groups hit most heavily by the food and energy crisis, as well as the extent to which they are affected, based on household livelihood studies. Here, China's case is used to illustrate the issue because of the ample data available to the author for the period of 2006–2007.

The National Bureau of Statistics of China reported that in 2007 per capita annual disposable income of urban residents amounted to RMB13,786, while per capita annual net income of rural residents was RMB4,140 (NBS, 2008). The consumption price index was estimated at 4.5 percent for the urban sector and 5.4 percent for the rural sector. The income ratio (after price deflation) between rural and urban residents was 1:3.36 (rural = 1). The annual food price rose by 12.3 percent. Among the food items, the prices of food grain, meat, edible oil and eggs increased by 6.3, 31.7, 26.7 and 22.9 percent, respectively. Noticeably, the pork market led the price surge. In December, the prices of pork, beef and mutton increased by 57.7, 48.0 and 44.5 percent, respectively (Ministry of Agriculture, 2008), compared with the same period in 2006. However, the price for fresh-water fish remained almost unchanged. The information stated above does help to explain the changes in household income and consumption, shown in Tables 5.1–5.3.

First, as illustrated in Tables 5.1 and 5.3, allowing for the price rise per capita, disposable incomes of the urban sample households generally increased, whereas per capita net incomes of the rural households declined across all three groups. In other words, the income growth of farmers' households fell behind the price increase in the rural sector.

Second, the bottom twentile income group in the urban sample apparently changed its food consumption pattern: less rice, wheat flour, cooking oil, pork,

Table 5.1. Changes in Per Capita Food Consumption of Urban Sample Households in China

Income group	Bottom twentile		Third quintile		Top twentile	
Year	2006	2007	2006	2007	2006	2007
Per capita annual food consumption	Quantity (kg)	Changes (%)	Quantity (kg)	Changes (%)	Quantity (kg)	Changes (%)
Rice	43.19	−13.57	40.97	1.32	35.35	13.21
Wheat flour	15.67	−7.28	11.89	7.74	5.17	15.28
Edible oil	8.23	−6.44	9.82	2.34	8.06	15.26
Pork	15.01	−19.85	20.55	−9.05	20.76	3.13
Beef	1.36	14.71	2.65	3.77	2.43	24.69
Mutton	0.81	8.64	1.49	−1.34	1.22	18.85
Chicken	2.84	14.79	4.76	16.60	5.77	31.20
Duck	1.05	−9.52	1.68	3.57	1.73	35.26
Eggs	7.52	−6.91	10.91	0.46	9.85	8.32
Fish	5.67	0.53	9.61	6.24	12.73	14.30
Shrimp	0.28	71.43	1.23	26.83	2.74	20.07
Vegetables	102.47	−9.50	121.16	0.73	109.08	10.48
Sprit	1.89	1.06	2.45	−1.63	1.74	1.72
Fruit wine	0.06	16.67	0.23	0.00	0.61	−13.11
Beer	2.61	20.69	6.69	−3.29	6.21	6.44
Soda beverage	0.70	30.00	2.21	4.52	3.66	−9.02
Bottled water	2.26	66.81	10.84	−1.38	28.91	−11.52
Tea leaves	0.13	23.08	0.26	7.69	0.32	21.88
Fresh fruits	18.53	24.34	40.00	7.50	51.46	6.10
Fruit melon	11.78	−17.32	23.35	−18.03	27.78	−9.36
Cookies	1.93	25.39	4.61	10.85	6.52	3.37
Fresh milk	7.32	11.07	19.16	0.00	25.76	−0.39
Milk Powder	0.21	14.29	0.55	−12.73	0.71	−25.35
Yogurt	1.02	52.94	3.87	9.04	6.42	−4.52

Source: NBS (2007).

Notes: The sample size: 56,000 households in 2006 and 59,000 households in 2007.

Table 5.2 Changes in Per Capita Consumption Expenditures of the Urban Sample Households

Income group	Bottom twentile		Third quintile		Top twentile	
Year	2006	2007	2006	2007	2006	2007
Per capita annual disposable Income						
At same year price (RMB)	2838.87	3357.91	10269.70	12042.32	39408.26	44961.34
At 2006 price (RMB)		3213.31		11523.75		43025.21
Total consumption expenditure per capita						
At same year price (RMB)	2953.27	3447.68	7905.41	9097.35	25320.72	27738.16
At 2006 price (RMB)		3299.22		8705.60		26543.69
Food spending						
At same year price (RMB)	1387.7	1672.36	3019.37	3538.3	6351.32	7070.85
At 2006 price (RMB)		1497.19		3167.68		6330.21
Share (%)	46.99	48.51	38.19	38.89	25.08	25.49
Clothing spending						
At same year price (RMB)	225.02	288.5	884.74	1017.66	2245.84	2439.66
At 2006 price (RMB)		291.12		1026.90		2461.82
Share (%)	7.62	8.37	11.19	11.19	8.87	8.80
Education spending						
At same year price (RMB)	256.18	278.87	587.93	614.32	1401.59	1468.82
At 2006 price (RMB)		280.84		618.65		1479.17
Share (%)	8.67	8.09	7.44	6.75	5.54	5.30
Energy spending						
At same year price (RMB)	254.98	271.66	406.92	433.88	693.58	708.4
Share (%)	8.63	7.88	5.15	4.77	2.74	2.55
Health-care spending						
At same year price (RMB)	213.39	250.27	590.45	646.52	1427.39	1655.21
At 2006 price (RMB)		246.09		635.71		1627.54
Share (%)	7.23	7.26	7.47	7.11	5.64	5.97
Transport and communication						
At same year price (RMB)	205.6	243.21	859.87	993.43	5886.19	6353.91
At 2006 price (RMB)		247.16		1009.58		6457.23
Share (%)	6.96	7.05	10.88	10.92	23.25	22.91

Source: NBS (2008).

Note: Figures on per capita income and expenditures have been adjusted according to the Statistical Communique of the People's Republic of China on the 2007 National Economic and Social Development (NBS, 2008), where the urban CPI is 4.5 percent, price index for food: 11.7 percent, clothing: −0.9 percent, entertainment and education/service: −0.7 percent, healthcare: 1.7 percent, transportation and communication: −1.6 percent. An energy price index is not available, related consumption is not adjusted.

Table 5.3 Changes in Food and Energy Consumption of Rural Sample Households in China

Income group	RMB 1000 and below		RMB 3500–4500		RMB 6000–10,000	
	per capita		per capita		per capita	
Year	2006	2007	2006	2007	2006	2007
Number of households	784	534	3091	2764	3112	3807
Per capita annual net income						
At same year price (RMB)	660.73	675.62	3978.2	3977.73	7473.08	7582.27
At 2006 price (RMB)		641.01		3773.94		7193.8
Per capita annual consumption expenditures						
At same year price (RMB)	1469.31	1611.97	2804.71	2898.67	4822.96	4895.74
At 2006 price (RMB)		1529.38		2750.16		4644.91
Food spending						
At same year price (RMB)	659.75	743.06	1126.94	1192.61	1644.91	1713.54
At 2006 price (RMB)		654.1		1049.83		1508.4
Share at same year price (%)	44.9	46.1	40.18	41.14	34.11	35
Clothing spending						
At same year price (RMB)	76.34	73.66	172.85	168.24	284.06	277.96
At 2006 price (RMB)		73.51		167.9		277.41
Share at same year price (%)	5.2	4.57	6.16	5.8	5.89	5.68
Energy spending						
At same year price (RMB)	82.48	89.91	120.07	116.88	164.85	163.07
Share at same year price (%)	5.61	5.58	4.28	4.03	3.42	3.33
Per capita annual food consumption (unit)	*Quantity (kg)*	*Changes (%)*	*Quantity (kg)*	*Changes (%)*	*Quantity (kg)*	*Changes (%)*
Grain	191.23	–4.07	201.92	2.27	190.66	9.16
Vegetable	81.14	11.49	109.98	5.75	115.77	2.78
Edible oil from crops	5.8	15.61	7.73	4.33	8.26	1.73
Edible oil from livestock	2.04	4.64	2.51	5.57	2.18	0.89
Pork	10.98	29	14.74	13.94	16.81	10.72
Beef	0.92	34.8	1.31	12.03	1.96	24.32
Mutton	0.72	16.51	1.06	23.73	1.4	18.85
Domestic fowl	2.51	27.98	3.36	4.29	4.4	6.45
Eggs	3.62	7.57	5.41	15.51	7.2	16.31

Source: Ministry of Agriculture. In 2008, a nation-wide sample survey on farmers' households was undertaken by the Rural Long-standing Observation Network under the Ministry of Agriculture.

Notes: The sample size: 20,351 households in 2006 and 18,255 households in 2007. In the year 2006, 93 percent of the sample households had annual net incomes per capita below 10,000; the proportion in 2007 was 88.7 percent. According to the report of the State Statistics Bureau, the national average per capita rural net income in 2006 was RMB3587, and was RMB4140 in 2007. Accordingly, we take the level of RMB1000 (and below), RMB3500–4500 and RMB6000–10 000, as the criteria to classify the low, the middle and the high income groups. Figures on per capita income and expenditure have been adjusted according to the Statistical Communique of the People's Republic of China on the 2007 National Economic and Social Development (NBS, 2008), where the rural CPI is 5.4 percent, the food price index is 13.6 percent, and clothing 0.2 percent. The energy price index is not available, and related consumption is not adjusted.

duck and eggs, fresh vegetables and melon, and more chicken, beef, fruit and dairy products. This is a manifestation of the food price impact through a "substitution effect" in people's diets. A similar variation can be found with the third quintile income group in terms of meat combination, but it is not seen in the consumption behavior of the top twentile income group (see Table 5.1). What is found in the top twentile group is a reduction in consumption of soda beverages and an increase in consumption of tea, seemingly in adopting a healthier diet.

Third, although Table 5.2 does not reveal the entire composition of the consumption expenditures of the urban sample households, it points out a few of the consumption items most fundamental to meeting such households' basic needs. The urban residents, except those in the top twentile, expended more on food in 2007, compared with that in 2006. No significant change in the value of the Engel coefficient (the percentage of expenditure on food in total consumption) was found for the third quintile (less than 1 percent), but for the bottom twentile, an increase in the Engel coefficient of 1.52 percentage points was found. Perhaps because the incomes of those in the lowest urban income group increased by 13.2 percent (in real terms) at the same time that prices of non-food consumer goods and services fell slightly, they spent more on non-food consumption items (but slightly less than previously on education and energy).

Fourth, Table 5.3 contains certain information regarding the decrease in the number of households specified in the same income group, if we keep the nominal income standard as 2006 and 2007 unchanged; that is, the income distribution curve has moved to the right. In addition, the households in the group with per capita net incomes of less than RMB1000 fell below the official poverty line. These households' total consumption expenditure exceeded their incomes. In this group, the income of more than 40 households was negative; that is what they earned was less than zero, but the value of capital and savings that these households possessed was higher than the average.

It implies that such a type of household belongs to the transit poor and they are able to smooth the household consumption with their assets. The chronically poor households (i.e. those with lower incomes and fewer assets than average) tend to rely on loans for some of their consumption. Furthermore, the value of average annual income and total consumption in real terms both decline, after being deflated by price. Farmers' livelihoods are generally hit by food price inflation and even the high income group is adversely affected. This is evident from the variation of their spending on basic need items: substitution among food, clothing and fuel took place; spending on education and medical care fell (not listed in the table). All three groups shifted towards less balanced diets in cutting down food expenditure. The quantity of the non-staple food that the poor consumed was originally at a low level. It substantially declined in 2007: the poor consuming pork, poultry and eggs decreased by 29, 28 and 8 percent, respectively, which will undoubtedly lead to deterioration of levels of nutritional intake.

Table 5.3 is worked out based on the sample data collected from a nation-wide survey of approximately 20,000 households. The network of the long-standing observation points set up in 273 sample villages has been run by the Ministry of Agriculture since 1986. There is also a nation-wide sample database managed by National Bureau of Statistics of China (NBS), with approximately 68,000 households selected from 7100 villages. However, the current NBS data available for the author relates to the year 2006, which is unsatisfactory for the use in a comparison study.

First, food price inflation hit rural households more forcefully than urban households. This finding is significantly different from the main stream opinion in China (Lu and Xie, 2008). The grain specialists in China generally hold that farmers' households rely mainly on their own farm output, while urban households rely on the market for food supply. Therefore, the latter are more vulnerable in terms of food security than the former. However, the fact is that farmers produce limited items of food and what the poor produce is not sufficient to meet their energy intake. Now farmers purchase more food from the market to meet the diversified needs of their family members. The indication of "food security" is more than just calorie intake; it incorporates the diversity of food consumption that supplies sufficient micronutrients and enables a balanced diet. If we look back on Tables 5.1 and 5.3 with this notion in mind, then it is clear that the urban middle and low income groups could manage to shift between different meats and between different starches and sustain their food diversity, but the rural poor and the middle income groups considerably cut their meat consumption to cope with price hikes. This indicates how vulnerable rural people are in terms of food security.

In addition, urban people enjoy higher incomes and better social security, which results in better food security conditions. Moreover, the government intervention on prices has resulted in a slower pace of food price inflation in the cities than in the countryside. In 2007, food prices increased by 13.6 percent in the countryside, which was 1.9 percentage points higher than in the cities. The intervention on food prices has reduced farmers' access to food in two ways: as producers they do not gain from price inflation; however, as consumers, their purchasing power falls when prices in rural food markets rise steeply.

Neither of the two samples described above include rural–urban migrants. The author finds through several interviews with migrant workers in a few cities in south China that their monthly food expenditure has grown by RMB150, while monthly wages have risen by only RMB80 since the beginning of 2007. The food security issue for rural migrants has as yet been ignored in food and nutrition policy in China.

5.3 Proposed strategies to cope with the crisis

International organizations and governments have responded speedily to the current food crisis, for example, by pooling resources, extending humanitarian aid to the countries threatened by hunger, and by increasing investment in international public goods such as R&D for agriculture, and so on. In addition, policy-makers are aware that the excessive speculation in the futures market on food and energy commodities is in essence a response to the decline in foodstuff storage, and to the declining spare capacity for back-up energy production. Therefore, international and regional cooperation, adjustment in biofuel policy, elimination of trade distortions, strengthening investment in agriculture and energy production, and promotion of energy-saving and emission-reduction measures are all becoming the foci in UN conferences and various summits. Whether or not the suggestions from those conferences will be put into practice depends on the governments of all countries, and whether they can create feasible policies and take action appropriate to their specific socioeconomic conditions.

The following strategies are proposed to cope with the crisis. First, the level of the minimum living standard guarantees program should be raised in proportion to CPI in both rural and urban sectors, together with provision of food aid to target groups. The two projects that the central government is ready to implement, that is, the "Mid and Long-term National Food Security Programming," and "Capacity Building for Jilin Province to Increase 5 Million Ton Food Grain Output" (Xinhua News, 2008), will undoubtedly promote food grain production in China. However, this will not necessarily strengthen the purchasing power of the poor, nor will it definitely "satisfy their present thirst with future accessible water." Therefore, it is necessary to issue food stamps in the cities to deliver food aid to the poor, including the migrant families. In the countryside, the existing aid procedure could be used to deliver meat and food with fortification to the poor, to help increase the intake of quality protein and micronutrients. Because of the irreversibility of damage caused to health by malnutrition at early stages of life, sustained nutrition intervention programs could be a highly cost-effective measure if such projects, for instance school feeding, could be implemented in rural low-income regions.

Second, the first priority in public resource allocation should be given to food security. The government has already stopped issuing new licenses for biofuel projects, which use foodstuff as inputs. However, there are still biofuel factories operating.

Third, "smaller steps with a faster pace" should be taken to release the government's control on prices and food exports, and to re-establish the function of prices in balancing supply and demand. The government puts limits on foodstuff exports and subsidizes energy prices, with the purpose of securing domestic food and energy supply while controlling price inflation. However, the history of the planned economy has shown that such measures suppress supply and stimulate demand to make shortages even worse. However, in the transition towards becoming a market-oriented economy, whenever the imbalance between supply and demand reemerges, the government is likely to apply price intervention. However, suppressed prices distort the supply–demand relationship, which eventually leads to price hikes. With a discrepancy between government-controlled prices and market prices, rent-seeking behavior and corruption are encouraged. Recently, there has been uncontainable foodstuff smuggling because of the cheap prices attainable within China; when coal is artificially undervalued, the related enterprises tend to increase exports and cut down domestic supply, leading to frequent power shortages; when the gasoline price is subsidized, the international airliners and shipping vessels try their best to fill up their tanks in China. All these cases tell the same story, that it is domestic consumers' welfare that is sacrificed under price control and bans on food grain export.

Fourth, the government must take urgent action to curb monopolies and to improve competition. The oil industry has the highest level of monopoly of all industries in China. The three giant companies are all state-owned. Such firms do not necessarily cope under market-oriented economic conditions. Their own interests are a stronger driving force to guide their behavior. When lacking fair competition rules, monopoly enterprises grow into interest groups with monopolistic positions. These oil giants are acting under the name of the "state" in doing business, excluding private investment from accessing petrol-deposit regions, from developing, trading, processing and retailing business. Therefore, the development of the oil and gas industries as a whole has been stunted. It is obvious that monopoly in the industry has not only reduced the efficiency in supply of goods and services, but has also narrowed the space for consumer choices.

Fifth, correct the price formation mechanism for production factors, and transform the pattern of economic growth. China's fast economic growth and the subsequent increases in employment and income are closely connected to the process of globalization. In the 1990s, China could only enter the lower end of the global value chain because of constraints on capital, technology and human resources. High energy consuming and high polluting firms have shifted from industrialized countries into China. One of the most important reasons is that the supply of undervalued labor, land, environment and water resources have enabled low production costs. The low production costs have driven the fast expansion in the manufacturing sector in mainland China and the huge demand for energy and raw materials. As an outcome, China has become a net importer of petroleum since 1993. The International Energy Agency predicted in the World Energy Outlook 2007 that the global daily demand for energy in 2030 will grow by 38.9 percent over the year 2005. Approximately 43 percent of this increase will come from China and India alone. Clearly, China's energy consumption has grown to a significant size in terms of the world energy market. China has become a net energy embodied export country (and is still growing in scale), with increasing carbon emissions.[1] The issues of environmental pollution, warming global weather and worsening terms of trade have been influencing policymakers and the general public to see the necessity of transforming the growth pattern of the economy. The notions of "saving energy and reducing emissions" and "building a society with thriftiness" have become targets in the national socioeconomic development planning. However, as long as the price formation mechanism remains unchanged, scarcity in resource endowments will not be presented in either the domestic or foreign trade, and the existing misallocation of resources will continue and the growth pattern will remain unchanged. At the present time, the worldwide food and energy crisis makes external-oriented development more difficult. Readjustment of the factor price formation pattern is necessary to endow farmers and workers by law with collective bargaining power for trading and making wage contracts. In addition, it is important to lift environmental-protection related tax rates according to world standards, including those relating to mining, water resource development and pollution emission. This will surely put a huge number of enterprises under great pressure. However, this is the right way to cope with the global food and energy crisis. This also fits China's long-term strategy of sustainable economic development.

Among the above stated policy options, the first two are emergency-response steps, the third and fourth are for mid-term readjustment, and the fifth is aimed at mid-term and long-term socioeconomic policy reform. It is vital that a check be placed on the power of the government and enterprises to foster a factor price formation mechanism that empowers workers and farmers. We can anticipate a transition toward a more balanced social structure in China by doing so.

Note

1 According to estimation by Chen et al. (2008), in 2002, the net export of embodied energy was about 240 million tce (tons of coal equivalent), which occupied about 16 percent of primary energy consumption in the same year, increasing about 150 million tce in China. In 2006, the net export of embodied energy went up to about 630 million tce, 162 percent higher than that of 2002.

References

Chen, Ying, Jiahua Pan and Laihui Xie, 2008, "Energy embodied in goods of international trade in China: Calculation and policy implications," *Economic Research*, Vol. 7, pp. 11–25.

Earth Institute (The Earth Institute at Columbia University), 2008, "Food crisis: A global emergency," [online; cited June 2008]. Available from: www.earth.columbia.edu/.

FAO (Food and Agriculture Organization), 2008, Special Programme for Food Security: "What is food security?," [online; cited July 2008]. Available from: www.fao.org/spfs/en/.

Houssin, Didier, 2007, "Security of energy supplies in a global market," [online; cited July 2008]. Available from: www.iea.org/textbase/speech/2007/Houssin_Prague.pdf.

Lu, Feng and Xie Ya, 2008, "Dynamics of grain supply-demand and prices (1980–2007): A discussion about prices fluctuation, macro-stability and grain security," *Xinhua Wenjai* (*Xinhua Digest*), No. 13, pp. 51–5.

Ministry of Agriculture, 2008, "Analyses on price fluctuations in wholesale market for the products covered under the food basket program in December 2007," [online; cited July 2008]. Available from: www.agri.gov.cn/pfsc/fxbg/t20080117_956379.htm.

NBS (National Bureau of Statistics of China), 2007, "The nation-wide sample survey on urban household," [online; cited July 2008]. Available from: www.stats.gov.cn.

NBS (National Bureau of Statistics of China), 2008, *Statistical Communique of the People's Republic of China on the 2007 National Economic and Social Development*, Beijing: China Statistical Press.

Xinhua News, 2008, "Mid and long-term national food security programming" and "Capacity building for Jilin Province to increase 5 million ton food grain output," [online; cited July 2008]. Available from: www.news.sina.com.cn/c/2008–07–02.

6 Food security and agricultural changes in the course of urbanization

China's small farmers face increasing challenges because of land and water resource constraints and the effects of climate change. With the strengthened agricultural stimulus policies, poverty reduction and social protection programs, as well as the expanding international food trade, up to now China has achieved food security through small farm agriculture. During intensive economic restructuring, smallholders still coexist with large sized farms and industrialized agricultural businesses, but are in a vulnerable position in market transactions. Oriented to 2050, China's agricultural development and food security policies should work to improve domestic market structure, to further release international trade control and to empower smallholders.

6.1 Introduction

Food security has always been a general concern for China, the most populous country in the world. The food grain supply, to a large extent, still relies on small farm agriculture. At the end of the last century, Lester Brown's book *Who Will Feed China* (1995) aroused heated debate and discussion on the issue of the macro-level balance of food supply and demand (Lin, 1998). Micro-level household and individual nutrition security, in contrast, were not yet on the radar of mainstream economics research or the focus of agricultural policies in China. After this time, however, China embarked on a decade-long boom. China's rapid industrialization and urbanization have come at a cost, with diminishing farming land, a brain drain in rural areas, increased pollution and water shortages.

In response to the macro-level food supply problem, the Chinese Government increased public investment in agricultural technologies and infrastructure, as well as provided more incentives for farmers to improve productivity. These measures have led to robust growth momentum in agriculture. In addition, China adjusted its import and export policies to support a domestic supply and demand balance without causing significant pressure on the international market. Furthermore, several social assistance programs have been implemented for alleviating poverty (the smallholders are mainly poor people). For the chronic poor, the

(Originally published in *China and World Economy*, No. 2, 2011.)

Chinese Government has adopted a minimum living standard guarantee system while continuing with existing poverty reduction schemes. For the transit poor (such as those hit by natural disasters and financial crisis), emergency relief systems are in place to free them from hunger.

Since 2008, the central government has made urbanization and agricultural and rural development a tactic to counter the global financial crisis and economic slowdown, as well as a long-term strategy for sustained economic growth.[1] It is foreseeable that China's urbanization will continue in a similar manner over the coming three or four decades. It is with such an understanding that the present paper's discussions will focus on the following research questions. First, how has China achieved food security in the course of industrialization and urbanization over the past 10 years? Second, what has changed in terms of the allocation of resources, the size of farming land, the commercialization of food production and the level of incomes of peasant farms? Finally, how will China's small farm agriculture meet increasing food demands with future urbanization against the background of climate change and increasing resource constraints?

Data and information used in the present paper are taken from the following sources: first, statistical information released by the Ministry of Agriculture and other government agencies; second, household book-keeping data that has been collected by long-term monitoring stations at the Research Center of the Rural Economy, Ministry of Agriculture; third, women and children's nutrition information provided by the Food and Nutrition Monitoring Team of the Chinese Center for Disease Control and Prevention; fourth, predictions on population trends and on agricultural development for the years 2020 and 2050 conducted by the Institute of Population and Labor Economics and the Agricultural Strategic Research Panel of the Chinese Academy of Sciences, respectively; and, fifth, findings from case studies carried out by the author herself.

Section II describes the status of China's food security. Section III presents the structural changes in the small farm economy and Section IV deals with institutional arrangements to enhance small farms' income as well as food security.

6.2 China's fragile food security

Because grain accounts for the highest proportion of the diet of most Chinese households and is the biggest source of feed for the livestock sector (such as corn), this section will first address the availability of food, particularly grain, using production, consumption and international trade statistics. Then, this section will explore food accessibility using data monitoring the nutrition of children living in poor rural areas. Finally, constraints to the growth of food production will be discussed, as well as the countermeasures that the Chinese Government has taken, and the characteristics of China's food security.

The year 2009 marks the sixth consecutive year of growth in China's grain production, with total production reaching more than 530 million tons (NBS, 2010a). This represents an increase of approximately 13.1 percent from 2004. During 2000–2009, total output of paddy rice, wheat and corn accounted for 85–89 percent of total food production. In 2005, production of the three cereals surpassed consumption, and inventory piled up (see Figure 6.1). The same year, corn exports plunged. After global food prices soared at the end of 2007, in particular, the Chinese Government increased grain reserves and raised prices for public procurement while imposing a temporary tariff on grain exports. Domestic food prices approached and even surpassed international market prices, putting an end to the net export of grain (Ministry of Commerce, 2010). In contrast, the import of soybean and edible oil surged, and China became the biggest importer of soybean. In 2009, China imported 42.55 million tons of soybean and 8.16 million tons of edible vegetable oil. China's food supply and demand balance is maintained through self-sufficiency in staple grains, meat, eggs, milk, fruit and vegetables, with imports of soybean and edible oil.

Against this backdrop, the proportion of malnourished rural children under the age of 5 years has gradually declined (see Table 6.1). Compared to children

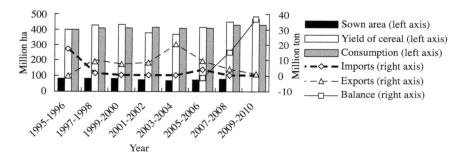

Figure 6.1 Yield and Consumption of Cereals (Rice, Wheat and Corn) during 1995–2010
Source: www.cngrain.com (news release on 9 February 2010, cited 15 August 2010)

Table 6.1 Nutrition Status of Rural Children under 5 Years during 1990–2009

Year	Low-weight percentage			Stunting percentage		
	Rural China	Non-poor Areas	Poor areas	Rural China	Non-poor areas	Poor areas
1990	16.5	–	–	40.3	–	–
1995	14.1	–	–	40.8	–	–
1998	9.8	7.0	14.5	27.9	23.4	36.4
2000	10.3	7.4	15.8	25.3	19.1	36.9
2005	6.1	4.4	9.4	16.3	13.9	20.9
2008	5.1	3.9	7.3	13.7	10.9	18.9
2009	4.9	3.7	6.6	13.0	9.7	18.3

Source: The table is sourced from Chen et al. (2010).

Notes: Sample size: 5341 children during 1990–1995, of whom rural children account for 65 percent; and some 16,000 children during 1998–2009, of whom 10,400 are rural children. The samples for 2008–2009 only include rural children because malnutrition was almost eliminated in cities by that stage. "–" No data available.

of other age groups and those of the same age group but living in cities and non-poor areas, the nutrition indices of children under 5 years living in poor areas are more sensitive to household food security. The nutrition status of this age group, therefore, can be used to deduce the food accessibility of their families. From 1998 to 2009, the low-weight ratio of this age group dropped from 14.5 to 6.6 percent, and the stunting ratio dropped from 36.4 to 18.3 percent. According to analyses by nutritionists, the decrease in child malnutrition in the poverty-stricken countryside is primarily due to the rising incomes of rural households and the growing share of meat, eggs and milk in children's meals (Chen et al., 2010). This also indicates an improvement in the food accessibility of poor households.

Despite improvements in China's food security, vulnerability in the system cannot be overlooked. First, at the micro-level, food security is unstable for the poor. During the global financial crisis from 2008 to 2009, the stunting ratio of children below 6 months old and from 6 to 12 months old increased from 5.7 to 9.1 percent and then to 12.5 percent, respectively. For poor households, the anemia ratio of infants less than 1-year-old reached as high as 40 percent, returning to a similar level as that in 2005. The anemia ratio of poor women went up to 47.6 percent, which is worse than the 2005 level. The nutrition status of children less than one year old worsened due to mothers' malnutrition during pregnancy.

Second, malnutrition remains serious for rural families at the bottom income level. In 2009, for the bottom decile of income groups (with average per capita annual incomes of RMB829), the low-weight ratio and stunting ratio of children below 5 years were 7.3 and 21.3 percent, respectively. Improvement in their nutrition status has been much slower compared to the children of other income groups.

Third, the children of the rural women working in the cities are more likely to become malnourished due to lack of care. No matter whether living in poor or non-poor areas, the stunting ratios of female migrants' children are 20–30 percent higher than for other children of the same age. This is a reflection of both poverty and food insecurity for a considerable number of rural households. However, it also reflects the lack of integration of China's urbanization in that migrant workers have to leave their families behind in villages.

At the macro-level, China's food supply and demand balance is also fragile. First, agricultural resources are becoming scarce, which makes it difficult to promote further growth of grain production. Arable land is being encroached upon by industrialization, urbanization and desertification. In 2009, China's arable land area was roughly 121.73 million hectares, a decrease of 7.47 million hectares since 1999. Water and soil erosion, misuse of fertilizers and soil pollution have led to serious soil degradation (Ye, 2010). A shortage of irrigation water is another constraint to grain production. Due to rapid industrial development and urban expansion, agriculture is facing increasing competition for water from industries and households. The annual shortage of irrigation water is as much as 30 billion cubic meters. The proportion of agricultural water consumption to national total declined from 70.4 percent in 1997 to 62.0 percent in 2008 (Ministry of Water Resources, 1997, 2008). However, only 40 percent of water in agriculture is effectively used in China due to lack of up-to-date technologies, while this figure is 80–90 percent in Israel (Han, 2010). A more crucial problem is that due to inappropriate treatment of waste water, solids and gases, China's major rivers have all been polluted to various degrees. Lake water has deteriorated, and the poorest quality water accounts for 23.1 percent of surface water in China (Ministry of Environmental Protection, 2009). Various forms of pollution have presented threats to potable and agricultural water in south China, an area that has been reputed for its numerous water towns since ancient times.

Second, a weakening agricultural labor force restricts the use of new technologies and the enhancement of agricultural intensity. In 2009, approximately 230 million of the rural labor force worked in non-agricultural sectors, and 145 million of them were rural–urban migrants. Among these migrant workers, men accounted for 65.1 percent, those aged below 40 years accounted for 83.9 percent, and those who have junior–middle school education and above accounted for 88.3 percent. Apparently, industries and services attract the best quality rural laborers into cities. However, these workers are unable to access urban social security. Therefore, farmland bears a function of securing the subsistence of rural people. As a result, some 80 percent of migrant workers leave their parents and women in the home village taking care of families and farmland (NBS, 2010b). According to a report by the Division of Crop Farming Administration of the Ministry of Agriculture, agricultural workers were aged 45 years on average in 2009.

Third, natural disasters and climate change have increased grain production risks and the incidence of farmers falling into poverty. From 1980 to 1993, natural disasters (flood, drought, wind and hailstorm, frost, pest and disease) accounted for grain output reductions of 15 percent on average. Forty percent of such losses were caused by weather disasters alone (Shi et al., 1997). From 2004 to 2009, weather disasters caused an annual average grain loss of 41.55 million tons, which is equivalent to 7.8 percent of total grain output in 2009. Due to the global warming and changes of farming systems, farmland areas affected by disease and pests have increased from 2 million hectares in the 1990s to 4 million hectares in the 2000s (Xia, 2010). The altitude where stripe rust disease of wheat lasts through summer has increased by more than 100 m, and the pandemic begins 2 weeks earlier than that in the 1990s. Cnaphalocrocis medinalis and paddy rice planthoppers, as well as locusts, are expanding their reach to higher latitudes and altitudes. Loxostege sticticalis Linnaeus has been rampant in north China for many years. During 2000–2009, grain losses caused by biological disasters annually amounted to 17 million tons, up by 13.3 percent over the period of 1990–1999.

Finally, changes in the above-stated agricultural production conditions, as well as rapid rises in the prices of inputs, particularly imported chemical fertilizers, have pushed up costs of grain production and cut profits. In 1995, the material costs of paddy rice, wheat and corn were RMB2674.5/hectare and labor costs were RMB1741.5/hectare. In 2008, these prices increased by 61.4 and 50.7 percent, respectively. In the same year, the net profits were RMB2796/hectare, down by 5.4 percent over 2004 (Ye, 2010). No doubt, these changes would dampen the enthusiasm of farmers to plant grains. However, demand for food keeps expanding due to population and income growth.

Under these unfavorable conditions, government intervention and public services have played a pivotal role in promoting food production. In 2003, grain production declined for the fifth consecutive year, resulting in an undersupply. This was due to the previously declining grain prices followed by a bumper harvest, which led farmers to restructure their planting. Another cause of the decline in grain production is the encroachment of development zones into farmland. To reverse this situation, from 2004, the Chinese Government launched a series of policies to protect and promote agricultural development (Chen, 2010), including:

1   Farmers have been made exempt from agricultural tax to reduce their tax burdens by RMB130bn.
2   Grain growers have been provided direct subsidies, in addition to the subsidies for their purchase of high quality seeds (and animal breeds), machinery and tools, and agricultural inputs, such as diesel and chemical fertilizers. Total subsidies amounted to RMB127bn in 2009.
3   Policies have been adopted to set minimum purchase prices for public procurement and temporary reserves on major cereals (paddy rice and wheat), so as to prevent extreme price volatility.
4   Key demonstration zones have been expanded for agricultural technology extension and to promote high-yield varieties and planting technologies.
5   Disaster prevention and mitigation capabilities have been strengthened. Farming techniques are improving in response to climate change, so as to reduce the impact of weather disasters. Monitoring and early warning systems are being developed to reduce losses caused by pests and disease.
6   Land consolidation and amelioration are being invested in, and farming area protection of 120 million hectares has been established.

The implementation of the agricultural stimulation policies has brought about rapid growth in farmers' investments. In 2008, the total power of small tractors in China reached 166.48 million kW, up by 27.5 percent over 2003. This led to apparent improvement in farming productivity. Output elasticity of agricultural labor for paddy rice was 0.183 during 1980–2004, and increased to 0.337 during 2005–2008 (Wang, 2010). As a result, grain production returned to the track of growth. During the global food price crisis of 2008, China's food prices avoided sudden hikes.

6.3 Divergence of smallholders

The fragile balance between food grain demand and supply at the macro-level reveals the vulnerability of smallholders in terms of both their production and livelihood at the microlevel.

According to the World Bank (2008), approximately 150 million rural people still live under the poverty line. The poor mainly consists of small-scale farmers and their family members. These families are facing food insecurity.

By processing sample survey data on rural households over the past 10 years, this section reveals the structural changes of the farm economy. Such changes essentially reflect development in China's macroeconomy, particularly the impact of urbanization. This section describes the situation of smallholders in terms of the allocation of market gains using the results of existing analyses on the value chain of agricultural products.

Time series data in Table 6.2 reveals the socioeconomic characteristics of the smallholders during 2000–2009. First, there was a decrease in the average size of rural households, while the labor-dependent ratio rose slightly, from 0.67 to 0.7. Second, the proportion of workers from farming households employed in non-agricultural sectors increased by 15.7 percentage points. Third, farmland cultivated by smallholders includes rented land, but, even so, the average area of farmland per household slid from less than 0.50 ha to less than 0.46 ha. Fourth, the average ratio of commercial sales of cereals (commodity food) per household increased nearly 20 percentage points. This is partly to do with increasing unit area yield, and partly to do with the increase in farmers working in cities and the result-ing reduced food consumption in the countryside. Fifth, with growing numbers of people taking non-farming jobs, non-farming income becomes increasingly important to family income growth. This is reflected in the yearly decline of the proportion of family income from crop farming and animal husbandry.

Table 6.2 Profile of Average Peasant Farms in China during 2000–2009

Year	Household size (person)[a]	Family labor (person)[a]	Non-agricultural labor[b] (%)	Cultivated area (mu)[b]	Commer-cialization rate of grain out-put (%)[b]	Annual income per capita (RMB)[a]	Income from crops and livestock[a] (%)
2000	4.2	2.8	29.7	7.43	44.8	2253	46.2
2001	4.2	2.7	30.2	7.42	41.3	2366	45.5
2002	4.1	2.8	31.3	7.38	46.4	2476	43 5
2003	4.1	2.8	33.7	7.25	52.1	2622	43.2
2004	4.1	2.8	34.3	7.15	53.7	2936	45.2
2005	4.1	2.8	37.9	6.99	62.3	3587	39.7
2006	4.1	2.8	40.3	6.87	62.5	4140	39.6
2007	4.0	2.8	40.3	6.87	62.5	4140	39.6
2008	4.0	2.8	41.0	6.86	63.9	4761	38.3
2009	–	–	45.4	6.84	64.7	5153	–

Source: [a] The Ministry of Agriculture of China (2009; In this table, the proportion of crop farming and animal husbandry to per capita net income is calculated using the data from p. 150). Base data are taken from the national rural household sample survey conducted by the National Bureau of Statistics with samples covering more than 68,000 households.
[b] This is calculated using national rural household sample survey data from the Research Center of the Rural Economy, Ministry of Agriculture. The sample size of this survey system covers fewer than 20,000 households.

Note: "–" No data available; 15 mu = 1 ha.

According to the cross-section data (Figures 6.2 and 6.3) for 2002 and 2009, there has been a divergence of farmers in terms of the size of farmland. The proportion of landless farmers and those with less than 3 mu of land (mu = 1/15 hectare) apparently grew. In 2009, their proportions were 15 and 28 percent, respectively, both up by 4 percentage points over 2002. Smallholders with less than 3 mu of land only possess 7 percent of total farmland. Most of them are part-time farmers whose primary jobs are non-farming jobs. Crop farming for them is only carried out to provide family food and vegetables. The number of landless farmers has increased for two reasons: land has been encroached upon by industries and expanding cities; and farmers have leased their land to others because they have taken non-farming jobs or are too old to grow crops. In addition, there has been a shift of farmland to the largest farmers. In 2009, the proportion of farmers with more than 30 mu of land remained the same as in 2002, which is 3 percent. However, they possess 27 percent of total farmland, up by 1

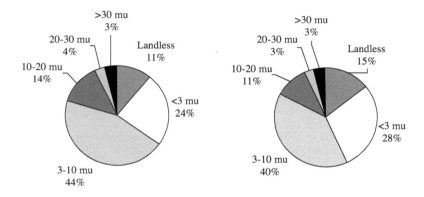

Figure 6.2 Distribution of Peasant Farms by Size of Farmland in 2002 and 2009

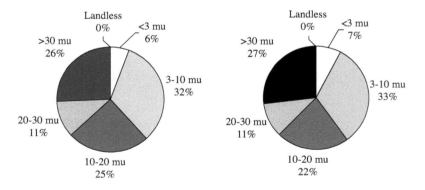

Figure 6.3 Distribution of Areas of Farmland by Size of Peasant Farms in 2002 and 2009

Source: Dataset of the national sample survey on farmers, Research Center of Rural Economy, the Ministry of Agriculture.

Table 6.3 Average Commercialization Rate of Grain Production of Peasant Farms in 2009

Farm size (mu)	Commercialization rale of grain production (%)
<3	38.9
3≤, ≤10	62.8
10≤, ≤20	74.8
20≤, ≤30	79.5
>30	90.3

Source: Dataset of national sample survey on farmers, Research Center of Rural Economy, the Ministry of Agriculture.

percentage point. However, even these large-size farms in China can be seen as "micro-farms" compared to the family farms in countries like Brazil and Russia.

State-owned farms are an important group of commodity food grain producers in China. In 2008, 54 percent of China's food grain output was for commercial sale, while this figure was 86.5 percent for state-owned farms, which is much higher than the national average (Ministry of Agriculture, 2009; State Administration of Grain, 2009). However, individual farmers account for the lion's share of total commodity food grain production. According to a Circular on Improvement of State-run Farms issued by the Ministry of Agriculture in 2006, commodity food grain provided by state-owned farms accounted for 10 percent of the national total in 1990. This ratio declined to 7.3 percent in 2008, which means a greater proportion of commercial food grain sales were provided by farming households. In 2009, for farmers with more than 10 mu of land, in excess of 70 percent of food grain output was for commercial sales. For those with more than 30 mu of land, as much as 90.3 percent of food grain output was for commercial sales (Table 6.3), which is much higher than the commodity food grain ratio of state-owned farms (87.1 percent) (Zhao, 2010).

When the average commercialization rate of grain production in different provinces is taken into account (Table 6.4), it is evident that food grain producing areas have experienced regional shifts. It was normal practice to transport food grain from China's south to north 30 years ago. However, now, Heilongjiang, Jilin and Liaoning Provinces in the north-east boast the highest percentage of commodity food grain production (86.7–92.4 percent). Table 6.5 reveals that the highest percentages of household non-agricultural labor are in Guangdong, Fujian and Zhejiang Provinces in the south-eastern coastal regions, excluding Beijing and Shanghai. In fact, the south-east coastal region has achieved the most rapid progress in terms of industrialization and urbanization. The region has attracted tens of millions of rural migrants from inland provinces. Therefore, the south-eastern region is experiencing an increasing gap in food grain supply, which is filled by rice imports from north China and neighboring south-eastern countries. To save on transport costs, surplus food grain in the north-east (primarily corn) has even been exported to South Korea and Japan.

Table 6.4 Distribution of Peasant Farms in Different Provinces by Commercialization Rate of Grain Production and Region

	Provincial commercialization rate of grain production				
	[0, 30%]	[30%, 45%]	[45%, 60%]	[60%, 75%]	[75%, 100%]
Northern region			Inner-Mongolia	Shanxi, Beijing Hebei	Tianjiin
North-eastern region					Jinlin, Heilongjiang, Liaoning
Eastern region		Zhejiang	Fujian, Hubei, Hunan	Anhui, Jiangsu, Shandong, Shanghai, Jiangxi	
Central–southern region	Guangdong	Hainan, Guangxi		Henan	
South-western region	Chongqing, Tibet, Sichuan, Guizhou	Yunnan			
North-western region	Xinjiang	Gansu	Ningxia, Qinghai, Shaanxi		

Source: Dataset of the national sample survey on farmers, Research Center of Rural Economy, the Ministry of Agriculture.

Table 6.5 Distribution of Peasant Farms in Different Provinces by Non-agricultural Labor Ratio and Region

	Provincial non-agricultural labor ratio				
	[0, 30%]	[30%, 40%]	[40%, 50%]	[50%, 60]	[60%, 100%]
Northern region	Inner-Mongolia	Shanxi, Hebei	Tianjin		Beijing
North-eastern region	Jilin, Heilongjiang		Liaoning		
Eastern region			Shandong	Jiangsu, Anhui, Jiangxi, Fujian	Zhejiang, Shanghai
Central–southern region	Hainan		Henan, Guangxi	Huei, Hunan	Guangdong
South-western region	Yunnan, Tibet	Guizhou	Sichuang, Chongqing		
North-western region	Qinghai, Xinjiang	Gansu, Ningxia	Shanxi		

Source: Dataset of national sample survey on farmers, Research Center of Rural Economy, the Ministry of Agriculture.

For most farmers in the north-west and north-east, the ratio of non-agricultural labor and the commercialization rate of grain production are below national average levels. This is a reflection of the backward socioeconomic development of China's western region. Because of harsh natural conditions, frequent disasters and weak infrastructure in these regions, the progress of industrialization and urbanization has been slow, and non-agricultural jobs are lacking. In addition, this region has low crop farming productivity and nomadic farming practices, coupled with the highest occurrence of poverty in rural China.[2] For instance, the poverty rate in Gansu Province reached 21.3 percent in 2008 (the poverty line is RMB785 net annual income per capita) (Liu and Du, 2010). There are a considerable number of agricultural and nomadic people in the west who do not have stable food security. Such people should be the target of poverty reduction schemes.

Farmers must have greater bargaining power in the market and a higher share in the value chain of agricultural products. This is one of the measures included in the poverty reduction schemes and a key goal in the government's efforts to promote income growth of farmers. Existing agricultural supporting policies include steps to develop professional large-size farms and cooperatives, together with actions to promote so-called "corporation plus peasant farms," where companies work with individual farmers. This has transformed the organization of agricultural production, processing and marketing, and increased diversity in the business patterns of farmers. First, smallholders still comprise the majority of farmers. They include part-time farmers whose primary jobs are farming or non-farming activities, as well as households specializing in small-sized farming, animal husbandry, processing or marketing. The second group includes large-size farms that have come about from specialized smallholders. Commodity grain farmers with more than 20 mu of land, as shown in Figure 6.2, for instance, belong to this category. This category of farmers accounts for 6 percent of the sample. The large livestock farmers (with annual pork sales of more than 500 kg or poultry and egg sales over 80 kg) accounted for 3.7 and 4.0 percent of the total sample in 2000 and 2009, respectively.

The third group includes agricultural enterprises that have assumed industrialized operations. They include companies located near farmers, partnership companies, businessmen who have made their fortune in cities and returned to their hometowns, as well as non-local industrial and commercial corporations. Through village committees, they have leased land for integrated agro-business activities from production and processing to sales. At the end of 2007, the author visited agro-businesses of this type during a rural survey in south Fujian Province. It was noticed in the case study that these companies share one common feature: they produce food for domestic and international markets, turn farmers into agricultural workers and receive preferential government policies. Apart from receiving monthly salaries, hired local farmers can also receive land rent dispensed by village committees.

Although industrialized agro-corporations are popular in the eastern part of China, in the central and western regions they have the "firm plus farmers," which performs in such an operational way that the firm engages in product processing and marketing while small farmers individually provide the preliminary products according to the technical criteria set by the company. In this type of practice, farmers are still at an auxiliary status and get little from product value chain. The government has attempted to strengthen the bargaining power of the smallholders by developing cooperatives, and through adopting the Law on Specialized Cooperatives for Farmers, which went into effect as of 1 July 2007. According to the statistics of the Ministry of Agriculture, there are more than 150,000 specialized cooperatives nationwide, with 34.86 million members, accounting for 13.8 percent of total farming households in 2008. According to the Law, farmers' cooperatives are entitled to tax deductions for agricultural activities such as production, processing, distribution and services. However, the first to enjoy such preferential treatment are firms and large-size specialized farms, in the following ways. First, cooperatives have been rapidly established with the "company plus farmers" model. Second, cooperatives have been established but led and controlled by large farmers. Finally, village officials have organized and led the cooperatives and acted as the middleman between farmers and companies. There has been no substantial change in the vulnerable position of smallholders in economic decision making and in the distribution of earnings (Zhang, 2009). Smallholders as suppliers of preliminary products are at the bottom of the value chain of agricultural products. Their share in the value chains of vegetables and fruit was no more than 20 percent during 2005 and 2007 (Huang and Rozelle, 2006; Zhang et al., 2010). According to a survey carried out around mid-January 2008 by the Research Center of the Rural Economy, the Ministry of Agriculture, vegetable growers obtained 5–32 percent from the value chains of eight vegetables transported from farm gate to well-established supermarkets in Beijing, with an average share of 18.4 percent (Research Group at the Research Center of Rural Economy, the Ministry of Agriculture, 2008). The same vegetable growers obtained 22.7 percent, on average, from the value chain of the farm-gate to the informal market in Beijing (Figure 6.4).

6.4 Future of smallholders: Suggested institutional arrangements

This section highlights the challenges presented by urbanization to China's food security and smallholders, and recommends institutional arrangements for responding to these challenges. Population growth and urbanization remain the major challenges confronting China's food supply. According to recent predictions made by the Institute of Population and Labor Economics, Chinese Academy of Social Sciences (Cai, 2010), China's population will surpass 1.4 billion by 2020 based on the national demographic census of 2000. Presuming that the total fertility rate remains at 1.8, the total population will decline to 1.38 billion by 2050. According to conservative estimates, China's urbanization rate will reach 54.5 percent by 2020. By 2050, this figure will rise to 70 percent. By that time, China will have 965 million urban residents and 410 million rural residents. This will result in heavier environmental pressures, increased scarcity of land and

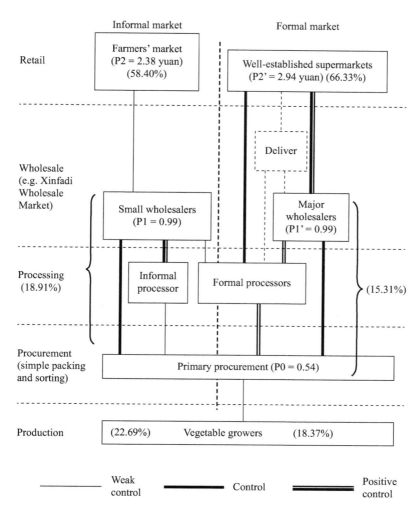

Figure 6.4 Value Chain of Vegetable Production and Distribution: Formal versus Informal Market

water resources, as well as an increased food supply gap. According to the Strategic Agricultural Research Panel of the Chinese Academy of Sciences (2010), except for rice, vegetables, fruit, poultry, aquatic products and pork, China's self-sufficiency rates for the main agricultural products will have noticeably declined by 2020 compared to 2004 rates. By 2050, a gap in the supply of rice, wheat and corn as major cereals will reach 15 percent (Table 6.6).

There is no fundamental difference between this scenario and China's current fragility of food security. In order to strengthen food security at the macro and

Table 6.6 Prediction of 2020–2050 Self-sufficient Rate of Major Agricultural Products (%)

Products	2004	2020	2030	2050
Three major cereals	103	93	90	85
Rice	101	102	104	104
Wheat	99	94	92	90
Corn	107	84	79	71
Soybean	49	41	39	38
Edible oil	67	62	60	58
Cotton	85	71	64	58
Sugar	91	85	79	75
Vegetable	101	104	105	106
Fruit	101	106	105	104
Pork	101	102	100	98
Beef	100	94	92	89
Mutton	99	94	92	89
Poultry	100	104	105	105
Milk and milk products	96	87	84	79
Aquatic products	102	103	104	104

Source: Strategic Agricultural Development Research Panel of Chinese Academy of Sciences (2010).

micro levels, the Chinese Government should continue to practice and enhance some of the existing key policies.

First, it needs to stimulate public and private investments in agricultural technology. China currently has only 3.3 million hectares of reclaimable land, while consumer demand for food is growing. On the supply side, the only option is to make agriculture more productive and sectors of processing and distribution more efficient. This requires public investment in long-term agricultural research. Meanwhile, patent protection must be improved to provide incentives for the private sector to increase investment in agricultural R&D.

Second, the targeting mechanism of the extension system on agricultural technologies must be further improved to serve the end users so that appropriate technologies can be applied more effectively. Currently, industries and cities are still attracting the best brains from agriculture. As a result, most of those who stay in agriculture are low-income smallholders, mostly women. Agricultural technological extension services should thus aim at low-income and poor smallholders, focusing in particular on women. In addition, priority should be given to resource-saving technologies, especially water conservation and efficient use of land and chemical fertilizers.

Third, rural social protection programs must be expanded and improved. In 2009, the coverage of the rural cooperative medical system surpassed 92 percent, and a rural pension insurance pilot program covered 10–20 percent of rural people. Current payment levels of the two insurance schemes are not sufficient to protect insurants from major economic shocks that disease and old age would bring to their families. Furthermore, migrant workers do not have equal access to urban social security and public services, although they live and work in cities. In this sense, land still provides security to rural people. The extent of land leasing and concentration depends not only on the social inclusion of cities, but also on improvement in social protection for rural people. Judging by the current level of social security in China, part-time smallholders, specialized large-size farms and industrialized agricultural businesses will coexist for a long time into the future.

Fourth, agricultural human resources should be better trained and educated. This requires the introduction of a "two-track" education system to the rural sector and additional resources for vocational education. Meanwhile, funding should be increased for students of agricultural vocational schools, which will provide skilled farmers for modern agriculture to replace the aging work force.

Fifth, international cooperation should be stepped up. Forecasts regarding China's self-sufficiency in agricultural products by 2020 and 2050 suggest a tendency of increasing food imports. Because an increase in global food supply will increase China's food security, China's participation in international agricultural cooperation, particularly its commitment to agricultural development in the least developed countries, is consistent with the its own interests and those of the international community at large. The China–African Agriculture Cooperation Forum held in Beijing in August 2010 can be seen as part of this effort.[3]

Furthermore, with the purpose of avoiding extreme price volatility and protecting small farmers from being placed in an unfavorable market position, existing policies should be improved, especially in the following areas.

First, market structure should be improved and the grain reserve system should be modified. Since China's domestic market for grain purchase and sales was deregulated in 2004, prices have been formed primarily based on market supply and demand. However, the national grain reserve system and state-owned grain purchase and marketing enterprises still have an overwhelming market share, which grants them a decisive influence on pricing (State Administration of Grain, 2010a, b). Taking advantage of receiving priority in obtaining licenses and contracts from the government for public procurement at guaranteed minimum prices, these enterprises have continued to hold monopolies. They occasionally underpay farmers for grain purchases, as reflected in the documents of annual inspections organized by the National Development and Reform Commission (General Office of NDRC, 2010). Fiscal subsidies for grain reserves have provided the motivation for grain enterprises to increase purchases. Some have even falsified purchase papers for additional amounts of subsidies or engaged in rent-seeking using purchase funds. Over the past 3 years, the annual grain reserve has accounted for more than 35 percent of total national grain consumption, which is much higher than the safety line of 17–18 percent defined by the Food and Agricultural Organization of the United Nations. Excessive reserves have led to a wasteful use of resources and compromised the effect of subsidies. According to the Ministry of Finance, the efficiency of China's grain subsidy is only 14 percent, which means that for RMB10 in state subsidies, only RMB1.4 goes to farmers, with the majority falling into the hands of grain purchase enterprises. Moreover, distorted grain pricing has also led to misallocation of agricultural resources. Current public grain procurement and reserve systems are inefficient and lack social justice. According to the experiences of South Asian countries like India, Pakistan, Sri Lanka, Bangladesh and Nepal, the solution is for the government to treat state-owned and private grain buyers as equals. The monopoly must be broken to increase competition and to engage the role of market pricing as a signal for resource allocation (Ganesh-Kumar et al., 2010).

Second, China should loosen government regulations, remove barriers to international grain trade avenues, and eliminate distortions in foreign trade and product pricing. During 2006–2007, the food price in China was lower than the average price level at the international grain market. During the global food price crisis of 2008, China imposed an export tax on grain trade and even banned rice exports. However, due to significantly low domestic food prices, smuggling persisted (Chen, 2008). Since 2009, however, China has unexpectedly had a higher price level than that of the global food market (NDRC, 2010). The great price disparities between domestic and international markets will ultimately damage the welfare of domestic producers and consumers.

The weak position of smallholders in economic restructuring, in the value chain and in terms of policy incentives, as well as their exclusion from sharing the benefits of industrialization and urbanization, reflects their marginal social position. In fact, there is reciprocal causation between their economic plight and marginal social status. The only opportunity to break this vicious cycle is for smallholders to become organized and to increase their political, economic and social influence. Empowerment of smallholders, although not entirely within the scope of agricultural policies, is an essential institutional condition for China's agricultural sector to develop in a sustainable way.

Notes

1 Refer to "Decisions of the CPC Central Committee on Advancing Rural Reform and Development" (adopted by the Third Plenum of the Seventeenth CPC Central Committee on 12 October 2008) [online; cited 13 August 2010]. Available from: http://www.china.com.cn/policy/txt/2008–10/20/content_16635093.htm.
2 According to the information provided by the Poverty Reduction Office of the State Council in January 2010: "during the period of 2006–2008, the poor in the five ethnic minority autonomous regions plus Yunnan, Guizhou and Qinghai account for 39.6 percent of the total number of poor people. . . . In the state designated key counties for poverty reduction scheme in western region, ethnic minorities account for 46 percent of the poor people."
3 See the "China-Africa Forum on agricultural cooperation, Beijing declaration," at Xinhua.net (cited 12 August 2010). Available from: http://news.xinhuanet.com/2010–08/12/c_12439928.htm.

References

Brown, Lester R., 1995, *Who Will Feed China? Wake Up Call for a Small Planet*, Washington DC: World Watch Institute.
Cai, Fang, 2010, *Report on China's Population and Labor* (Green Paper on Population and Labor 2010), Beijing: Social Sciences Literature Press (in Chinese).

Chen, Chunming, Wu He, Yuying Wang and Lina Deng, 2010, "Nutrition during rapid economic development, and nutrition status in China under the global economic crisis," Nutrition Policy Research Report, Food Nutrition Monitoring Work Panel, China Center for Disease Control and Prevention, Beijing (unpublished research report).

Chen, Jialin, 2008, "Signals of grain smuggling," 4 July 2008 [online; cited 25 August 2010]. Available from: finance.people.com.cn/GB/1045/7468338.html (in Chinese).

Chen, Xiwen, 2010, Current situation of agriculture and the rural economy: A speech at a seminar at the Chinese Academy of Social Sciences in Beijing on 5 January 2010 (in Chinese).

Ganesh-Kumar, A., Devesh Roy and Ashok Gulati, 2010, *Liberalizing Food Grains Markets*, New Delhi: Oxford University Press.

General Office of NDRC, 2010, "Circular on the inspection of guaranteed minimum price grain purchase," 23 June 2010 [online; cited 24 August 2010]. Available from: www.sdpc.gov.cn/zcfb/zcfbtz/2010tz/t20100701_358365.htm (in Chinese).

Han, Changfu, 2010, "Steadfastly transforming the growth pattern of agriculture," [online; cited 17 August 2010]. Available from: www.gov.cn/jrzg/2010–05/17/content_1607473. htm (in Chinese).

Huang, Jikun and Scott Rozelle, 2006, "Small farmers and agri-food market restructuring: The case of the fruit sector in China," [online; cited 10 August 2010]. Available from: iis-db.stanford.edu/pubs/21703/FAO_small_holders_horticulture_2006.pdf.

Lin, Yifu, 1998, "Can China feed itself in the 21st century?," *Liao Wang* (*Journal of Outlook Weekly*), No. 33 (in Chinese).

Liu, Xuemei and Dehua Du, 2010, "The highest poverty incidence is in Gansu Province," [online; cited 31 July 2010]. Available from: www.chinanews.com.cn/gn/news/2010/03–15/2170685.shtml (in Chinese).

Ministry of Agriculture, 2009, *China Agriculture Development Report*, Beijing: China Agriculture Press (in Chinese).

Ministry of Commerce, 2010, "Report on China agricultural product analysis," [online; cited 16 August 2010]. Available from: wms.mofcom.gov.cn/accessory/201005/1272939548240.pdf (in Chinese).

Ministry of Environmental Protection, 2009, "National environmental quality status," [online; cited 17 August 2010]. Available from: jcs.mep.gov.cn/hjzl/hjzlzk/200901/t20090121_133715.htm (in Chinese).

Ministry of Water Resources, 1997 and 2008, "China water resources communiqué," [online; cited 17 August 2010]. Available from: www.mwr.gov.cn/ztbd/zgszygb/19970101/15238. asp, and www.mwr.gov.cn/zwzc/hygb/szygb/qgszygb/201001/t20100119_171051.html (in Chinese).

NBS (National Bureau of Statistics of China), 2010a, "Statistical communiqué on the national socioeconomic development in 2009, P.R. China," [online; cited 15 August 2010]. Available from: www.stats.gov.cn/tjgb/ndtjgb/qgndtjgb/t20100225_402622945. htm (in Chinese).

NBS (National Bureau of Statistics of China), 2010b, "Monitoring and survey report on migrant workers in 2009," [online; cited 18 August 2010]. Available from: www.stats. gov.cn/tjfx/fxbg/t20100319_402628281.htm (in Chinese).

NDRC (National Development and Reform Commission), 2010, "Wheat price rise in the international market has a limited impact on grain prices in the domestic market," 13 August 2010 [online; cited 24 August 2010]. Available from: www.sdpc.gov.cn/xwfb/t20100813_366175.htm (in Chinese).

Research Group at the Research Center of Rural Economy, Ministry of Agriculture, 2008, "An investigation on distribution processes and price setting in vegetable markets in Beijing," (unpublished survey report), 17 January.

Shi, Peijun, Jing'ai Wang, Yun Xie, Ping Wang and Wuguang Zhou, 1997, "Preliminary research on China's climate change, agricultural natural disasters and grain production," *Natural Resources Journal*, No. 3 [online; cited 18 August 2010]. Available from: irs. bnu.edu.cn/SPJBook/paper percent5CJP199705.pdf (in Chinese).

State Administration of Grain, 2009, *China Food Yearbook 2009*, Beijing: Economic Management Press (in Chinese).

State Administration of Grain, 2010a, "Catalogue of enterprises with grain purchase permit issued by State Administration of Grain," 12 January 2008 [online; cited 24 August 2010]. Available from: www.chinagrain.gov.cn/n16/n1122/n2127/n1378378/n1448784/1480334.html (in Chinese).

State Administration of Grain, 2010b, "Response of officials with State Administration of Grain to questions on current grain and edible oil supply and demand status," [online; cited 24 August 2010]. Available from: www.china.com.cn/policy/txt/2008–02/02/content_9638835.htm (in Chinese).

Strategic Agricultural Development Research Panel of Chinese Academy of Sciences, 2010, *Roadmap for China's Agro-Technology Development till 2050*, Beijing: Science and Technology Press (in Chinese).

Wang, Meiyan, 2010, "Can migrant workers go back to agriculture?" A presentation at the Conference on Labor Migration held in University of St Andrews, UK on 12–14 June 2010.

World Bank, 2008, *Poverty Data: A Supplement to World Development Indicators 2008*, Washington, DC: World Bank.

Xia, Jingyuan, 2010, "Plant protection goes green," [online; cited 18 August 2010]. Available from: www.farmer.com.cn/hy/spaq/spdt/200911/t20091123_500674.htm (in Chinese).

Ye, Zhenqin, 2010, "Stronger agriculture is essential for increasing grain output," speech presented at the China Rural Development High-Level Forum on 22 May 2010 (in Chinese).

Zhang, Xiaoshan, 2009, "Trends of specialized farmers' cooperatives," *Guanli Shijie* (*Management World*), No. 5, pp. 89–96 (in Chinese).

Zhang, Xiaoyong, Huanguang Qiu and Zhurong Huang, 2010, "Apple and tomato chains in China and EU," LEI Report 2010–019. The Hague: Wageningen University and Research Centre.

Zhao, Guangfei, 2010, "Overview on farming system development and modern agriculture of stateowned farm system," [online; cited 21 August 2010]. Available from: www.chinacoop.com/HTML/2010/06/10/47227.html (in Chinese).

Part III
Nutrition and health

7 Changes in rural basic health system

Despite their enormous success, there's no denying the fact that market oriented reforms in China have also led to a widening of rural-urban gaps, increasing regional disparities, and income inequalities adding to poverty. Individuals and households are now under greater risk and uncertainties that cannot be mitigated by the existing informal protection systems. The process of restructuring the social protection system in response to the socioeconomic transition lags behind marketization that proceeds unhindered. As a result, those outside the formal security systems, save those in the high-income group, have become more vulnerable to economic forces.

The growing health vulnerability of the rural people is becoming increasingly apparent and although a booming medical market has emerged during the transition, medical services and drug markets remain far from well regulated. Corruption is rampant in the process of drug procurement, leading to costlier medicines and poorer access to health services. The vicious circle of poverty and illness has evoked wide public concern and calls for prompt policy intervention.

This chapter focuses on the health insecurity problems faced by the rural people during the current socioeconomic transition in China. We first introduce the changes in basic health care system and financing, and review the socioeconomic impacts of the current transition drawing on macro-level information. Section 7.2 identifies health vulnerable groups through household livelihood analyses. This part also draws heavily from sample data on the use of medical services to identify residual insecurity under the existing health risk-pooling systems. We end with a discussion of the necessary policy interventions, looking at the Indian experiences related to these issues.

7.1 Health care system and financing

7.1.1 Tracking the changes

As early as the mid-1960s, a three-tier (county, township and village) health service network had the responsibility of providing both medical treatment and health care in rural China. In the highly centralized planning system, public health

(Originally published in *China and World Economy*, 2014 with the title "Restructuring the Basic Health Protection System in Rural China".)

programs sponsored by the government could be implemented rather smoothly in the countryside through this network. Rural health workers, widely known as 'bare-foot doctors', played a major role in providing easy and quick access to primary health care for the rural population. These rural health workers received work points from their respective production teams and received cash from the villagers for the cheap medicines.

The so-called cooperative health care system, operating in most parts of China at this time, was the grassroots public health service system closely associated with the functioning of the commune system (Zhu, 2006).The government retained firm control over medicine production and sale so as to guarantee reliable and inexpensive supply. These institutional factors and strong government financial support for public health made a decisive contribution to the improvement of rural health conditions despite the overall low level of health services.

Since the early 1980s, China's rural health care system has gone through far-reaching reforms. Government was the prime mover in this case, roping in the market to tackle the problems of public health financing and contain health care costs. Pursuing financial decentralization, higher government levels often delegated the responsibility of health care financing to the lower levels that were in financial difficulties and likely to leave the responsibility to health care institutions. This actually meant that the problem was left to the market. Such a policy orientation became visible as early as in 1985 when the health care reform program was announced (China, State Council 1985).[1] This policy document neither tried to encourage government authorities at various levels to increase investment in public health, nor did it find a way to rein in medical costs. Instead, it allowed medical institutions to collect fees at their will to deal with the shortfall in government financing.

As a result of financial decentralization, the three-tier health service network in rural China was challenged by the decline of public investment. One of the manifestations is the notable decline of the share of public health expenditure in total expenditures. The share of public health spending declined from 2.5 percent in 1980 to 1.7 percent in 2000. The cooperative health care system virtually disappeared following the collapse of the People's Commune System, and the overwhelming majority of village health clinics were privatized. Subsidies for public health services at and above township levels were reduced[2] and rural health services were commercialized but the lack of well-functioning medical services and drug markets as well as corruption in drug procurement resulted in cost increases. For example, the cost of hospitalized treatment for appendicitis increased by 37.2 percent in 2000 compared to what it was in 1995, and the cost of hospitalized treatment for pneumonia increased by 83.2 percent, at a time when the net per capita income of rural households increased by just 25.9 percent (Figure 7.1).

These changes resulted in a turnaround from the pre-reform policy that had effectively combined basic biomedical intervention and public health care. In order to reverse such a trend, the Chinese government has been making efforts to re-establish the cooperative health care system and at the same time carrying

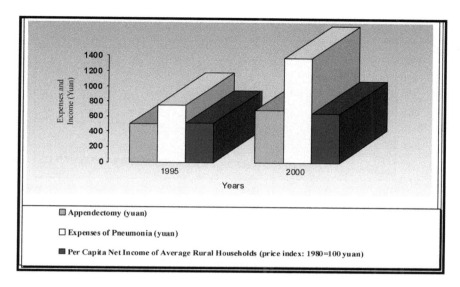

Figure 7.1 Expenses and per capita net income of average rural households in China, 1995 and 2000

Source: Editorial Committee of Health Yearbook, 2001, *zhongguo weisheng nianjian (China Health Yearbook)*, p.474 and 501, Beijing: renmin weisheng chubanshe (People's Health Press).

out experimentation of various forms of health risk sharing systems in different regions at varying development levels, making investments in upgrading public health care facilities, and addressing the problems of health care and drug markets. However, the trend has not yet been reversed partly because the intervention is far from adequate.

7.1.2 Impact of changes: Growing inequality and vulnerability

The impact of changes in health care financing on health vulnerability of rural people has not been directly discernible in the overall health outcomes since such outcomes are also influenced by other factors such as nutrition, clothing, housing, jobs, education, living environment, behavior and lifestyle etc. Nevertheless, one can feel the impacts in the following areas:

1   *Increasing medical costs borne mainly by patients.* In the 1980s, the total health expenditure in China was 3 percent of GDP. Figure 7.2 show that in the early 1990s, health spending was in the range of 100–200 billion yuan or 4.1 percent of GDP and increased to more than 400 billion yuan, or 5.1 percent of GDP in 1999 (Editorial Committee of Health Yearbook 2001). The increase in health care expenditure (in nominal terms) during these years was mainly and directly borne by patients.

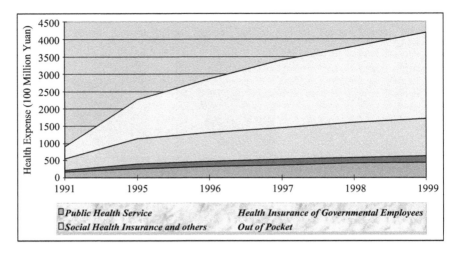

Figure 7.2 Total health expenditure in China during the 1990s

Source: Editorial Committee of Health Yearbook 2001

2   *Declining utilization of health care resources.* A report by the Ministry of Public Health pointed out that '. . . compared with 1990, in 1998 the average patients per doctor declined from 1683 to 1178; the utilization of hospital beds declined from 80 to 60 percent . . .', and that '. . . insufficient health resources co-exist with their wasteful use . . .' (China, Ministry of Public Health, 1999: pp. 188 and 190).

3   *Widening rural-urban gap in health resource allocation.* The urban population, especially the unemployed and their families have also suffered from the market-orientation of health services, although investment in health care by both central and local governments was concentrated in the cities. Social medical insurance and social aid systems were also mostly developed for the cities. Under these conditions, health care services have been biased against the rural population. By the end of the 1990s, rural dwellers accounted for more than 70 percent of the total population in China, but rural health care expenditure accounted for only about 20 percent of the total government expenditure on health care (China, Ministry of Public Health, 1999: pp. 188 and 190).

4   *Notable reduction of access to medical services by rural people.* The state health service survey organized by the Ministry of Public Health found that in 1993, 58.8 percent of the rural patients needing hospitalization did not go to a hospital because of personal economic difficulties. In 1998, this percentage increased to 65.3 percent (China, Ministry of Public Health, 1999: pp. 188 and 190).

5   *Aggravation of the vicious circle of poverty and illness.* According to one calculation, poor households[3] accounted for 7.2 percent of the total rural households in 1998, whereas the non-poor households falling into the category of poor households due to medical expenses accounted for 3.3 percent of the

total households. This means that due to family medical expenditure, more people slipped into poverty and the poverty rate went up to 10.5 percent.

6   *Preventive health service reduced at the grassroots level.* This problem exists despite the fact that the government has neither given up its management role in public health[4] nor forgotten to insist that village clinics should continue to take the responsibility of epidemic prevention, maternity and childcare, and family planning. The government's document of health care reform announced in 1985 stipulated that any institution or individual could run village clinics if the village provided appropriate subsidies for the labor input by rural doctors/health workers in the area of public health work. In the poor areas, local governments were also required to provide assistance and subsidies for such activities (China, State Council 1985). These requirements, however, were too difficult to be met in the economically less developed areas. As a result, in most rural regions, especially the poor ones, preventive services either remain deficient in terms of service supply, or are starting to charge fees. This makes it more difficult for the poor to obtain preventive services creating greater health vulnerability among them.

7.2 Identifying rural health insecurity

None of us can know beforehand when we'll fall seriously ill, but the poor, pregnant, children and the elderly are definitely more prone to health risks than the rest. However, even the high-risk groups at low-income level are not unavoidably vulnerable when they are protected by social security systems or are supported by other forms of safety nets. The health care services that increase accessibility through public support can also alleviate the insecurity of the high-risk groups. Based on this understanding, this section gives an overview on the portfolio of the social security coverage in China based on recent national statistics. Subsequently, the health vulnerable segments are identified mainly based on individual and household level information.

7.2.1 Institutions of rural health security

The institutions that help and support rural people during illness or suffering from illness-related income and expenditure shocks in China are as follows:

1   Formal health insurance systems including commercial health insurance programs; social health insurance programs; and community-based cooperative medical insurance schemes (effectively functioning only in a few well-off counties).
2   Health relief and assistance including:

   •   Medical relief in the case of the major income earners falling seriously ill (cases found within the rural health project financed by the World Bank covering a number of poor counties in southern Shaanxi Province) (World Bank, 1997b);

- Social assistance with cash transfer to the aged confronting catastrophic illness or injuries (cases recorded in Shaoxing townships of Zhejiang Province); and
- Subsidized maternity services to women of poor households (cases found from the rural health project financed by the Chinese Poverty Alleviation Foundation for Lijiang County, Yunnan Province).

3   Selective health service provision with budgetary subsidies for rural health education schemes; and targeted preventive health plans including pre-natal and maternal care program and immunization for children aged below seven.
4   Informal risk pooling among family members, relatives, friends and neighbors.

The formal Chinese social protection system for the rural people, however well-established it may have been in the past, is currently extremely limited in coverage. Health relief and assistance have functioned only in a few developed regions. In those poor areas where health promotion projects were carried out with the aid of poverty reduction funds, the assistance was only for the duration of the projects.

The budgetary subsidies allocated to rural health education and targeted preventive health plans are often not sufficient to support the full operation of the programs. For example, the immunization plan was designed to be free of charge for children under the age of seven, but the central government disposed funds for the vaccine and left the payment for services to be met by the local governments, the majority of whom have not paid the cost either due to unwillingness or inability. The parents have to pay at least 1–3 yuan for every shot of vaccine, so some of the rural poor cannot afford to have their children participate fully in the program. Due to the financial and geographical constraints to accessing reproductive health care, around 40 percent of pregnant women from the poor rural households did not receive pre-natal care. A similar proportion of rural pregnant women in poor areas could not have deliveries at a health center or a hospital.

With regard to health insurance programs, people covered by health insurance schemes in China accounted for only 27 percent of the total population in 1998, with the coverage rate at 55.9 percent and 12.7 percent for urban and rural people respectively. The elderly with declining earning abilities belong to a high health risk group with the coverage of pension scheme determining their ability to cope with enlarging medical expenditures. The coverage of pension schemes in 2001 was estimated at 29.5 percent for urban dwellers and 7.5 percent for the rural. Thus there is a considerable proportion of the population outside the coverage of the two most important schemes in both the urban and rural sectors. The uncovered portion is substantially larger for the rural group than the urban segment (figures 7.3 and 7.4).

As the average rural income is lower than the urban and poverty in most part of the countryside is more severe than in urban areas, rural people are more vulnerable to health threats. The insurance schemes covering urban people are essentially related to the labor force employed in the formal economy, and are similar to those in any developing countries. The rural people covered by the

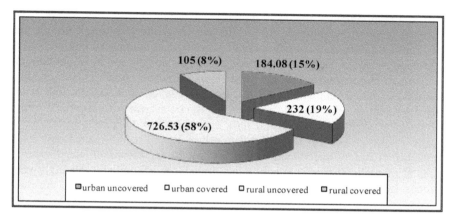

Figure 7.3 Coverage of health insurance in China in 1998 (million people)
Source: National Health Survey 1998; China Statistical Yearbook 1999.

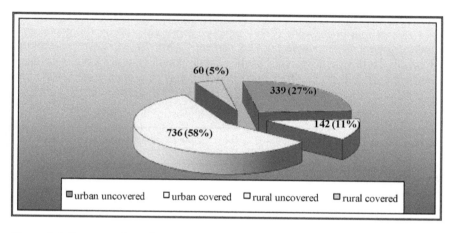

Figure 7.4 Coverage of pension system in China in 2001 (million people)
Source: Labour and Social Security Development Statistics Report 2001; China Statistical Yearbook 2002.

two formal social support systems are primarily those working in rural industries and services. Farmers and their family members account for the major part of the uncovered and are only secured by the entitlement to land. Thanks to the great improvement in land productivity, most farming households have achieved food security even with very small land plots measuring on average only 0.6 ha per household. However, the deficit of the basic needs that were met by the income generated from land-related activities is growing bigger with marketization. This is particularly true for health care and education, which have become increasingly expensive since the government started shifting financing responsibilities to individuals.

To overcome the problems of insufficient investment in public health and the limited coverage of health insurance systems, a number of counties/cities in the eastern rural regions took the lead in re-establishing village public clinics, integrating township and village medical prevention services, and creating community-based cooperative medical insurance schemes or social health insurance systems. In other regions especially in the poor areas, similar efforts rarely produced successful results (Zhu, 2006). The majority of the rural people have to rely on informal systems to protect themselves against health-related risks even though it is widely understood that the informal mechanisms of social security such as mutual assistance via family ties, friends, neighbors, and rotating saving groups etc. are unable to provide adequate protection and support to the rural people in the context of increasing marketization.

7.2.2 Health-risk groups and use of medical services

The characteristics of rural health insecurity can be more precisely presented with descriptive statistics deriving from a sample survey[5] by the author. In a total of 1,989 sample households (7,900 people), those covered by the cooperative medical programs accounted for 11.8 percent (Table 7.1) while school children of ages 8–16 (nearly 13 percent of the sample population) are insured for accidents and hospitalization. These two categories may have some overlaps in terms

Table 7.1 Mean household assets possessed by the poor and the non-poor*

Asset	Total sample n = 1989	Low income n = 266	Middle n = 671	High n = 1052
Human capital				
Household size (person)	3.91 (1.7)**	4.19 (1.6)	4.3 (1.7)	3.6 (1.6)
Labor ratio (Number of labor/ household size)	77 percent (55.0)	54 percent (26.8)	63 percent (26.8)	81 percent (68.0)
Years of schooling of household head	6.63 (2.2)	5.63 (2.3)	6.50 (2.7)	6.97 (2.0)
Natural capital				
Area cultivated (mu/per household)***	6.19 (7.4)	6.84 (5.7)	6.59 (5.0)	5.77 (8.8)
Area contracted****	3.89 (4.3)	3.34 (3.8)	4.69 (4.2)	3.51 (4.4)
Financial capital				
Bank savings and cash at end of the year	9,654 (25776)	1,538 (3411)	3,654 (6531)	15,534 (34201)
Bonds and others	34 (859)	0 (0)	8 (193)	59 (1170)

Asset	Total sample n = 1989	Low income n = 266	Middle n = 671	High n = 1052
Physical capital				
Value of production assets	6,118 (29081)	2,877 (6781)	3,608 (7392)	8,539 (39251)
Value of non-production assets	23,381 (41135)	8,767 (8671)	13,249 (15179)	33,538 (53028)
Health insurance coverage (%)	11.80	6.80	7.50	15.80

Source: Author's survey.

* In this Table and Table 7.2 the poor are the low income group with annual per capita net income below 1,000 yuan; non-poor above 1,000 yuan; and middle income 1,000–2,000 yuan
** Figures in brackets are standard deviation
*** 15mu = 1 ha
**** Area that a household received from the process of land distribution in its village

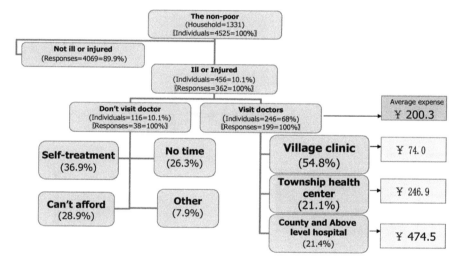

Figure 7.5 Types of health service providers chosen by the non-poor
Source: Author's survey

of participation by the sample population as the benefit packages of the two are very different. The findings underline the fact that the majority of the rural people remain health insecure.

Figures 7.5 to 7.8 show the incidence of sickness in the two weeks prior to the survey and the choices that the patients made in dealing with it. Figures 7.5 and 7.6 show that the poor suffered from a higher incidence of sickness. About 70 percent of the people who fell ill and visited a doctor chose to get medical treatment from the local village clinics that generally receive nothing from government budgets. There were also a remarkable number of patients from both the poor and the

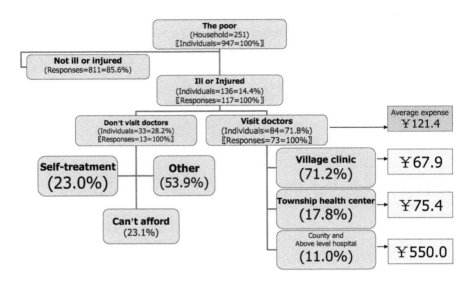

Figure 7.6 Types of health service providers chosen by the poor
Source: Author's survey

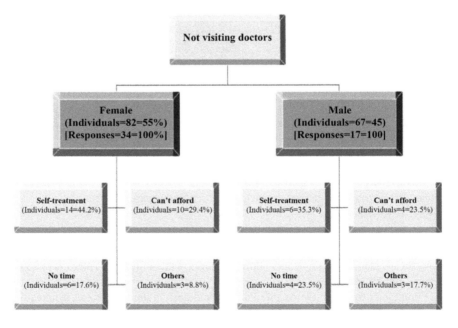

Figure 7.7 Reasons for not visiting doctors by gender
Source: Author's survey

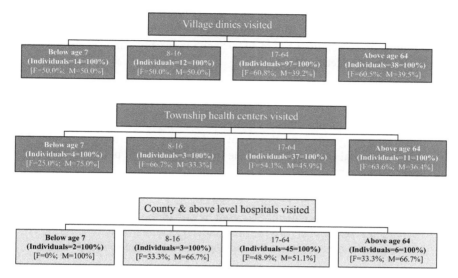

Figure 7.8 Types of health service providers chosen by age and gender
Source: Author's survey

non-poor groups that bought medicine on their own for self-treatment. Such practice apparently helps to reduce the cost of medical treatment but it contains health
risks that cannot be ignored. To buy and take medicines without a doctor's exami-
nation and prescription may well result in incorrect and indiscriminate use. This
is even more risky for those who do not have much knowledge: a concern borne
out by the fact that less than 30 percent of the heads of the poor households in our
sample said they'd received health education services, compared to 35–41 percent
in the non-poor category.

About 10 percent of the total sample reported being ill, with the sickness incidence of females at 12.6 percent, 3 percentage points higher than the sickness
incidence of males. Roughly 28 percent of the ill included those over the age of
64 while pre-school children under the age of seven accounted for 13.3 percent.
The group of school children between the ages of 8–16 had the lowest share of
5.2 percent. Ironically, only this age group is covered by commercial insurance,
due to the campaign launched by insurance companies throughout the school system. The companies ruled out the group over the age of 60 by requiring a much
higher premium than the other age groups, thereby inducing the majority of those
who most require it to give up buying commercial insurance.

7.2.3 Residual health insecurity

Residual health insecurity can be generally defined as the situation of an individual
or a group of people who are outside the coverage of health security institutions.

For well-targeted policy intervention, it is crucial to identify the residual inse-curities at both the country as well as regional levels since there are significant differences in security institutions between countries and regions. Groups in rural China living under conditions of residual health insecurity can be identified based on the following criteria:

1   Those excluded by social health insurance schemes or/and by commercial insurance programs;
2   Within these groups, those outside community-based cooperative health insurance programs, and those covered by the cooperative programs but whose medical expenses exceed the limit of the benefit packages offered by the cooperatives;
3   Those who are eligible to receive subsidized provision of targeted health care services but for various reasons are not covered;
4   Among those who are neither covered by any of the insurance programs nor by targeted health plans are the poor, elderly, and major income earners suf-fering from serious sickness but lacking access to relief or assistance.

The above categories can be ranked according to the degree of insecurity and a visual picture is presented in Figure 7.9. However, it must be pointed out that the rural migrants are working in urban areas without health protection under the urban security institutions. Although they are better off in terms of income in the city than in their home villages, most of them have to face greater health risks and more expensive medical services due to the institutional barriers against rural-urban migration. The migrants play multiple social and economic roles as they are

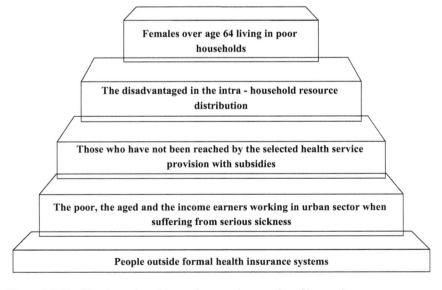

Figure 7.9 Health-wise vulnerable rural groups by severity of insecurity

the major income earners for their rural families, while in the city they belong to the most vulnerable group of the society.

Among the rural residents falling in the aforementioned categories, those who have less control over household assets, weak family ties, kinship and community, and low income-generating capacity are regarded as the residual health insecure in relation to the informal institutions. The most vulnerable in the insecure groups are those who are most disadvantaged in the intra-household resource distribution. Because of the survey limitation, the data set cannot shed light on the informal risk-pooling arrangements between the sample households and the intra-household resource distribution amongst individuals. Nevertheless, it can be used to describe the economic characteristics of the health vulnerable groups through household livelihood analyses.

Tables 7.1 to 7.3 compare the poor and non-poor sample households with regard to two aspects: (1) assets and (2) composition of consumption and total expenditures. Apparently, the non-poor households have fewer members but they enjoy wider labor ratios. The heads of the non-poor families received higher formal education than the heads of the poorer households. These imply that the non-poor households are able to put more labor force in income generating activities.

The non-poor owned much larger amounts of financial and physical assets, which partly reflects access to more remunerative non-farming activities. Given that all village households are only eligible to usufruct land rights and that land is by law unmarketable, the possession of financial and physical capital is indicative of substantial differences in wealth between households. The value of productive and non-productive assets of the poor sums up to 11,644 yuan, which is

Table 7.2 Composition of household expenditures of the poor and the non-poor

Per capita Net Annual Income	Statistics	Total Annual Expenditure	Production	Consumption	Others
Below 1000 yuan (Poor)	Mean (yuan)	7,190	2,775	3,719	696
	Percentage	100	39	52	10
	SD	12753	11464	3216	1141
	Number of HH	266	266	266	266
Above 1000 yuan (Non-Poor)	Mean (yuan)	17,952	7,406	9,050	1,495
	Percentage	100	41	50	8
	SD	37587	30302	14049	5058
	Number of HH	1,723	1,723	1,723	1,723
Total sample	Mean (yuan)	16,513	6,787	8,337	1,388
	Percentage	100	41	50	8
	SD	35480	28554	13253	4733
	Number of HH	1,989	1,989	1,989	1,989

Source: Author's survey

SD = Standard Deviation

Table 7.3 Household consumption expenditures of the poor and the non-poor

Per capita Net Annual Income	Statistics	Total annual Consumption Expenditures	Food	Health	Education	Others
Below 1000 yuan	Mean (yuan)	3,719	2,094	178	239	1,208
	Percentage	100	56	5	6	32
	SD	3216	1220	451	608	2453
	Number of HH	266	266	266	266	266
Above 1000 yuan	Mean (yuan)	9,050	3,910	432	692	4,017
	Percentage	100	43	5	8	44
	SD	14049	3223	1786	1489	12264
	Number of HH	1,723	1,723	1,723	1,723	1,723
Total sample	Mean (yuan)	8,337	3,667	398	631	3,641
	Percentage	100	44	4.7	7.6	43.7
	SD	13253	3095	1672	1412	11490
	Number of HH	1,989	1,989	1,989	1,989	1,989

Source: Author's survey

equivalent to about 40 percent of the average asset value of a sample household (Table 7.1). Household assets can be used to cope with economic risks, but the assets of the majority of the sample households are far from sufficient to deal with income shocks resulting from catastrophic illnesses. This is particularly true in the case of the poor. For instance, hospitalization because of cancer cost a patient in rural areas about 5,092 yuan on average in 1998. The cost of hospitalization would be double in urban areas. This happened to be equivalent to half of the total value of assets of the poor in the survey sample.

The health vulnerability problems of the poor can be further identified by the following features of the subsistence economy that largely characterize poor areas:

1   Consumption had considerably more weight than production in total house-hold expenditures. They constituted 50 and 41 percent of total expenditure respectively. The proportion of consumption in total expenditure of poor households was larger than that of the average, although the poor spent a noticeably smaller amount on consumption in absolute terms that accounted for about 45 percent of the average (Table 7.2).

2   The poor households were under very tight budget constraints in meeting their non-food basic needs since their food expenditure already took 56 per-cent of total consumption (Table 7.3). While the shares of health and educa-tion in the total consumption of the poor did not differ very much from those of the non-poor, the non-poor actually spent as much as 2.4 and 2.9 times what the poor spent respectively on health and education.

In terms of health resource distribution within a poor household, the sample results showed that under financial constraints household members were generally ranked in the following order of priority: major income earners, children, and elderly. At each level the male usually ranked better than the female due to traditional gender inequality. Frequently in extended families, the elderly of over 60 years would prefer to renounce medical treatment for themselves and use the resources so saved to pay for the health care of their children and grandchildren. During the current socioeconomic transition, the majority of extended families were separated into nuclear families leading to a rapid increase in the number of the 'vacant nest families' with only an old couple or a single elderly person. In our sample, there were 75 vacant nest families with their household head aged over 60. Such households accounted for 3.8 percent of the total sample households with one third falling in the poor category. Since most rural residents were not covered by pension schemes, the livelihood of the elderly in poor households became noticeably insecure. The aging couples without working capacities were supported by their children for food and other basic necessities while the children cultivated the land plots of the parents. For the aged without children, the village committees took care of them in the same way. However, constrained by the lack of cash income, the elderly people in poor areas often confronted difficulties in accessing medical treatment while ill.

This information indicates that all rural groups without formal social security coverage tend to become more vulnerable when access to preventive and curative medical services deteriorates because of changes in health care financing. Among these, the poor, elderly, women, and pre-school children are more at risk. The elderly in poor households were the most vulnerable amongst all groups owing to deficiencies in both public and family support for their health care.

7.3 Options for policy intervention

We have seen that market reforms in the health sector and lack of sufficient government intervention in health service and insurance cannot overcome the difficulty of financing and cost control. The market-oriented transition leads to low efficiency in resource allocation and utilization, and hence results in increasing inequality and reduced capability of the poor to access health care services. It has also increased the vulnerability of the already-vulnerable, those who were not under the coverage of social protection. These problems were revealed during the recent outbreak of SARS that encouraged the government and the public to make more efforts to restrict this tendency in the health sector.

Currently the government still uses a few instruments employed under the planned economy to control the health sector, those that resulted in serious price distortions and monopoly of the public hospitals. For example, the authorities set the ceilings for the pharmaceutical prices high enough to leave remarkably huge margins for rent-seeking activities by those who are involved in the process of delivering drugs from producers to final consumers (patients). Also, the services of doctors are so undervalued in the administrative price system that it is an incentive for the hospitals and doctors to compensate for it by providing patients with excessive treatments and drugs. The administrative barriers put up by the health authorities against the entry of private hospitals have allowed public hospitals in most counties and cities to function as a monopoly, making it virtually impossible for farmers to see doctors and seek even the low quality yet high-cost medical services (Bureau of Health in Shuyang County, 2004). This implies that "market failure" and "government failure" have been coexisting in the health sector of China during the period of the economic transition. Indeed, recommendation of government intervention should include demands for further reforms of the health systems by way of change in the way of governance and functioning of health authorities.

Based on this understanding, it is suggested that the rural health protection system be restructured systematically to meet the basic health needs of the rural population. The provision of health security does not depend as much on the demand or the supply of health resources as it does on the political decision of the members of the entire society (Walford, Pearson, Eliya, and Fernando, 2006). To achieve basic health security for all rural people, joint efforts are needed by the government at different levels as well as village communities, households and NGOs.

7.3.1 *Improving planned immunization programs*

The first priority in restructuring the basic health protection system is to improve and extend the rural immunization programs. It is financially feasible for the central government to inject additional funds into preventive institutions targeting children so that the programs can be implemented free of charge. Here, China should learn from the experience of India where free immunization has been provided for many years.[6] China shares with India similar characteristics such as a huge population and a similar level of development. This also implies that the decision to either take or not take up the necessary costs of immunization services is as much a matter of fiscal capacity as of political will.

Since the government did not pay a fee to the service providers in the planned immunization programs and only financed the production and distribution of the vaccines, they collected fees from the parents of the children covered. This situation has substantially changed in the developed regions since the outbreak of SARS. For example, the local governments at county level in Zhejiang province have given township hospitals a public health service fund for implementing the preventive activities including immunization programs. The size of a fund is corresponding to the number of the residents living in a township. The poor county, for instance Chunan County, receives a transfer from the provincial government annually of 15 yuan per capita. In this way, free immunization services are realized in Zhejiang province. This experience provides a solution for the central government to extend the free immunization services by taking the responsibility of the transfers to the poor counties located in the less developed provinces, the western regions in particular.

7.3.2 Investing in village clinics

At the village level, health care services most frequently used by the rural residents, especially the poor, are provided by private doctors or health institutions (Zhu, 2006). In current China, the regular services that village health stations provide consist of diseases prevention, public health intervention and basic medical services. But health stations can hardly be able to cover the costs of those services, which have a great externality such as diseases prevention and public health intervention. In the small and medium sized villages, the stations are usually unable to achieve economy of scale in the provision of basic medical services. This implies that the provision of health services at the village level can be an area in which market failure occurs and therefore public support is needed. The welfare of the rural health vulnerable groups can improve substantially if the government prioritizes its financial support to village clinics. The Indian government has already implemented such policies. For example, health workers in village clinics were paid salaries by the government in the state of Gujarat. In this area, a feasible step for China is to adapt the Indian practice to local conditions with special emphasis on providing strong incentives for village health workers to improve the quality of service.

The experiences in financing and managing the village health stations in rural Changshu of Jiangsu Province also serve as a valuable model for the central government. The cases from the rural areas around Changshu City suggest that the following factors are necessary if the stations are to provide sufficient services with reliable quality and reasonable prices. First, the county government, township government and village committees invest in village health stations with both physical and human capital. Second, local health authorities provide management and supervision for village health stations. Third, the township government and village committee rationalize incentive mechanisms following the changing socioeconomic framework to affect the behavior of health workers. Finally, villagers take active part in health financing. The village committees, township and county governments in less developed regions certainly need fiscal transfer from the upper level governments to support the health service providers in villages either with the Indian or Changshu model, or with their own institutional innovations. In any case, there are three aspects worth noting: First, health workers should be paid an amount sufficient to act as incentives for them to provide villagers with the best possible services in health education and disease prevention.

Second, the pre-reform tradition of budgetary resources being used to finance periodic training for village health workers should be restored. Most training courses are now funded by the trainees themselves. As a result, village health workers have reduced their demand for basic training courses in poor areas since they cannot afford them.

Third, under the framework of the cooperative medical system, an incentive structure should be designed to stimulate health operators to offer villagers inexpensive and reliable medical services. The remuneration of the health professionals, that is a basic salary plus a registration fee practised in the village clinics of well-developed regions, can be integrated with a monitoring system by a regulatory institution of public health at the township level to ensure transparency of medical costs.

7.3.3 Linking social and commercial insurance programs

Government intervention prior to the SARS pandemic, including for example the experiments of the community-based cooperative health insurance programs, achieved only limited success in well-developed regions and little in the middle and less developed regions. It was found that sustainability of social medical insurance or health care cooperatives in the more developed regions depends on a relatively high rural average income, the willingness of farmers to take a more decisive stance in avoiding health risks, efficient provision of health care services, reliable management of insurance funds, and social mobilization with government involvement and financial support. These are all important preconditions but unfortunately most of them are lacking in large parts of rural China. Moreover, the community-based cooperative health insurance system faced two kinds of difficulties: one, the risk pool is so small that it is not capable of sharing risks of catastrophic diseases without running a deficit, and the second relating to high management costs.

To overcome these difficulties, a new type of rural cooperative health insurance program designed to cope with risks of catastrophic illness was launched in the fourth quarter of 2003. This system is, in essence, a quasi-social medical insurance system. The central government has provided unprecedented strong institutional support and financial subsidies to provinces trying the system in the mid and western parts of the country. The minimum funding raised is 30 yuan per rural resident per year to be shared equally among the central government, local government and farmer households participating in the program. The money raised is mainly used to subsidize farmers and their family members when they are hospitalized. The risk pool of the new program is county-based and a management system was established in corresponding to the administrative hierarchy within a county. Apparently, the design concept of the new system is based on the insurance principle of healthy groups and infirm groups sharing disaster risks, with the prerequisite of the broadest participation of the rural population.

The health insurance coverage for the rural people has been then rapidly scaled up based on the government intervention with a strong administrative power since the end of SARS pestilence. Up to the end of 2005, there were 678 counties, nearly accounting for one third of the rural counties, approved to undertake the new program. Some 179 million rural residents that made up 75.7 percent of the rural population in the experimental counties, participated (Statistical Information Center, Ministry of Health, 2006).

According to studies that the author conducted in Wuxing County in Zhejiang province, one of the factors affecting the farmers' willingness to participate in the program is that only the in-patients accounting for about 3 percent of the participants in a year were eligible to get a partial reimbursement for their medical expenses since the program mainly covers the risks of catastrophic illness. Using the fund to compensate the outpatients for 15–20 percent of the medical fees immediately enlarged the proportion of the beneficiaries to 52.4 percent in a year. This is because most Chinese farmers do not have enough to spare financially. If they have to pay the insurance premiums, but the probability of receiving benefit is low, they are less likely to participate. For similar economic reasons, the low-income groups in the rural areas often do not see the doctor when they have minor diseases, thus by delaying treatment, increasing the likelihood of minor diseases evolving into major ones. So the positive effect of using the cooperative medical fund to compensate for a small portion of medical fees is that it encourages farmer families to increase health budgets and use more medical services.

However, the use of the fund in this way not only complicated reimbursement but also increased management cost. If the size of funds raised remains unchanged, it would inevitably lead to lower compensation for medical expenses incurred due to catastrophic illness. This is what is really happening in all of the experimental counties including the rich areas. A possible solution to this is to establish a linkage between the commercial and social health insurance programs. Besides the practice of channeling a small portion of the fund to the medical account of the individual households in the experimental counties, it will also help to channel a part of the fund in a county to pay a premium to the commercial insurance companies operating cross-county as an additional health insurance program sharing risks of catastrophic illness for all the participants.

The local government in Jiangyin County in Jiangsu province has set up a partnership between the government and a commercial insurance company to manage the rural cooperative health insurance program. The practice of Indian production cooperatives and NGOs in linking informal and formal insurance programs can be a good point of reference. For example, the Malabar Regional Cooperative Milk Producers Union in Kerala implemented its Mediclaim Insurance program in conjunction with Oriental and New India Assurance Companies. The member farmers of the Union paid premiums of Rs.130 per annum[7] in full and were entitled to receive the benefit of hospitalization treatment up to Rs.15,000 per year. Acting as a facilitator, the Union organizes the farmers and reaches a contract with the commercial insurance company. In this way, the two contractors benefited from the organizational advantages of each side. By such a group insurance arrangement the commercial insurance company won the enlargement of its pool of participants. Even the individual farmers obtained access to the formal insurance program that the commercial insurance companies usually refuse to offer them due to high transaction costs.

7.3.4 Health relief and health pension

Toward the end of 2003, the central government earmarked 300 million yuan a year for use as medical relief to households enjoying the "five guarantees"[8] and to poor farmer families with catastrophic illnesses. In addition, the government requested the provincial governments to allocate fiscal resources also for the same purpose. The policy makers anticipated that both the new rural cooperative health insurance program and health relief programs could help the poor break the vicious circle of poverty and illness. Nevertheless, under the principle of a minimum payment out of one's own pocket and co-payment for meeting the medical expenses over the minimum, the poor often use less medical services than the non-poor. Therefore, the health relief fund has been used in three ways; one, by subsidizing the poor for paying premiums to cooperative health insurance programs as a form of health relief. Without such subsidies either the poor households would be excluded from insurance programs or the programs cannot be implemented in the first place in villages and poor areas. Second, it is transferred to the insurance fund for sharing the minimum payment and co-payment of the poor to enable them to access medical services with a higher proportion of reimbursement than the non-poor are eligible for. Third, a part of the fund is directly transferred to the poor households suffering from economic crises due to catastrophic illness of their members. According to rough statistics, the fund was used to pay the insurance premium for a total of 8.68 million poor people while those who received direct transfer from the health relief fund amounted to 2.44 million people till the end of 2005 (Ministry of Civil Affaires, 2006).

There are two major problems in the ongoing health relief program. One, the size of the fiscal resources for pooling into the health relief fund in a county is periodically fixed, but the number of the needy and eligible for relief and the amount of subsidies to a specific beneficiary fluctuate because of the uncertainty in incidence and severity of diseases. Therefore, persons with the same income and similar diseases can receive different amounts from the fund in different years because of the lack of standardization of health relief. This problem would be solved in the near future when the health risks of the low-income groups including the poor are better estimated and the resources available for the relief goes up.

The other problem is that the mode and the time of delivering the relief have not matched the emergent needs of the poor, often reaching them after the misfortune has happened, for instance in the case of illness affecting a family member. This problem can be avoided with the introduction of publicly financed coupons or special accounts with which the poor will be able to visit doctors or get hospitalized. The system of relief through medical coupons has been practiced in the city of Shanghai since the beginning of reforms of state-owned enterprises, allowing even the unemployed to purchase basic health care services. This is supported by the experiences of the county government in Yuexi, a poor county in Anhui province, of delivering medical assistance to "five guarantees households". The county government injects annually 100 yuan per capita of the five guarantees households into a specific account to meet the medical expenses of these households. Under this system, the members of these households are exempted from users' fees when they see doctors within the county while the hospitals acquire transfers from the specific account as well as from the cooperative insurance fund after the delivery of the services.

Though a majority of the five guarantees households are the elderly, there is a need for specific social assistance and relief programs targeting the rural elderly. One policy option would be to set up a pension scheme starting with the health component, encouraging rural residents to save during their working years so that the accumulated pension funds can be used to meet their basic health care needs after they retire. During my field studies, I learnt that most elderly people tried their best to save for this purpose and wished to be exempted from the interest tax levied on their small savings. Thus, the health pension program can be operated as a supplement to family and community care services aimed at meeting the basic needs of the elderly for food, clothing, shelter etc. The welfare funds of Kerala have similar institutional design, where the labor union within different informal sectors collects a small amount of savings from member workers. Those who make contributions are eligible for a certain amount from the fund for specific needs.

7.3.5 A health insurance program for rural migrants

At present, the insurance plans are operated locally and are far from adequate to promote and protect labor mobility to the extent required by industrialization and urbanization. A basic health insurance program with universal coverage is certainly the right solution. Yet, for a big country like China with 1.3 billion people living in a dual society, to establish a sustainable universal social health insurance system will no doubt require tremendous efforts in terms of social mobilization and organizational work. Change may gradually begin with a health insurance program for the rural migrants as they form a strong link between the rural and urban society and face greater health vulnerability than other working people in China.

Most migrants are the breadwinners for their families in the villages. A national sample survey the by the State Statistics Bureau says that around 118 million rural people left their home village to work in cities and towns in 2004. Those commuting inter-provinces every year made up 51 percent of them. A majority of migrants engage in unskilled work in environs that are bad for health, like noisy or dusty working spaces, poisonous materials and other dangers related to industrial sectors. At the same time, their employment is less stable and their wages on average lower compared with those of workers with permanent urban residential registration. The weak human capital of the migrants, such as the low level of educational background and lack of occupational training, which leads to unskilled and low-paying jobs, could also be attributed to discriminations in the past. But the social protection systems in cities to a large extent exclusively benefit the permanent urban residents, especially the permanent employees. Though the rural cooperative health insurance program has covered those migrants, the medical expenses in cities are much higher than in their home counties. This implies that the rural sector has to share a part of the disease burden that the urban sector ought to undertake since the migrants contribute their labor to the latter. In other words, the transfer of the disease burdens to the rural sector implies that the low income groups subsidize the better-off and the poor pay more.

One way to avoid this is to integrate the rural migrants into the urban social health insurance program. In reality, the barriers to prevent migrant participation arise from two factors. On the one hand, the urban program requires a high premium that neither migrant workers nor their employers are willing to pay (Meng and Yuan, 2006). On the other, a large number of the local governments in the urban sector have not been willing to extend the coverage of health insurance to the migrants mainly due to financial difficulties.

One innovative model is found in Shenzhen City where about 6 million rural migrants work in factories. In 2005, the city government started to implement a health care program targeting the rural migrants. Each enterprise pays 8 yuan per worker per month into the insurance fund while each worker matches 4 yuan to it. The participating workers are eligible to receive around 50 percent of reimbursement for both the outpatient and inpatient medical expenses. The ceiling set to one's annual reimbursement amounts to 60,000 yuan. Till the end of 2005, there were 5500 participating enterprises and the participating workers numbered 1.24 million people (Meng and Yuan, 2006). Another model is in operation in Zhangjiagang City in Jiangsu province since 2004. The local government administers an area covering 854,000 people. Nearly 80 percent of the permanent residents are registered as rural people. In addition, over 200,000 rural migrants coming from outside of Zhangjiagang work in the non-agricultural sector. From a field study in 2005 I found that migrants working in factories were integrated into the local rural cooperative health insurance program. They were treated as equal in terms of premium payment, government subsidies and the reimbursement arrangements.

From my interviews with the migrant workers, I can conclude that the health protection programs established for the rural migrants will not only contribute to public health security and economic security, but also promote nationwide labor mobility, leading to the narrowing of urban-rural and regional disparities. This would serve as a crucial step in getting socioeconomic policies to aid the integration of the society, currently marked by a wide chasm between the cities and the countryside.

Notes

1 This policy document considers the severe shortage of investment in public health, low medical fees, and the financial loss of medical institutions as the main causes for the slow development of health enterprises. Further, strict government regulations are regarded as being not conducive to stimulating private investment. The document therefore encourages collectives and individuals to set up medical institutions and allow existing medical institutions to increase user fees, and charge labor and cost recovery fees for preventive and supervisory services.

2 According to the author's investigation in Nong'an and Yongji counties of Jilin Province in November 2001, the government no longer provided subsidies to township hospitals, and subsidies were being provided to county hospitals only for their investment program.
3 The rural poverty line set by the Office of the Leading Group for Poverty Alleviation, under the State Council, was 625 yuan per capita annual net income at the end of the 20th century. The exchange rate is 8 Yuan for a dollar.
4 Since the beginning of the reforms, the National People Representatives have passed 9 laws; the State Council announced or rectified 25 administrative regulations; and public health authorities promulgated over 400 departmental rules concerning health care issues.
5 The author organized the sample survey in 1999–2000 in collaboration with colleagues from the Research Center for Rural Economic Policies under the Ministry of Agriculture, China. The survey included 2,500 households in 34 villages, 34 counties and 6 provinces (Guangdong, Jiangsu, Hebei, Jilin, Sichuan and Gansu) in 1999.
6 The information about the Indian experience in public health care and innovative insurance programs for informal workers was acquired from the training programs in which the author participated in Gujarat and Kerala, India, in February–March 2003.
7 The exchange rate was about Rs.50 to a dollar in India during February–March, 2003.
8 "Five guarantees" means guarantee in the supply of food, clothing, medical care, housing and burial expenses.

References

Bureau of Health in Shuyang County, 2004, *A Compilation of Health Reforms (Weisheng Gaige Wenjian Huibian)*, printed by the county government, Shuyang. Cai, F. and Gu, eds. 2006, *Reports on China's Population and Labor No. 7 (zhongguo renkou yu laodong wenti bao gao No. 7)*, pp. 44–47, Social Sciences Literature Press (shehui kexue wenxian chubanshe), Beijing.

Meng and Yuan, 2006, Shenzhen: Health Insurance for Migrated Workers, in *Health News (Jiang Kang Bao)*, published on 4th of April, p. 7, Beijing.

Ministry of Civil Affaires, 2006, *Information about the Performance of Rural Medical Relief Program (nongcun yiliao jiuzhu gongzuo de qingkuang)*, an unpublished working report in March, Beijing.

Statistical Information Center, Ministry of Health, 2006, *Statistical Bulletin on Development of Health Sector in China in 2005, (2005 nian zhongguo weisheng shiye fazhan qingkuang tongji gongbao)*, issued on 25th of April, download on 1st of May from: www.moh.gov.cn/uploadfile/200642584823110.doc

Walford, Pearson, Eliya and Fernando, 2006, *Future Policy Choices for the Health Sector in Asia*, a background paper prepared for the conference for *Asia 2015 □Promoting Growth, Ending Poverty*, held during 6–7th of March, 2006, in London, www.asia-2015conference.org.

Zhu, L., 2006, Creating a Competitive Mechanism in Medical Services at County and Township Levels: A Case Study from Rural Jiangsu, forthcoming in the journal of *Management World (Guanli Shijie)*, Beijing.

8 Effects of rural Medical Financial Assistance in China

This paper presents research results from the evaluation of the Medical Financial Assistance (MFA) program, supported by the World Bank, to extremely poor rural residents. It is found that MFA can help to improve the ability of the poor to make use of medical services, and especially their ability to receive services from township clinics. The present study also shows that adoption of the MFA mechanism helps to reduce the impact of disease on the economies of poor families, and prevents the poor afflicted with serious illnesses from being marginalized. However, as the beneficiaries often suffer from serious, complicated and lasting illnesses, the financial assistance is often insignificant in relation to medical expenses. Furthermore, the MFA plays no significant role in restoring a patient's income-earning ability.

8.1 Introduction

In 2004, the research team[1] of the Institute of Economics, of the Chinese Academy of Social Sciences, was entrusted by the Foreign Loan Office of the Ministry of Health to evaluate the effects of the Medical Financial Assistance (MFA) program for extremely poor rural residents, a component of the Health VIII Project, which was enabled by a World Bank loan to China. This project aims to strengthen basic medical services in the poor areas of rural China. The purpose of the present study is to identify problems and to discuss the experiences of those involved so as to provide policy advice and a decision-making reference for improving the efficiency of the current MFA system nationwide. Using an empirical approach, the researchers selected two project counties from each of the provinces of Shanxi, Chongqing and Gansu for fieldwork. In 2005, the research team completed a sample survey of 1206 rural households in the six project counties, including 24 townships and 48 administrative villages. To examine the impact of fundraising on MFA implementation, three of the six selected project counties were recipients of grants from the UK Department for International Development (DFID), because counties with grants had more funds for the purpose of assistance. In addition, to

(Originally published in *China and World Economy*, No. 2, 2007.)

ensure that the size of the sample of households covered by the MFA program was big enough for statistical analysis, the MFA beneficiary households and non-MFA recipient households were selected in the ratio of 2:8.[2]

While the research was under way, the Chinese Government extended the MFA mechanism nationwide, and increased the number of experimental counties using new types of cooperative medical schemes. Consequently, MFA programs in Health VIII Project counties joined with the MFA programs under the charge of the Ministry of Civil Affairs, and some project counties even combined the MFA mechanism with the cooperative medical scheme. The research team kept track of such changes. In the first quarter of 2006, the team conducted fieldwork in provinces including Anhui, Zhejiang, Yunnan, Shandong, Sichuan, Shaanxi, Hubei and Hunan, using the latest information in nine counties for representative case studies.

During 2005 to 2006, while conducting sample surveys and field work, the team also interviewed the following institutions and individuals: (1) Health VIII Project managing agencies from central to local levels; (2) functional departments in township and county governments as well as villagers' committees; (3) rural three-level disease prevention and medical services institutions; and (4) rural households at different levels of income, as well as individuals different in terms of gender, age and health condition, especially households and individuals that received MFA. In addition, the team collected large amounts of literature with respect to medical insurance and assistance both in China and overseas, from books, journals and the Internet.

8.2 Effects of Medical Financial Assistance

Based on the processing of collected information and data, the research primarily focused on three issues. First, is the MFA program really aimed at the present beneficiary groups? Second, to what extent has the MFA program improved the ability of the poor to make use of medical services? And third, to what extent has the MFA program alleviated the burden of disease on the economic security of the poor households?

In the design of the Health VIII Project, the target groups for MFA are a certain percentage of the poorest in certain areas. Therefore, the logit possibility model is applied to the statistical analysis of sample household data (Jin, 2006). It is found that rural households at the lower level of income and with member(s) in the poorer conditions of health, especially households with members who have lost their ability to work all year round, are more likely to be covered by the MFA program. This indicates that primarily two factors determine whether a household or an individual receives MFA: poverty and illness. Taking the government-designated low-income criterion for rural residents (annual net income of 924 yuan per capita) as a poverty line, and the scenario of some member(s) in the family being long laid up or disabled or suffering from serious illness over the past six years as the indicators of illness severity, the results from the cross-tabulation reveal that 46.5 percent of MFA program-covered households are non-poor households. Such a phenomenon can be interpreted from three aspects. First, to prevent or to reduce "poverty caused by illness, either falling into poverty for the first time or getting rid of poverty but falling back to poverty later", in granting MFA, project managing agencies do not necessarily exclude the non-poor from the MFA program. Second, taking into consideration the limits of cross section data, it may be understood that some of these non-poor households are still entitled to financial assistance although they are not living in poverty. Finally, traditional values and social preferences in villages also influence the determination of MFA recipients. To determine MFA beneficiaries, two indicators, poverty and health, must be applied simultaneously to potential households or individuals. It is stipulated in the MFA mechanism that the determination of beneficiaries' entitlement depends on the recommendation of the villagers' group and the villagers' committee, or selection by representatives of the villagers. The deviation of actual beneficiaries from preset target groups indicates that villagers and village leaders are inclined to assist households with sick members rather than poor households without sick members.

Disregarding the indicator of the poverty line and only observing other socioeconomic characteristics of the MFA group and the non-MFA group, the following is noted in regards to the MFA group: men, especially unmarried male adults, make up a large proportion; non-laborers, mainly the disabled and aged, also make up a large proportion; average education level is low; a large number of the laborers are involved in farming; family property and area of farming land are small; and there are big loans because of illness. This shows that the MFA project tends to cover highly vulnerable households and individuals. Inquiries about whether the sampled individuals were ill or injured in the past four weeks reveal a much higher level of health risk in the MFA group than the average. Whereas incidence of illness in the contrast group is 29.1 percent, the incidence of illness in the MFA group is up to 37.6 percent. Undoubtedly, the MFA group needs more medical services.

In our sample, approximately 80 percent of patients in both groups have seen a doctor. This difference is so insignificant that it can be ignored. To find out the factor that significantly affects the patient's decision-making in seeing a doctor, the linear possibility model is used to estimate the sample data of poor patients 15 years and above, as well as that of all patients. These estimations indicate that both MFA and cooperative medical schemes help to increase the rate of patients going to see a doctor, but the effect is statistically insignificant. It is worthwhile mentioning that for patients living in poverty, the estimation coefficients of two dummy variables, whether entitled to MFA or in the cooperative medical scheme, are much higher than that of the entire group of patients. Moreover, the estimation coefficient of whether patients are entitled to MFA is much higher than that of whether patients are in the cooperative medical scheme. This means that the two basic healthcare schemes exert much more influence on the capability of the poor to make use of medical services than of the entire population; and compared with the cooperative medical scheme, MFA can better enhance the capability of the poor to make use of medical services. When the multinomial logit model is used to further analyze how the poor choose medical service providers, it is found that the MFA program encourages them to choose township clinics (Wei, 2006).

The MFA program stipulates that medical expenses occurring in township clinics can have a higher percentage of reimbursement than in other medical institutions. This stipulation plays a decisive role in a patient's choice of medical institution, because the poor are particularly sensitive to the percentage of reimbursement.

To evaluate the effect of the MFA project in alleviating poverty, first, the research team conducted descriptive statistical studies on the composition of medical expenses among individuals suffering from serious illnesses during 1998–2004.[3] Individuals with serious illnesses covered by the MFA program spent an average of 4653 yuan on medical services, of which 347 yuan was not out of their own pocket because of cost reimbursement, price discount or expense exemption, accounting for 7.5 percent of the total expenses and hospitalization expenses. In terms of absolute volume or relative amount, MFA only constitutes a tiny part of total medical expenses (see Table 8.1). Second, a Working-Lesser expenditure function is used for a comparative analysis on the consumption structure between MFA recipients and non-MFA recipients. The results show that the adoption of

Table 8.1 Medical Expenses, Reimbursement and Loans Resulting from Serious Diseases of the Sample Individuals

Unit: yuan

	Those without insurance	Those with CMS*	Those with MFA**	Those with commercial insurance and others
Total medical expenses	3724.9	5245.5	4652.7	18814.3
Direct medical expenses	3397.2	4353.9	4239.5	17574.8
Drug purchase	1104.7	1029.5	1034.9	2040.0
Outpatient expenses	913.9	1202.7	1632.3	3214.8
Hospital bed and medicine expenses	1378.6	2121.8	1572.3	12320.0
Indirect medical expenses	327.7	891.6	413.2	1239.5
Living in hospital and accompanying cost	182.0	415.0	296.0	834.1
Transport expenses during treatment	93.0	106.3	64.7	269.7
Other expenses during treatment	52.6	370.3	52.5	135.7
Reimbursement and/or price discount	1.8	556.1	347.0	7164.9
Percentage in hospitalization expenses (%)	0.1	26.2	22.1	58.2
Out of own pocket	3723.1	4689.4	4305.7	11649.4
Self-funded payment	1788.7	1369.0	1686.1	5738.3
Borrowing status owing to diseases and injuries				
Total fund collected from others	1934.4	3320.4	2619.6	5911.1
Money not needed to repay	134.6	373.3	489.2	1925.9
Money needed to repay	1799.9	2947.2	2130.4	3985.2
Money already repaid	814.0	1014.6	661.6	1888.9

Source: Wei (2006).

Notes: CMS, Cooperative Medical Scheme; MFA, Medical Financial Assistance program.

the MFA mechanism plays a positive role in reducing the replacement of medical expenditure by non-medical expenditure and in rationalizing the distribution of medical resources among family members. However, in the case where a resident suffers a serious disease or a major injury, the current MFA mechanism cannot substantially eliminate the impact of the burden of disease on the resident's consumption behavior. Third, as the cooperative medical scheme and the MFA mechanism are combined in some localities, those in poverty suffering from serious illnesses can benefit from the two schemes, having their medical expenses reduced and exempted. Therefore, the income function is applied to analyze the impact of a family member's poor health conditions on income, and the relationship between the percentage of medical subsidies and family income. The calculation shows no obvious impact of the two schemes on restoring a resident's income-earning ability. This is mainly a result of the fact that the principle of compensation in the current medical care system concerns the amount of medical expenses rather than the loss of a resident's income earning ability as a result of illness (Luo, 2006).

To sum up, there are three findings: (1) the MFA program covers the poor groups and the groups with vulnerable health; (2) the program helps to improve the ability of the poor to make use of medical services, especially the services of township clinics; and (3) MFA helps to lessen the negative impact of illness on the finance of poor households and helps to prevent communities, families and individuals inflicted with disastrous illnesses from being marginalized or those who are ill from dying. However, as the beneficiaries often suffer from serious, complicated and lasting illnesses, the financial assistance is insignificant in relation to medical expenses, and the current financial assistance system plays no significant role in restoring a patient's income earning ability. The MFA program can do little to prevent transitory poverty from turning into long-term poverty, or to prevent light poverty from reaching severer levels.

8.3 Management problems

Rural MFA programs are complicated in their implementation, because there are numerous parties involved, including various government departments at different levels, health service providers, self-governing village organizations, rural households, and individuals. The operational costs of these programs are rather high, because it is difficult to achieve smooth coordination among these stakeholders. Our case studies reveal that a considerable number of management offices tried to pass some management costs onto other participating institutions because of a shortage of program funds and management outlay. In particular, the matching funds from the local governments are seldom in place on time (see Table 8.2). This led to various distortions of the management system in practice and reduced the effectiveness of the programs.

Shortages of funds have caused the county governments and management offices in poor areas to face financial difficulties. Under administrative pressure from the superior government and management office regarding implementation of the project plan, seeking and adopting alternative ways to perform the project has almost become the only choice for the grassroots program outfits. It appears to

Table 8.2 Profile of the Medical Financial Assistance Program in Yunyang County under Chongqing Municipality during the Period of 1999–2003

Year	MFA card recipients		MFA card recipients/ rural population (%)	Matching funds of MFA program (1000 Yuan)		Number of MFA funds recipients	Reimbursement of hospitalization expenses (1000 Yuan)
	Number of households	Number of people		Amount of funds in plan	Amount of funds actually in place		
1999	1467	4436	2.68	91.6	47	5	3
2000	4971	15,190	4.20	227.6	187	81	8.9
2001	8794	24,776	4.32	350.8	322.5	167	24.5
2002	15,802	47,051	3.92	483.6	164.8	469	59.6
2003	16,968	58,902	5.19	1247.5	480.4	2985	573.6
Total	–	–	–	2401.1	1201.7	3707	669.6

Source: Health VII Project Office in Yunyang County, 2004.
Information on Implementation of MFA Program (A Working Report).

Note: MFA, Medical Financial Assistance program.

be a government priority to reduce the project scale and to simplify management procedures as follows.

8.3.1 Reduced size of project coverage

If the project coverage is to be calculated by the percentage of beneficiaries in the whole agricultural population, the preset target should be at least 5 percent of the rural population in a project county. Table 8.3 shows that the scale of coverage in Zuoquan and Yushe counties is smallest as the project offices of the two counties had to raise funds themselves for carrying out the MFA program. According to the survey conducted by the Bureau of Civil Affairs in Zuoquan County, in 2003, there were a total of 25,754 rural residents living below the poverty line, defined as having an annual net income lower than 625 yuan per capita, including the households encountering catastrophic difficulties (2323 households, 6459 residents), the residents covered by the Five Guarantee program (609), and those in poor households (7763 households and 18 686 residents). In the rural population of approximately 145,000, poverty incidence is calculated as 17.8 percent (Bureau of Civil Affairs in Zuoquan County, 2004). However, the MFA program coverage under the Health VIII Project reaches less than 3 percent of the rural population. During the period of the program implementation, the number of those having obtained reimbursement for medical expenses was remarkably small. During 1999–2004, the actual number of beneficiaries, including both outpatients and inpatients receiving treatment, made up only 0.2 percent of the rural population in the county. Meanwhile, in Yushe County, only 39 patients in total had received

Table 8.3 Profile of the Medical Financial Assistance Program in the Sample Counties

County	Zuoquan	Yusbe	Wuxi	Yunyang	Minxian	Kangle
Year	2004	2004	2003	2003	2003	2004
Total population (1000 people)	162	137	510	1259	448	243
Rural population (1000 people)	145	115	468	1133	409	230
MFA targeted people	3878	–	31,976	58,902	20,895	14,133
MFA targeted people/ rural population (%)	2.95	–	6.83	5.20	5.11	6.14
Period	2000–2004	1999–2004	1998–2003	1999–2003	1999–2003	2000–2004
Planed amount of appropriation (1000 yuan)	–	200	–	2401.1	–	–
Actual appropriation (1000 yuan)	120	60	3298.6	1201.7	560	–
The World Bank loan	–	–	–	–	–	355
DFID donation	None	None	2204.1	None	–	755
Matching funds of local governments	120	60	–	–	–	–
Number of outpatients receiving MFA funds	176	–	237,967	None	6153	39,988
Amount of MFA funds spent for the outpatients (1000 yuan)	12	–	1977.8	None	44.7	237.5
Accumulated number of inpatients receiving MFA funds	149	39	2678	3707	640	1558
Accumulated amount of MFA funds spent for inpatients (1000 yuan)	37	12	1075.3	669.6	101.9	365.7

Sources: (1) Figures referring to the counties of Zuoquan and Yushe in Shanxi Province were acquired, respectively, from the county project office under the Health VIII Project and the author's interviews with the project officers. (2) Bureau of Health in Chongqing Municipality and Chongqing Office of Health VII Project, 2004, the Annual Analysis Report on the Project Supervision and Appraisal Indicators in 2003; Statistics on the Implementation of MFA Program. (3) Zhang and Long (2004). (4) Project Office in Yunyang County in Chongqing Municipality, 2004, Implementation of Ongoing MFA Program. (5) Minxian Government in Gansu Province, 2003, Implementation Plan of MFA Program at the Second Stage under the Health VIII/H8SP Project; Health VIII Project Office in Minxian, 2004, Design of the Appraisal on the Factors Affecting the Use of Medical Service under the MFA Program. (6) Project Office in Kangle County in Gansu Province, 2005, Statistics on Implementation of the MFA Program in Kangle County; A Report of Monitor and Appraisal on Health VIII/H8SP Project in Kangle County.

Notes: DFID, UK Department for International Development; MFA, Medical Financial Assistance program; "–" Data not available.

reimbursement from the MFA fund. This number is negligible in relation to more than 110,000 rural residents. In the extremely poor counties, it is apparently hard to realize the preset target of "improving the capability of the poor to make use of medical services" with such a project scale. Comparison of the data in Table 8.2 with that in Table 8.3 shows that before 2003, the scale of the project coverage in Yunyang county was lower than that in Wuxi, Minxian and Kangle counties, which had more funding sources. Only in 2003 had the total fund in Yunyang County increased by almost 200 percent from the previous year and, accordingly, the project coverage improved from less than 4 percent to 5.2 percent. In fact, as a result of funds donated by the UK Department for International Development, project coverage in the experimental townships is above 5 percent to Wuxi, Minxian and Kangle counties. In fact, in a couple of years, the percentage in a few experimental townships in Wuxi County reached 11.3 percent (Zhang and Long, 2004). A reduced project coverage scale appears to be a direct response of management offices to the shortage in the MFA fund.

8.3.2 *Weaken the intensity of financial assistance to the poor*

Regulations relating to medical expense reimbursement, especially the setting of minimum payment out of one's own pocket, the percentage of co-payment and the ceiling to reimbursement, are the usual tools applied to adjust the intensity of medical financial assistance. In experimental counties receiving DFID funds, the assistance recipients can obtain partial reimbursement for their outpatient and hospitalization expenses. The reimbursement percentage of medical expenses incurred in different levels of medical institutions varies from 30 to 80 percent. The outpatient reimbursement per household per year should not exceed 60 yuan, and the ceiling of hospitalization reimbursement falls between 220 and 1360 yuan. In counties with no DFID funds, outpatient expenses are commonly not reimbursed, and the reimbursement of hospitalization expenses is limited to within 40 to 50 percent, or even less. Although these regulations help to prevent the total amount of reimbursement from exceeding the volume of available funds, reduced assistance intensity has certainly occurred. In our sample, 145 cases of serious diseases or injuries occurred during 1998–2004. The average amount of reimbursement, price discount and medical expense exemption for those patients covered by the MFA program accounted for only 22.1 percent of the hospitalization expenses per case. This is low when compared to the initially designated amount of 40 to 60 percent.

8.3.3 *Extensive management*

In the small sized projects, with sophisticated regulations, complicated management and lack of funds, simplifying procedures and even extensive management have become the preferred means of cost reducing by the local project offices. Although these countermeasures are partly reasonable, distortion of the project design and extensive management lead to reduction in effectiveness of the MFA program. The distortion manifests itself in two ways in particular. First, some project management participating institutions adopt the usual administrative measures to replace the qualification assessment procedures for assistance targets. According to the project design, the required procedure for identification of beneficiaries is reporting the applicants from the grass roots (villagers) to the top (the county project office) and approving from the top to the grass roots. In fact, a large number of beneficiaries are determined by the townships' cadres in consultation with village leaders or the representatives of the villagers. In some localities, the project offices have simply copied the name list of the Five Guarantee Households and the beneficiaries under other financial assistance programs from the County Bureau of Civil Affairs, but do not really notify them. Hence, a considerable section of the poor in the list do not know they are beneficiaries of the MFA program, neither have they any idea about their rights (Jiang, 2005). Second, in the counties with very small sized projects, the management offices almost give up any supervision over the medical service provision controls, and instead merely use co-payment rates and ceilings of expense reimbursement as an instrument to control spending of the MFA fund. However, although these two tools could help to limit patients' spending behavior, they have almost no influence over the medical service providers. Such extensive management could only offset the benefits brought to the beneficiaries by medical assistance, with an increase in medical expenses incurred by excessive medical service.

8.3.4 Integration of the Medical Financial Assistance program with the regular relief system

At the end of 2003 when the MFA program within the framework of the World Bank Health VIII Project was not yet completed, the rural medical assistance system, in the charge of the Ministry of Civil Affairs, commenced establishment nationwide. Counties with the Health VIII Project were facing a situation whereby the regulations of the MFA program were to be integrated with the rules set up by the Ministry of Civil Affairs, with the remaining funds of the MFA program to be diverted to the account of the County Bureau of Civil Affairs. Therefore, some project offices took the chance to suspend the MFA program and wait for a handover by the County Bureau of Civil Affairs while the others simply released the MFA fund based on the regulations of the conventional relief system. Apparently there are shortcomings with such a practice. First, it implies a principle of post-disaster-relief, or the rules themselves exclude instant relief to those who suffer from income shocks brought about by ongoing events. As regulated, the one who applies for medical assistance must submit copies of his or her personal identification card, income certificates, diagnosis records made by medical institutions above the township level, and receipts for medical expenses (Government Office of Zuoquan County, 2003). Under these regulations, when seriously ill patients are in the greatest need of money, the medical relief fund cannot be used in a timely way to help them to deal with their emergency. As a result, the program goal of "improving the capability of the poor to use medical services" might not be well targeted. Second, the medical relief funding that the poor person receives is no different from the living subsidies they have acquired in the past, which is used either to repay a debt or to subsidize daily consumption expenses, rather than being invested in health.

Within the management system of the Health VIII Project, there is concern for the sustainability of the MFA program: Are other sources to be introduced to support the program when the foreign aid project is completed? The solution to the question of program resources is now already quite positive. The rural medical relief system put forward by the Chinese Government can be considered either a continuation or an extension of the MFA program under the Health VIII Project. Although the shortage of funds has played a crucial role in affecting project efficiency, it is surely not the only determinant. Our analyses show that the feasibility of the institutional arrangements and the incentive structures designed for the management offices and staff members of the MFA system also determine the success or failure of the program in practice. Undoubtedly, extensive management would result in a lower efficiency. This does not imply that the more sophisticated the management system is, the higher the efficiency of the project operation, because the more complicated a system is, the less feasible it is in the poor areas because of the weak financial and administrative abilities of the local governments. This argument is actually supported by the actions of the county project offices in simplifying the project design during the implementation process. Moreover, the design of the Health VIII Project is embedded with a concept to involve the poor in the decision-making and supervision process. However, the poor are more likely to be excluded from the process if it is too complex. In Chinese grassroots societies, poor people usually have a weak voice in the decision-making process in village affairs because of their poor educational background and lack of access to information. Certainly, it is even less possible for the poor to have their say if the complexity of the project design far exceeds the ability of the poor to manage the way of participation, and if the concept of the project design is in direct conflict with the existing order in the decision-making processes and politics of rural grassroots societies. For this reason, the present design of the MFA program should not be seen as a permanent model. The top-level decision-makers should encourage the stakeholders to innovate further in the management of the program to establish a system that is not only consistent with the expected goals of the MFA for the poor, but that is also more cost-effective and more easily executed than has been to date.

Of course, no matter how rational a project design is, supervision and inspection are definitely necessary for the project implementation. At the test stage of the program, supervision is crucial. So far, the performance of all regulation systems through the implementation of the Health VIII Project has largely depended on intensive supervision of the funding institutions. Take the experimental county Wuxi as an example. During 1998–2003, the World Bank, the UK Department for International Development, the Foreign Loan Office of the Ministry of Health and the Project Office of Chongqing Municipality conducted 11 joint inspections on the project sites (Zhang and Long, 2004). The performance of the MFA program in Wuxi County was so satisfactory that the practice there was designated as a model demonstrating to all other counties with the MFA program under the Health VIII Project. Nevertheless, the organizational costs of such intensive outside supervision are so high that it could neither cover all the project counties nor remain sustainable in the long term after completion of the Health VIII Project. Therefore, it is necessary to identify a regular supervision mechanism with a broader coverage and lower cost, as a replacement. The approach of the Public Expenditure Tracking and Survey adopted by the World Bank in African countries (PETS Task Team and Ministry of Finance, 2004) could be applied to the MFA program. The results from public expenditure tracking and supervision could be used to evaluate the performance of government institutions, and as an instrument to stimulate improvement in program management.

8.4 Policy options

It is necessary to point out here that the MFA program provides an additional social protection device from which the poor gained benefit. Moreover, the program played a role of guidance and demonstration that contributed greatly to the efforts of the Chinese Government to build a nationwide medical assistance system. Problems that have occurred in the implementation of the MFA program under the Health VIII Project also exist in the Chinese current medical assistance program. The following policy options are proposed, based on our research results:

Realizing a smooth implementation process for medical financial assistant programs is urgently needed so that the problems of shortage in MFA funds and management outlays can be solved. The financial capacity of the poor counties in less developed regions is generally weak. Therefore, it is crucial that the central government strengthen the public transfer with joint input or supplementary matching funds from the provincial governments to the MFA programs according to the size of the beneficiary group covered by the Minimum Living Standard Guarantee program and the Five Guarantee Households program.

Operation of the MFA programs should be combined with that of the medical cooperative system and the minimum living standard guarantee system to reduce management outlays and to obtain economies of scale. For example, the target group of the MFA can be identified with the list of the recipients covered by the Minimum Living Standard Guarantee program, while preferential treatment can be given to the target group of the MFA through the management network of the medical cooperative system.

Different policy goals should be distinguished, and assistance rules specified. For poor people, medical assistance should be provided to increase the capability of the beneficiaries to make use of medical services. For major income earners, medical assistance should be used to alleviate "health poverty" through disease intervention. For those suffering from serious diseases and major injuries who are on the brink of poverty, medical assistance should be brought into play to reduce transitory poverty and to prevent the transitory turning into chronic poverty.

The implementation process of the MFA and medical cooperative programs should be constantly monitored with the Public Expenditure Tracking Survey.

The results from the survey can be used to evaluate the achievements of the government at different levels and as key reference materials to assist management institutions in improving their efficiency.

Notes

1 This paper is a project report based on the findings of the entire research team consisting of the following key members: Jiang Zhongyi (Rural Policy Research Center under the Ministry of Agriculture), Wei Zhong, Jin Chengwu, Luo Chuliang, Wang Jing, Zhai Pengxiao, Deng Quheng, Yao Yu, Wang Zhen and the author herself.
2 Appendix XI of the World Bank Qin-Ba Medical Project Documents stipulates: "It is required that the poverty-alleviating fund in each project county should at least cover 20 percent of the poorest households." Later, in implementation, it requires that MFA recipients should make up 5 percent of the agricultural population in the project county, while DFID project counties have a slightly higher percentage (usually up to 8 percent). The high percentage of MFA recipients in this sample is to ensure that the sample size can meet the needs of research.
3 The definition of a serious disease or a major injury is: (1) a disease or an injury that cost more than 1000 yuan or for which a patient received hospitalization during 1998–2004; and (2) a disease that has been treated but not cured since 1998.

References

Bureau of Civil Affairs in Zuoquan County, 2004, "Zuoquan county report on relief to rural extremely poor households," 3 September, (unpublished documents).

Government Office of Zuoquan, 2003, "Detailed regulations on implementation of medical assistance for the rural poor families with serious disease burden," Zuoquan Government Office Issue No. 69, 27 November, (unpublished documents).

Jiang, Zhongyi, 2005, "The medical assistance system for the rural extremely poor." A policy study report submitted to the Division of Rural Health, Ministry of Health, (unpublished documents).

Jin, Chengwu, 2006, "Identifying qualification of the MFA beneficiaries." An evaluation report submitted to the Foreign Loan Office, Ministry of Health, on the MFA program under the Health VIII Project of World Bank Loans, Beijing.

Luo, Chuliang, 2006, "Impacts of disease burden on households' income and consumption." An evaluation report submitted to the Foreign Loan Office, Ministry of Health, on the MFA Program under the Health VIII Project of World Bank Loans, Beijing.

PETS Task Team and Ministry of Finance, 2004, Sierra Leone Government Report of the Public Expenditure Tracking Survey (PETS) for Financial Year 2002 Selected Expenditure [cited on 2 June, 2006]. Available from: web.worldbank.org/wbsite/external/countries.

Wei, Zhong, 2006, "Effects of the MFA program on the use of medical services." An evaluation report submitted to the Foreign Loan Office, Ministry of Health, on the MFA Program under the Health VIII Project of World Bank Loans, Beijing.

Zhang, Deping and Yunzhi Long, 2004, "Review on MFA program implemented in Wuxi County, Chongqing Municipality, during the period of November 1998–December 2003," 16 February (unpublished documents).

9 Nutrition and healthcare for children from rural Tibetan households*

Three major programs have been implemented in rural Tibetan areas in order to improve children's nutrition and healthcare, namely antenatal care, infant and young child feeding, as well as school feeding. In terms of effectiveness of service provision, the school feeding program has been put into practice more effectively than the other two for two reasons. First, rural Tibetan families are accustomed to traditional infant and young child feeding practices. Secondly, the lack of incentives for healthcare workers and the shortage of funding have hindered the provision of healthcare to rural families. Therefore, this paper proposes an adjustment of the incentive structure for healthcare providers, a fortification of the village level network of healthcare services, an improvement in the approach to healthcare education for farmers and herders, and the coordination of training courses targeted at the officials and service teams of the healthcare system.

9.1 Introduction

Nutrition and healthcare are key factors for development, especially at early ages (Van der Gaag, 2011). Access to a nutritional diet and good practices of child raising and disease prevention will simultaneously reduce disease and mortality rates in addition to preventing malnutrition and stunted growth. Children having access to nutrition and healthcare services will not only have appropriate height, weight and cognitive and non-cognitive abilities (character and emotion) but also be less likely to suffer from chronic diseases. Adequate nutritional and healthcare for children will in effect improve the quality of the workforce, expand labor participation and contribute to economic growth.

In the early 21st century, international development organizations and scholars of various disciplines produced studies on early child development in relation to such factors as nutrition, healthcare and education.[1] Nutrition and healthcare

* The author would like to acknowledge the contribution of literature by Deng Quheng and Zhao Chen and discussion by Chen Chunming, Luorong Zhandui, Danzeng Lunzhu, Wang Dan and Zha Luo in the course of this study.

(Originally published in *China Economist*, No. 3, 2014.)

issues have received much less attention than education from Chinese policymakers and most scholars. Fortunately, the "12th Five-Year Plan" launched a nutrition improvement program impacting 26 million rural middle and primary school students across 669 impoverished counties. At the end of 2012, child nutrition intervention pilot programs began to provide nutrition allowance for children aged between 6 and 24 months in eight poverty stricken areas covering 100 rural counties across ten provinces and autonomous regions.[2]

Due to reasons mentioned above, over the past 30 years, very few Chinese scholars have carried out studies on child nutrition and healthcare in Tibet. Nutritionists at the Chinese Center for Disease Control and Prevention conducted multi-rounds sample surveys on the nutrition status of children in both urban and rural areas, but their samples did not include rural Tibet (Chen et al., 2010; Chen, Chunming et al., 2010). In the child development studies conducted by the China Development Research Foundation, only one survey carried out in Ledu County of Qinghai Province includes Tibetan families (Hao, 2012). Luorong Zhandui, a scholar from the China Tibetology Research Center, twice visited ten rural primary schools in Lasa (Lhasa) City, Shannan and Rikaze prefectures in 2000 and 2010. For each visit, he measured the height and weight of 300 ten-year old children. In the 2010 study, the average height and weight of children is 125.6cm and 23.5kg. Compared with the result of measurement in 2000, height and weight averages for children had increased by 5cm and 2.5kg respectively.[3] Unfortunately, the measurement records do not contain gender-specific data. In 2010, the women and children's healthcare system of Changdu (Qamdo) Prefecture conducted a survey on 3,887 children under the age of five yet without gender and urban-rural classification. The survey report did not state methodology of statistics and the stunting rate of the surveyed children. It only shows that the rate of low weight of the surveyed children below the average level of the poor region in China, which implies that the nutrition status of the children in Changdu is better in this respect.[4] Without access to original data though, it is difficult to assess the accuracy of such statistics.

Since the 1990s, international scholars have published the following findings on child nutrition and healthcare conditions in Tibetan Autonomous Region (TAR) and Tibetan areas of Qinghai Province:

> First, the altitude of Tibetan plateau makes an impact on childhood nutrition. Between 1994 and 1995, Nancy Harris et al. (2001) carried out a survey of the parents of 2,078 children from immediately after birth to seven years old in eleven counties of five prefectures through collaboration with local healthcare officers in Tibet Autonomous Region. Their results show that the ratio of stunted child growth is a staggering 51%. According to the location of sample towns and townships, Harris et al. believe that child malnutrition is not correlated directly with altitude but is correlated with community medical conditions. For instance, among children two years old and above, stunted growth ratio is 35% for children in urban areas and 60% for children in rural areas.
>
> (Harris et al., 2001)

According to a 1999 study conducted jointly by the medical school at Xi'an Jiaotong University and the University of Tokushima (Japan) in 29 counties and 145 townships in TAR, altitude has a major effect on the physical development of children in this region, particularly on their height. Their results indicate that among children under age three, the ratios of stunted growth and underweight are 39.0% and 23.7% respectively compared to 25.3% and 18.1% for urban children and 41.4% and 24.7% for rural children. Stunted growth and underweight ratios for children in herding areas are higher than those in farming areas (Dang et al., 2004, 2008). In fact, altitude is seen as a dummy variable affecting childhood nutrition and healthcare conditions. Urban, farming and herding areas are in an ascending order of altitude, and the higher altitudes frequently experience harsh environmental conditions and offer weaker infrastructure and social services, such as healthcare.

Second, the following socioeconomic factors affect childhood nutrition and health: maternal health, childhood feeding practices and integrated factors from living environment to healthcare offerings. First, in 2004, Mary Wellhoner et al. carried out a questionnaire survey on 402 women of childbearing age in Xiaosumang Township in collaboration with the Maternal Healthcare Institute of Yushu County, Qinghai Province. The study concluded that it was very difficult for local women and newborns to access institutionalized healthcare services, which results in high maternal and infant mortality (Wellhoner et al., 2011). Second, the aforementioned study by Xi'an Jiaotong University and University of Tokushima provided a questionnaire for mothers. According to the responses of 1,655 mothers, their breastfeeding period is averaged at 26 months. Of them, 20.1% had a pure breastfeeding period of four months and the others added roasted barley flour paste one month after giving birth. When an infant reached six months, less than 25% of mothers fed their children with egg and meat and 20% provided fresh vegetables. Scholars concluded that lack of variety in diet was a key problem in child feeding in rural Tibetan areas (Dang et al., 2005). Lastly, in 2003, Kunchok Gyaltsen et al. selected 10 villages in two townships and interviewed 280 women of childbearing age in two counties of Tibetan areas of Qinghai Province for a survey on their socioeconomic attributes, living conditions, community environment, medical services and childcare. Gyaltsen et al. discovered that diarrhea and respiratory infections were common among local children, particularly those suffering from malnutrition. The same was true for places with poor hygiene and sewage discharge facilities. They also emphasized that lack of maternal healthcare services were a major reason for infant and maternal mortality (Gyaltsen et al., 2007).

These sample survey results reflect childhood nutrition and healthcare conditions and their decisive factors in Tibet between 1994 and 2003. Afterwards, the central government introduced a series of major public healthcare programs and investment projects for improving livelihood of rural people, which have transformed Tibet's socioeconomic landscape. These efforts would have made an impact on child nutrition and health, but this policy intervention failed to draw adequate attention from researchers. Additionally, the existing reports provide only statistical data and analysis. The qualitative studies are not sufficient.

Based on field visits conducted in Gongjue County and Jiangda County in the TAR and Dege County in Sichuan Province in 2011, this report focuses on three research questions. First, what do maternal healthcare programs contribute to the improvement in women's and children's healthcare services? Second, have child and infant feeding practices changed in light of evolving living conditions for farmers and herdsmen? Third, what are the effects of school feeding programs on the diet and health of pupils?

Responding to these questions requires an observation and evaluation of relevant public policies, a review of the government's policy implementation and policy recommendations. Thus, this study has adopted the case study approach and visited the healthcare bureau of the Changdu Prefecture in TAR, the healthcare bureaus and county hospitals in the three studied counties, five township healthcare centers, three township primary school kitchens, six village committees, the healthcare workers, the pregnant women and the mothers with infant or young child in the villages. In 2005, this study conducted a healthcare service survey in the Ganzi Tibetan Autonomous Prefecture in Sichuan Province and Changdu Prefecture in the TAR. The first-hand information collected from that survey could be used as a reference.

In light of the recent policies for certain groups, this report discusses the improvement in nutrition and healthcare of pregnant and breastfeeding women, children aged between zero and two and primary school students. Commonly, nutrition and healthcare programs for children between three and six years old are executed at the kindergarten level, but the necessary facilities are lacking in rural Tibetan villages.

9.2 Maternal nutrition intervention and healthcare services

The 2007 report released by the World Health Organization put emphasis on a fact that appropriate nutrition is essential to a child's survival. Mothers must also acquire sufficient nutrition during pregnancy (Siddiqi et al., 2007). According to the Report on Nutrition Development for Chinese Children aged between zero and six released by China's then Ministry of Health, maternal and childhood nutrition in the first 1,000 days after inception will have long-term impacts on the health of the child. Malnutrition in this stage will lead to irreversible and irreparable damage. Short-term effects include retarded physical and mental development and an increased incidence of disease. Long-term effects include the loss of cognitive abilities and increased risk of chronic diseases such as cardiovascular disease, diabetes and hypertension (Chinese Ministry of Health, 2012). Maternal healthcare services not only ensure that a child can start his or her life well but also effectively reduce maternal and infant mortality.

The prenatal care program was launched in 2000 to reduce maternal mortality and eliminate newborn tetanus. Under this program, rural women are entitled to a 500-yuan allowance per person for the hospitalized childbirth. Under the defective-birth prevention program, free supplements of folic acid are provided to women three months prior to their due date and after their pregnancy to prevent neural tube defection. In rural Tibetan areas, the program provides vitamin A capsules.[5] As international experience suggests, these services can effectively reduce maternal and infant mortality as well as defective birth, thereby improving widespread access to healthcare. Free and subsidized access to maternal services provides an obvious benefit to rural Tibetan households. However, these very households did not respond actively to the programs due to lack of knowledge, information and services (Zhu, 2008).

First, maternal healthcare services in rural Tibetan areas did not fully reach the target groups. In townships and villages adjacent to public roads, some target women received free medicine, however, in less accessible places, pregnant women and their families reported that they had not known about free nutrition supplements. When asked about their pregnancy, most respondents said that they delivered their babies in their own home (or tent) with the assistance of their family members, relatives or female neighbors. A woman aged 34 delivered three times at home. Her husband cut off her umbilical cord using a thin rope, which caused excessive bleeding. She remained too weak to engage in outdoor work since she delivered her third child. Another respondent said that his wife cut off her own umbilical cord using an unsterilized knife and died less than one month later due to the resulting complications. Moreover, pre-delivery checkups, post-delivery visits and the use of sterilized instruments for non-hospitalized delivery were still uncommon. Healthcare statistics in surveyed areas also suggest that maternal healthcare services were yet to reach key policy targets. In 2010, the hospitalized maternal delivery ratio was 47.4% in the Changdu Prefecture; the rural women's hospitalized delivery ratio was 39.8% in Dege County. Second, communication efforts are insufficient. There are major gaps in the coverage of information dissemination. A maternal mortality reduction and newborn tetanus elimination program as well as a defective-birth prevention program have included the promotion of knowledge and service information. Banners are put up and leaflets are distributed in county areas on theme publicity days or on the occasion of holiday fairs. Township healthcare centers have also put up posters. These practices are useful, yet insufficient for reaching target groups.

Furthermore, the transmission of key information relating to maternal service provision was neglected. The new Rural Medical Cooperative, referred to as the Rural Tibetan Medical System in TAR, had become popular in studied counties.[6] The TAR government stipulated that the costs of the non-hospitalized childbirth service with disinfection measures provided by the healthcare workers can be reimbursed from the funds of the Rural Tibetan Medical System when the medical bills are verified with the signature of the delivery woman or her family members. The stipulation is apparently an appropriate arrangement favorable to the women and their families living in very remote villages. However, such key provisions were omitted in the implementation regulations issued by the Changdu Prefecture. Moreover, some recent supplementary provisions were yet to be informed to rural households, such as, for instance, if a pregnant woman from a Dibao household, one which is protected under minimum subsistence guarantee system, opts for hospitalized delivery, they are entitled to a subsidy of 100 to 500 yuan in addition to the regular reimbursement of healthcare costs, maternity benefits and transport allowance. Some households still benefit from certain services. For example, a nine-month pregnant woman in Hajia Township in Gongjue County asked a lama about her pregnancy-related discomfort, and the lama told her to see a doctor. She then received an inspection at a county hospital, where she was diagnosed with abnormal position of the fetus. Another pregnant woman in Tongpu Township in Jiangda County also went to the county hospital twice for prenatal check following the advice of the village healthcare worker, who also happened to be a village cadre. The village healthcare worker gave her nutritional supplements two or three times, and she asserted that she took them all. In order to determine the venue of delivery, she visited Wala Temple and was told by the Living Buddha to have a hospitalized delivery. As a result, her parents were prepared to escort her to the county hospital. These instances show that pregnant women and their families in rural Tibetan areas will seek information from their trusted sources. Sufficient dissemination of healthcare information to households is essential to the utilization of maternal healthcare services.

Third, the lack of effective information delivery is a reflection of inadequate management of healthcare services. Healthcare bureau officials in surveyed counties ascribed this problem to the following reasons. First, residences of rural Tibetan households were scattered, and healthcare workers were inadequate at the grassroots level. Furthermore, there had been a brain drain due to harsh living conditions in high-altitude regions and unattractive compensation. Tightening management would make healthcare staff even less willing to stay.

In fact, these circumstances can be ameliorated. As a growing number of Tibetan medical graduates are hired by township healthcare centers, healthcare quality at the grassroots level has been improved. Due to the scarcity of jobs in Tibet and the employment security in the public sector, these graduates take their jobs very seriously. Moreover, a steady increase in investment into Tibet's infrastructure and public service in Tibet has improved heath financing, medical equipment and buildings of public healthcare providers.

The lack of incentive for healthcare workers and management of healthcare services present areas with room for improvement. In fact, some excellent healthcare workers reported leaving Tibet because they felt unsatisfied regarding the lack of professional incentives. Township administrative officials were frequently appointed to be county-level healthcare officials without necessary training – they lacked experience in the healthcare sector and did not know much about good management practices from other parts of China. For instance, they were unfamiliar with the evaluation of healthcare services and the practice of compensating healthcare staff according to the quality of service.

Hence, it is necessary to adopt the following measures in order to improve the maternal healthcare management of women in rural Tibetan areas:

1   Management capacity training focusing on case studies of successful maternal healthcare management experiences for township and county officials should be a top priority for Tibetan assistance programs. For instance, the

China Foundation for Poverty Alleviation carried out a maternal and infant protection program in the mountainous areas of Yunnan Province to ensure delivery of services to households through the creation of a three-tier maternal and child healthcare network. Physicians at the township healthcare center of Chun'an County, Zhejiang Province were assigned to households in various areas at which they were to conduct regular visits as family physicians.

2   Maternal and child healthcare management responsibilities should be fulfilled at the household level and incorporated into the assessment of grassroots healthcare institutions and staff. Service providers should be subsidized for the maintenance and fuel costs of transport vehicles such as motorcycles.

3   Family planning and maternal healthcare services should be integrated. Although county healthcare bureau and family planning commissions in surveyed counties had been combined namely, the organizations operated independently. The family planning commission holds adequate funding and mobile healthcare equipment while healthcare institutions boast strong technical service capabilities. Their comprehensive integration will create a more effective system overall.

4   Village committee members should be involved in dissemination of health knowledge and information. These activities should also be supported with public finance.

9.3 Infant and young child feeding

According to the Global Strategy for Infant and Young Child Feeding (IYCF) adopted at the 55th World Healthcare Assembly (WHA) in 2002, a total of 10.9 million children below the age of five die each year. At this age, roughly 60% of mortality results from malnutrition, and more than two thirds are related to inappropriate feeding in the child's first year. The report explains that breast milk should be the only food and drink to infants for their first six months. After six months, infants will require safe and nutritious supplementary food in addition to the nutrition they receive from breastfeeding. The WHA called on member states to implement these baseline-feeding conditions for infants and young children to reduce malnutrition and risk of relevant diseases (the World Health Organization and UNICEF, 2003). The 65th WHA, held in 2012, adopted a comprehensive scheme on maternal and childhood nutrition, further requiring member states to elevate childhood nutrition to a key national priority and incorporate it into national development projects.[6]

In addition to proactive participation in the deliberation and voting of the WHA, the Chinese government has released the Infant and Young Child Feeding Strategy (MOH, 2007). This document has demonstrated that breastfeeding can provide all of the nutrition required for infants below six months of age. Breast milk contains abundant anti-bacterial benefits and breast-fed infants are less likely to suffer from diarrhea, respiratory and skin infection. Breast milk contains many amino acids necessary to the cerebral development of infants. Also a mother's voice, embrace and touch during the process of breastfeeding can stimulate her baby's brain response and stimulate early intellectual and psychological development. Infant and Young Child Feeding Strategy calls for the establishment of infant care standards for hospitals and health education avenues to extend strictly breastfeeding for newborns for the first six months after birth. Moreover, the report advocates pre-job and on-the-job training to enhance the knowledge and skills of healthcare staff regarding infant dietary supplements, continued breastfeeding and special infant feeding practices.

This part of the paper will discuss childhood feeding practices in rural Tibetan households. According to a survey on women and children in TAR conducted in 1999, roughly 80% of breastfeeding-period women provide roasted barley flour paste to their children one month after birth.[8] The Changdu Healthcare Bureau reported in 2011, 94.7% of the 4,066 breastfeeding women who were surveyed breastfed their babies under the age of six months, and of them, 51.1% fed their children only breast milk for the first six months.[9] It seems that more women had chosen to breastfeed their babies than ten years before. However, by our field visit in the same year it is found out that most of the interviewed rural women still adhered to the traditional baby feeding practices.

The duration of breastfeeding corresponds to the interval between two births. A 40-year-old pregnant woman in Shadong Township, Gongjue County mentioned that she had given birth to four children, one of whom had died. She breastfed each child for two years, added roasted barley flour paste after the first two months and included meat after one year. A woman at the same age in Hajia Township reported that she breastfed each of her children. She stopped breastfeeding her oldest daughter when she was one year old and her younger son around the age of four or five. Nevertheless, she added roasted barley flour paste, butter and milk soon after birth of each child. In the interviews, the respondents stated that they first chewed roasted barley flour paste then used their fingers to take out some to feed babies. Such feeding takes place three or four times a day, and each time a baby was fed only one or two mouthfuls. As an infant grows up, the quantity of feeding increased as well. Often, when a child reached two years of age, he/she would eat roasted barley flour paste by himself/herself and whatever else adults ate. Respondents indicated that they had not known or heard about the recommendation from the health service institutions that mothers should feed newborns only with breast milk for the first six months and then start to provide a supplementary diet.

The similar way of the infant and young child feeding is found in the counties of Jiangda and Dege. Nevertheless, it is noticed that the households with better living conditions and higher incomes provided their babies with a greater variety of supplementary food. Tongpu Township in Jiangda County is located near the public road No. 317 and is over 20 kilometers away from the county seat. A shuttle bus operated by the nearby Wala Temple provides service to and from the county town for RMB 12 yuan a one-way ticket. The author interviewed a 29-year-old pregnant woman in Xiawo Village, in which three generations of her family members shared the same house. With ten family members, four taught or worked outside the village and brought about a stable cash income. By the time her first daughter was four months old, her family added milk, roasted barley flour paste, butter, vegetables and meat to the infant's diet. In Lengcha Village of Baiya Township, 40 kilometers away from the county town in Dege, the health worker at the village was interviewed. His daughter and son in-law went to Lhasa city to work such that his grandchildren were weaned with breast milk at the age of six months, and their daily diet also consist of the five types of food indicated above.

According to the Infant and Child Feeding Strategy released by the Ministry of Health, the following three challenges remained present in the manner in which rural Tibetan households fed their infants. First, the duration of breastfeeding was too short and the provision of supplementary nutrition occurred at too young an age. Second, infants were fed with food chewed by adults, which presented risks for infection for the children's vulnerable immune systems. Third, the supplementary diet was not sufficiently diverse for far-located markets. The first two problems were directly related to the lack of knowledge in rural areas. The members of the households interviewed reported that children had been fed in this manner for generations. The explanation given by the Tibetan scholars interviewed in Beijing are as varied as follows:

- First, if breast milk was sufficiently available, roasted barley flour paste was usually not provided before a newborn reached six months of age, but butter was. In general, Tibetans view butter as a very nutritious food, but difficult to digest. Therefore, they diluted butter with roasted barley and tea when feeding it to infants.
- Second, roasted barley mixed with buttered tea can prevent diarrhea regardless of whether a mother has sufficient breast milk. Adults traditionally chew meat before feeding it to infants, and the parents themselves report being fed in this manner.
- Third, roasted barley flour paste is a warm food. It is nutritious, digestible and the only supplementary diet appropriate to babies in rural Tibetan villages.

These replies were based on conventional experience, and respondents were not familiar with the differentiation between "pure breastfeeding" and "breast milk feeding." The author consulted Professor Chen Chunming, a nutritionist at Chinese Center for Disease Control and Prevention, regarding the above explanations. Her responses are below. First, providing a newborn with only breastfeeding before he or she reaches six months of age ensures a comprehensive and safe supply of nutrition. The provision of supplementary food prior to the six months will be unfavorable for the development of the child's digestive system, and may even damage digestive functions and increase the risk of mortality. Second, traditional ways of feeding in rural Tibetan villages are neither safe nor nutritious, as asserted by a Tibetan physician in Boluo Township in Jiangda County. He said that the most common illness for local children is indigestion during the breastfeeding period. Improper ways of feeding can partially explain why the ratios of low weight and stunted growth of children under the age of five in rural Tibetan areas are higher than national average. In 1998, the ratio of low weight and stunted growth for children under the age of five were 9.8% and 27.9% respectively (Chen, Chunming et al., 2010). For comparison, in 1999, the low weight and stunted growth ratios of children below the age of three were 24.7% and 41.4% (Dang et al., 2004, 2008).

Based on the information above, we may suppose that in the distant past, there was no food security in the Tibetan region and women suffered from malnutrition. They were unable to provide sufficient nutrition to their infant children, and had to add adult food into their diet. Gradually, this feeding practice became a local custom, and young parents added supplementary food in the diet of newborns at the age of three to four months or younger. Infants had often suffered from diarrhea, and some had died as a result of this practice. The parents were not aware of the true reasons for their child's gastrointestinal diseases and did not realize that numerous fatalities of infants and young children resulted from improper feeding. For the same reason, government and healthcare institutions in rural Tibetan areas did not give sufficient attention to the hazards resulting from traditional ways of feeding.

In the households' visits, the author asked extensively about the diet of pregnant women and breastfeeding women. Respondents indicated that they had no problem of food variety; however, the level of diversity in their diet depended on the types of self-produced food, family income and distance to the nearest food market, which were usually located at the county towns. For instance, a 140 kilometers ride separates Geluo Village, Shadong Township in Gongjue County and the local county town, a three-hour ride in an SUV in good conditions. This village was specialized in growing staple food crops while vegetables were planted around each residence. A pregnant woman in the village said that she relied on butter and roasted barley and rarely ate meat during the pregnancy and breastfeeding period. Vegetables were not available until the weather became warm.

While feeding her baby, Bo Ga (a pseudonym), a woman in Bairi No. 2 Village of Yulong Township, Dege County stated that during her pregnancy for her sixth son who had been born three months before, she just had a bit more beef soup than her family members did. Her family received a Dibao subsidy (a minimum subsistence guarantee) and purchased roasted barley powder, butter, beef and vegetables from the nearby Mani Gange Market. In comparison, the pregnant woman of a rich family in Tongpu Township in Jiangda County ate a more varied diet – her diet included butter cooked with roasted barley, rice, potato, cabbage and occasionally beef. Since her pregnancy, she had eaten chicken meat and drank chicken soup, beef soup and fish soup. When asked about cost of additional food, she smiled and kept silent. It turned out that this family's money manager was her father-in-law (59 years of age). He replied "about RMB 2,000 yuan."

Short duration of only breastfeeding and a lack of nutrition and safety in the supplementary food provided to infants represent problems that are still prevalent among rural Tibetan households. Such feeding practices are closely related to the traditional customs of Tibetan society. It is then expected that health education would provide substantive improvements in childhood nutrition. One-on-one and face-to-face guidance must be provided to pregnant and breastfeeding women. In particular, nutrition and health knowledge should be included in primary and middle schools' health courses. These efforts will require public healthcare institutions to provide careful, solid and effective door-to-door service across remote areas of Tibet.

The statistics issued by the Changdu Health Bureau in 2010 indicated that health management services had covered 62.6% of children under the age of seven and 57% of newborns had received home visits. The dissemination of necessary information on infant and young child feeding, however, lacked strategy and effectiveness. In 2012, the health service system in TAR began to enhance child health management. For instance, the Health Bureau of the TAR requires at least two visits for newborns and at least four uses of child health services within the first year after birth. The scope of services ranges from physical checkups and growth monitoring to breastfeeding analysis, psychological development review, the prevention of accidental injury and guidance on the prevention and treatment of common diseases. Currently, the question is what kind of incentive should be provided to ensure that grassroots healthcare staff fulfill these requirements and promote the targeted groups to take action. This is consistent with resolving the challenges confronting maternal healthcare services. The policy measures identified in the previous section may apply as well.

9.4 Primary school feeding management

The policy of free meals for primary and middle school students has proven to be widely applauded according to the studies of our research team. In 2005, the team documented the efforts made by Changdu Prefecture, eye witnessing township officials and village leaders visiting each household to persuade parents to allow their children to attend school. By 2010, however, with the exception of the children who studied Buddhism in monasteries, enrollment of school-aged children in Tibet had already approached almost 100%, indicating the effectiveness of the policy on obligatory education. Government policies of free school lunches, free accommodation and no tuition fees have undoubtedly reduced the cost of raising children in rural Tibet. In particular, the school meals are often much healthier, safer and more delicious than the family meals, which has made attending school more attractive to rural Tibetan children. As also seen in international experiences, the free school meals have not only resulted in the increased cognitive abilities and academic performance of the children but also improved the nutrition and healthcare of the children. Therefore, free school meals represent a human capital investment with a long-term return (Bang Di et al.). In 2011 field visits of the team, the following became very noticeable.

First, the free school meals bring benefits in dietary hygiene and food safety to the children. In rural Tibetan areas, primary schools with kitchens and dining halls are all located near township centers with boarding facilities. These buildings are frequently newly constructed and not far from healthcare institutes. A health worker of Baiya Township in Dege County checks food hygiene of the adjacent primary school kitchen on a daily basis. Under his escort, the author interviewed Chef Bai Zhen and Principal Mr. Zou. The school has a tidy and bright kitchen and both the stove and the bench of schoolchildren are furnished with white tiles.

Shining stainless steel kitchen utensils were organized neatly. The kitchen of the central primary school in Hajia Township, Gongjue County was not as well organized but equally well-equipped. In addition to above-mentioned kitchen equipment, there was a stainless steel steamer and an electric butter tea mixer.

The school kitchens described above boasted a level of hygiene uncommon in ordinary rural Tibetan households encountered during the study. Both the kitchen and dining hall have access to tap water, which is convenient for the chefs and children to maintain hygiene standards. Of the 60 children in the school, 40 were boarding. Once ill, children are immediately sent to the township health center and if the condition becomes worse, parents are telephoned to take them home. Many villagers have telephones and can be reached in time.

Second, the school feeding program also provides an otherwise unavailable diversity to the students' diet. A small blackboard at the entrance of the dining hall specifies the menu for the three meals of the day. During an interview, the chef Bai Zhen reported that she had finished cooking for lunch, a meal of steamed rice and a mixed dish of fresh meat, lettuce, potatoes and cabbage. She said that every morning, she woke up at six o'clock to boil water for the schoolchildren and began to prepare breakfast. Breakfast included butter, roasted barley and milk tea. Lunch usually included rice or a fried dish, and supper was usually a noodle dish or porridge, possibly mixed with dishes left over from the day's lunch. At nine in the evening, she heated water for the schoolchildren to wash their face and feet. The interviewed pupils stated that the school meals are so tasty that they enjoy the food provided by the school kitchen. Slogans on the walls of the dining hall read "every grain of rice comes as a result of sweat of farmers." A small bucket in the corner of the kitchen was more than half full of buns, rice and vegetables thrown away by schoolchildren. The principal explained that he has not yet found an effective way to stop schoolchildren wasting food as they could eat as much as they wish without any payments. Third, the food procurement system and publicity arrangement on food expenditures demonstrate room for improvement. The school kitchens work for nine months each year as there are two months of winter vacation and one month of summer vacation. The education bureaus in the studied counties all made rules on food procurement, storage and consumption. According to the principal Mr. Zou of the primary school in Baiya Township in Dege County, authorities from the central government, the Sichuan provincial government and Ganzi prefectural government jointly provide funding for primary school meals at the level of monthly 120 yuan per student. County education bureaus are responsible for procuring rice, wheat flour, cooking oil and other ingredients while each school purchases its meat and vegetables. A teacher of the school is selected to be responsible for food storage. The principal himself is in charge of procurement while the chef only manages cooking. In 2010, the local price for rice and wheat flour per 500g is recorded as 1.7 yuan and about 1.6 yuan respectively. In 2011 the prices increased to 1.92 yuan and 1.8 yuan.

Most of the meat and vegetables come from Sichuan Province. Notably, Hajia Township in Gongjue County utilized poverty alleviation loans to build greenhouses and hired Sichuan farmers to lead local resettled households to grow vegetables. In this manner, schools purchase vegetables from nearby farms. In 2011, farmers from Sichuan were not available, and local resettled farmers were still unable to grow vegetables independently. As a result, the school and sur-rounding villagers had to buy vegetables transported from Sichuan. Households in the Yulong Township in Dege County used to be herdsmen and are now unable to grow vegetables so that the school procured it from Mani Gange Fair. The only foodstuffs produced locally were barley, beef and butter, therefore, diet diversity was primarily supplemented by non-local food products. The school feeding pro-gram had not yet significantly stimulated local food production.

To the question about publicity of the food expenditure and the supervision from the parents of the schoolchildren, the principals of the visited schools replied that although the parents cared more about what their children ate than the expenses resulting from the free meals program, schools still published monthly expenses on the blackboard. Deficits appeared in some of the accounts due to inflation of food prices. Each month the school accountant reports bills to the local bureau of education and the bureau is currently working on a solution.

Fourth, nutrition monitory system had not yet been established such that the author did not obtain access to the nutrition data of the schoolchildren covered by the school feeding program.

The free meals program has been effectively institutionalized across schools of rural Tibetan areas. It has increased the diversity of the diet of local children and been applauded by farmers and herdsmen. Shortcomings in the project's opera-tion are observed as follows: first, chefs lack nutrition education and cooking skill training; second, it has not yet been put on the policy agenda that funding for food procurement should be pegged to inflation of food prices; third, a third-party evaluation system has not been established; and fourth, parents have not been included in the decision-making and monitoring of the program.

9.5 Discussions and tentative policy conclusions

Early child development is a critical and sensitive period for capability formation in the life circle of human beings. Nutrition and healthcare in this stage provide a foundation for a person's development through the rest of his or her life. Lack of early nutrition may lead to irreparable damage to an individual's physical growth, cognitive abilities and emotional development. The existing cross-disciplinary studies indicate that investment in early child development such as nutrition, healthcare and education provides an indispensable and most effective tool for unlocking healthy human development. Moreover, the earlier a child is exposed to the investment the better the results will be. According to a 40-year study on African-American children, investment in pre-school age children has an annual return of 6% to 10% higher than annual return to investment in school education and on-the-job training, and even higher than the annual return of stock market in the same period (Heckman et al., 2010).

However, a society often faces the following problems: first, low-income parents may not be informed of the knowledge about early child development.

Second, even if a household's income increases, less productive expenses compete for priority with nutrition and health. As in financial decision-making, investment items with a short-term horizon will inevitably enjoy greater priority over those with long-term return. Returns made on early child development will not normally be realized until adulthood, so they are often neglected. Third, once investment on early child development is delayed, the best timing for such investment is missed. Moreover, poverty itself creates a negative impact on childhood development. Public action is thus necessary to care for poor children in their critical, early stage of development to alleviate the negative impacts on their growing up in impoverished conditions. These programs allow the poor schoolchildren to compete on a level playing field by reducing the potential for the inter-generation poverty transmission. The programs of antenatal care, infant and young child feeding and school feeding in rural China belong to the public actions undertaken for poverty reduction with investment in early child development.

The school feeding program carried out in Tibetan townships has been implemented much more effectively in comparison with the programs of antenatal care and infant child feeding for the following reasons. First, organizational cost is relatively low – there is only one school in each township and no more than a dozen in each county, which provides a manageable scope for county-level administrators in the bureau of education. Second, the primary school administrative network was already in place and the implementation of the feeding program just adds additional tasks to the existing administrative networks. Third, the schoolchildren as a target group are highly organized. Schoolchildren are one of the groups with the strongest desire for knowledge and sense of discipline among residents in rural Tibetan areas, and thus they welcome projects such as the free meals program. Despite a partial transformation of their traditional but less diversified diet, the substantial nutritional improvement is consistent with the aspirations of both the schoolchildren and their parents. Hence, the implementation of the program met almost no social obstacles. Fourth, as part of the public sector, schools are subject to a clear incentive system regarding policy implementation, which has, in this case, proven effective in encouraging the productive implementation of the feeding program.

The implementation of the maternal healthcare program and the infant and young child feeding strategy is different. First, the agencies responsible for implementing the programs are managing disparate rural Tibetan households. Delivering information in person to each household proves to be a high organizational cost relative to the school feeding program. Second, the target groups of these two programs are farmers and herdsmen with low levels of formal education. Their receptivity to new knowledge conflicting with traditional practices regarding infant and young child feeding requires long-term, careful and frequent health education to create a worthwhile behavioral change. Therefore, it is unlikely that this program will demonstrate significant results rapidly. Second, few officials in charge of health service administration at county and township levels are healthcare professionals and thus lack training in the sector of public health, providing another barrier to effective program operation. Third, the relatively poor performance resulted from the lack of a qualified professional team, funding shortage and a weak incentive structure.

Therefore, multiple actions must be taken to enhance the quality of the program. First, the government should stay in closer contact with the rural Tibetan community. The village committee, women's groups and primary school can be included in the healthcare program to enhance the healthcare service network and help close the contact between government and grassroots community.

Second, multiple avenues of information dissemination should be adopted to ensure that knowledge on child nutrition be conveyed to households, particularly to women of childbearing age, such as television programs popular with the rural Tibetan community, village meetings, posters in the homes of local citizens and basic healthcare courses for schoolchildren. In addition to providing the door-to-door delivery of healthcare materials and services, such as nutrients and health checkups, service staff could provide childhood healthcare knowledge to women of childbearing age and their family members. According to existing domestic and international experience, expanding the access to knowledge of rural Tibetan females will promote gender equality, which is favorable for the improvement of early child development (The World Bank, 2012).

Third, the incentive structure of healthcare institutions must be improved. In addition to pegging the salary of healthcare staff to their quality of service, efforts could be made to establish a healthcare monitoring system that incorporates grassroots public opinion and personal accountability into the evaluation of healthcare staff. Meanwhile, third-party assessments could provide a more independent review on performance of healthcare and health service administrators.

Fourth, training should be strengthened in the aid program for Tibetan areas. Knowledge and information about early child development should be included in the training curriculum. Besides the managerial training and health education targeting local officials and health service administrators, courses should also be provided to the healthcare staff, school principals and chefs who are critical for the program.

Fifth, the superior levels of government should allocate sufficient funding for the operation of the programs to ensure effective implementation. As this study was limited in its scope, an additional study assessing the operation of the programs in the Tibetan areas would be beneficial. Then, statistical analysis results could be compared with the costs of similar programs undertaken in other regions. In this way the differences could be identified for counties at different altitudes, with various accesses to modern transportation and varying levels of population density. These calculations will provide a basis for the allocation of funding.

Notes

1 See the World Bank webpage: Why Invest in Early Child Development (ECD), http://web.worldbank.org/WBSITE/EXTERNAL/TOPICS/EXTCY/EXTECD/0,,content MDK:20207747~menuPK:527098~pagePK:148956~piPK:216618~theSitePK: 344939,00.html, November 17, 2012.
2 Fan Xiaojian: Speech at the Opening Ceremony of the 3rd International Symposium on Poverty Relief and Child Development, Beijing, October 18, 2012.

3 For this survey on the weight and height of Tibetan children, I asked for measurement tables and results from Luorong Zhandui. Reporters with People's Daily also covered his survey but misstated the data about the change in children's weight. See people.com.cn: Tibetan Researcher Luorong Zhandui: Unprecedented Improvement in the Livelihood of Tibet, August 13, 2012, http://xz.people.com.cn/n/2012/0813/c138901–17351477.html, March 3, 2013.

4 There is the following statement in Analysis Report on Women's and Children's Health-care Annual Report 2010 for Changdu Prefecture: "nutrition survey included 3,887 children below five years of age, including 201 with median weight -2SD. Incidence of malnutrition is 5.17%, up 2.83 percentage points over the level of 2.34% in 2009". (Source: Qamdo Healthcare Bureau, March 2, 2011.) By the WHO standards, child nutrition indicator value $Z=(W-RM)/SD$. Where, W is the height or weight of sample under observation; RM is the WHO reference criterion (median value of height or weight); SD is standard error for the WHO reference criterion (height or weight). By such calculation, low weight rate of children under five years of age in rural poor regions of China in 2009 is 6.6% and stunting rate is 18.3% (Chen, Chunming et al., 2010).

5 Ministry of Health, People's Republic of China: Regulations on Maternal Healthcare and Good Maternal Healthcare Practices, June 23, 2011, http://www.moh.gov.cn/mohfybjysqwss/s3581/201107/52320.shtml, March 14, 2013.

6 In 2010, medical financing standard for rural Tibet is RMB 260 yuan per head and this figure is RMB 130 yuan for the new rural cooperative program of Dege County, Ganzi Prefecture, Sichuan Province. Contribution requirement for both regions is the same, i.e., RMB 20 yuan per person from rural households and the rest comes from government allowance. In addition, insurance participation for poor households is paid by civil affairs departments on their behalf. Insurance participation ratio for the three counties under survey are all above 90%.

7 65th WHA: Maternal and Infant Nutrition, June 2012, http://www.moh.gov.cn/wsb/01100214/201206/55094/files/e3b7441a4a274b0686b40bef9a8c7ca0.pdf, March 15, 2013.

8 Dang, S., H. Yan, S. Yamamoto, X. Wang and L. Zeng. "Feeding Practice among Younger Tibetan Children Living at High Altitudes", *European Journal of Clinical Nutrition*, 2005, No. 59, pp. 1022–1029.

9 Qamdo Healthcare Bureau: Report on Annual Data of Women and Children's Healthcare in Changdu Region 2010, March 2, 2011.

References

Changdu Health Bureau. 2011. Women and Children's Health Annual Data Analysis Report 2010 for Changdu Region, Changdu.

Chen, Chunming, Wu He, Yuying Wang, and Lina Deng. 2010. "Nutrition in Rapid Economic Development" and "Nutrition Status in China under Global Financial Crisis." Report on Nutrition Policy Research, Nutrition Monitoring Program Work Group, China Disease Control and Prevention Center, Beijing.

Chen, Chunming, Yuying Wang, and Suying Chang. 2010. "Effect of In-Home Fortification of Complementary Feeding on Intellectual Development of Chinese Children." *Biomedical and Environmental Sciences*, no. 23: 83–91.

Dang, S., H. Yan, and S. Yamamoto. 2008. "High Altitude and Early Childhood Growth Retardation: New Evidence from Tibet." *European Journal of Clinical Nutrition*, no. 62: 342–348.

Dang, S., H. Yan, S. Yamamoto, X. Wang, and L. Zeng. 2004. "Poor Nutritional Status of Younger Tibetan Children Living at High Altitudes." *European Journal of Clinical Nutrition*, no. 58: 938–946.

———. 2005. "Feeding Practice among Younger Tibetan Children Living at High Altitudes." *European Journal of Clinical Nutrition*, no. 59: 1022–1029.

Gyaltsen, K., C. Gewa, H. Greenlee, J. Ravetz, M. Aikman, and A. Pebley. 2007. "Socioeconomic Status and Maternal and Child Health in Rural Tibetan Villages." On-Line Working Paper Series, California Center for Population Research, UC Los Angeles, escholarship.org/uc/item/04d8b3mv, accessed on June 23, 2012.

Hao, Zhirong. 2012. "Analysis on Rural Family Education in China – Qualitative Study Based on Ledu County in Qinghai Province." In *Collection of Children's Program Research Outcomes*. China Development Research Foundation.

Harris, N. S., P. B. Crawford, Yeshe Yangzom, Lobsang Pinzo, Paldeng Gyaltsen, and M. Hudes. 2001. "Nutritional and Health Status of Tibetan Children Living at High Altitudes." *The New England Journal of Medicine*, 344, no. 5: 341–347.

Heckman, J., S. Moon, R. Pinto, P. Savelyev, and A. Yavitz. 2010. "The Rate of Return to the High Scope Perry Preschool Program." *Journal of Public Economics*, 94: 114–128.

The Ministry of Health. 2007. "Infant and Young Child Feeding Strategy," www.gov.cn/fwxx/jk/2007–08/01/content_703104.htm, accessed on March 16, 2013.

The Ministry of Health, People's Republic of China. 2012. "Report on the Nutrition Development of Children Aged between 0 and 6 in China," www.moh.gov.cn/mohbgt/s3582/201205/54990.shtml, accessed on February 22, 2013.

Siddiqi, A., L. G. Irwin, and C. Hertzman. 2007. "Early Child Development: A Powerful Equalizer: Final Report for the World Health Organization's Commission on the Social Determinants of Health," apps.who.int/iris/bitstream/10665/69729/2/a91213_chi.pdf, accessed on March 13, 2013.

Van der Gaag, J. 2011. *From Early Child Development to Human Development – Investing in the Future of Children*. Beijing: China Development Press.

Wellhoner, M., A. Lee, K. Deutsch, M. Wiebenga, M. Freytsis, Sonam Drogha, Phuntsok Dongdrup, Karma Lhamo, Ojen Tsering, Tseyongjee, Dawa Khandro, L. Mullany, and L. Weingrad. 2011. "Maternal and Child Health in Yushu, Qinghai Province, China." *International Journal for Equity in Health*, www.equityhealthj.com/content/10/1/42, accessed in 2012.

The World Bank. 2012. *World Development Report 2012: Gender Equality and Development*. Beijing: Tsinghua University Press.

World Health Organization, UNICEF. 2003. "Global Strategy for Infant and Young Child Feeding." Geneva, whqlibdoc.who.int/publications/2003/9241562218.pdf.

Zhu, Ling. 2008. "Preventing Inter-Generational Transmission of Poverty at the Starting Point of Life." *China Demographic Science*, no. 1: 30–36.

Part IV

Poverty reduction and social protection

10 Labor intensive public works in poor areas

Poverty in China is mainly concentrated in certain regions and in rural areas. Poverty is not related to unequal land distribution, since land reform and collectivisation more than 40 years ago levelled out differences in land ownership.

The market-oriented economic reforms begun in the late 1970s have given Chinese farmers decision-making powers in the management of agricultural activities. They also enabled many farmers to increase their incomes within a short period through better use of resources and by taking advantage of price increases, economic restructuring, and the development of non-farm industries. However, about one-tenth of the rural population has barely benefited from these institutional changes, and remains food-insecure (Chen Chunming, 1992; Zhu Ling and Jiang Zhongyi, 1994). This section of the population inhabits areas that are poor in resources and infrastructure (Tong Zhong et al., 1994). Hence, there is a widening gap between the socio-economic development of these areas and the national average.

To bridge this gap, the Chinese Government has carried out large-scale anti-poverty measures since 1985 to speed up development in poor areas and to ensure that the basic requirements of the poor for food and clothing are met. The criteria set at that time for identifying poor households and poor counties were an annual per capita foodgrain consumption of less than 200 kg and an annual per capita income of less than 200 yuans. Poor counties designated by the central and provincial governments total 699.

'Yigong-daizhen', which means 'to offer job opportunities instead of straightforward relief', is one of the Chinese Government's poverty-alleviation programmes. It consists mainly of government infrastructural construction investments (in kind) in poor regions. It supplies the material basis for regional economic growth and provides short-term job opportunities and incomes for the local population. The projects tried out are identical to those known internationally as 'labour-intensive public works' (von Braun et al., 1991).

This article considers the effects of Yigong-daizhen projects on the employment, income, and nutritional status of households in poor areas. The organisational

(Co-author with Zhongyi Jiang, originally published in *Development Policy Review*, No. 4, 1995.)

pattern of the Yigong-daizhen projects is described first. Data obtained from surveys of village communities and peasant households will then be presented and analysed to identify (1) the targeting mechanisms of Yigong-daizhen projects and (2) the impact of the projects on the income and consumption of poor rural households. Finally, problems will be assessed in the organisation and operation of the programme and measures for improvement will be explored.

10.1 The size and organisation of the Yigong-daizhen programme

The Yigong-daizhen programme started at the end of 1984. Public investment under this programme differed from the government's formal capital construction projects in the following ways:

1 The central government's investment took the form of in-kind financing of these projects. These in-kind goods were surplus products created during a certain period under the planned economy. The investment plan depended on the availability of surplus goods. In many cases, several schemes have operated during the same period (Table 10.1).
2 Regulations stipulate that in-kind goods allocated by the central government are distributed as wages to those involved in construction projects. Local governments are supposed to raise an equal or larger amount of supplementary funds to pay for project materials and other expenses. However, in practice,

Table 10.1 Chinese government investment in Yigong-daizhen schemes, 1984–93

Scheme number	Planned period	In-kind goods invested	Converted value of the goods (billion yuan)[a]	Project focus
1	1984-87	Cereals, cotton, and cloth	2.7	Roads and drinking water supply facilities
2	1989-91	Medium- and low-grade consumer goods	0.6	Roads and drinking water supply facilities
3	1990-92	Industrial goods	1.5	Roads and drinking water supply facilities, farmland improvement
4	1991-95	Foodgrains	5.0	Terraced fields, small-scale water conservation
5	1991-95	Foodgrains and industrial goods	10.0	Big rivers
6	1993-97	Cereals, cloth, edible oil, medium- and low-grade consumer goods	10.0	Infrastructure, including clinics, health care stations for women and children

[a] In 1993, 5.8 yuan equalled US$1.

Source: Documents issued by the State Planning Commission referring to Yigong-daizhen schemes, 1984–93.

Table 10.2 Major achievements of the Yigong-daizhen projects, China, 1985–90

Public roads	131,000 km
Bridges (number)	7,972
Dredged river navigation routes	2,400 km
Public roads connecting	1,500 townships
	10,000 administrative villages
Drinking water supply for	20,970,000 people
	13,560,000 animals

Source: Data from the State Planning Commission.

    apart from a few provinces with adequate resources, most provinces and counties have not been able to come up with the matching funds. To fill the gap, poverty-alleviation funds from other channels (such as from line ministries) were used and some of the goods transferred were monetised.

3   Local governments have also mobilised the rural population to provide part of their labour free of charge or at reduced wages. Such practices are not workable in the implementation of formal capital construction projects. But because the Yigong-daizhen programmes were aimed at reducing poverty, local governments and the poor accepted these practices and participated in the investment projects. This flexibility played a positive role in pooling resources to improve the infrastructure. However, employment of unpaid labour will reduce the current income of the poor.

4   Yigong-daizhen projects have mainly made use of simple, labour-intensive technology. Construction was normally carried out in the slack seasons, thus providing varying amounts of additional income. Between 1985 and 1990, projects focused on building roads and providing drinking water supply facilities (see Table 10.2). Thanks to this programme, both transport facilities and social services in the poor areas have improved, and human resources in the project areas have been enhanced. Specifically, farmers acquired technical skills on the job and administrative cadres learned construction management; a specialised technical work force has been trained in the area of infrastructure construction and water conservation.

10.1.1 Implementation rules of the Yigong-daizhen projects

Local governments at various levels tend to give priority to concentrating resources on the most important projects and those which can be easily implemented, and carry out projects in stages. For road projects, efficiency is stressed and priority in investment is given to the following categories of projects: (1) feeder roads linking villages and towns with main roads; (2) roads in areas with rich resources, but without accessible roads; (3) roads connecting existing public highways and transportation networks; and (4) renovation projects for existing roads that carry heavy traffic, but are of a low technical standard.

Drinking water projects are selected based on the availability of water sources. The following categories of projects have priority: (1) projects with greater labour input (large employment generation); (2) projects which match existing infrastructure works (favourable complementary effects); (3) projects proposed by villages where the leading body has comparatively good organisational ability and households volunteer to collect supplementary funds or to contribute their labour (low organisational and budgetary costs); and (4) supply projects in townships or villages suffering from serious water shortages (high public health and sanitation benefits).

10.1.2 Contractors, payment regulations, and compulsory work

Two types of labour are required for construction work: skilled and unskilled. The former includes masons, carpenters, blacksmiths, etc. In recent years, they have tended to organise themselves into crews of contractors to take on tasks of a higher technical standard, both locally and in more distant counties. Unskilled workers are local farmers who are recruited for manual labour, such as moving earth and stones.

Earthwork and stone work in road projects are usually contracted out by the project headquarters to groups of villagers along the roads. The heads of these groups usually distribute the task among households, according to the number of workers per household. The labour of farmers is, to some extent, compulsory; it is incorporated in the unpaid work which is converted into the matching 'funds' provided by the local governments. Those households with workers who are unwilling to work have to pay an amount to the villagers' group to relieve themselves of work obligations. However, because of the tradition of mutual enforcement of work obligations among members of village communities, especially with regard to projects for the public benefit, failure to work is rare. As for the drinking water projects, which belong to individual households or village communities on completion, all the unskilled labour input contributed by the villagers is unremunerated; only the skilled workers are paid.

Payments for labour are set by the project headquarters as task rates, with work quotas stipulated according to the amount and difficulty of the work contracted. The daily payment of a skilled worker is usually twice that of an unskilled worker. The mode of payment varies with the kind of materials allocated by the central government. When foodgrains, cotton, and cotton cloth are used as inputs, payments for project participants will be made in these materials. When stocks of industrial products are invested in construction work, workers receive 'industrial coupons' as wages. These have the same value as the official currency of the Renminbi but function as a kind of banknote which can be used only once. They have to be used within the county and in the shops run by government departments of commerce, agricultural machinery, and production materials, or in county and township purchasing and marketing co-operatives (Zhu Ling and Jiang Zhongyi, 1990).

10.1.3 Monitoring and planning

Monitoring and control for the approval of the projects are carried out by the professional departments in charge of engineering and technology operations. The whole process of project planning, controlling, organising, and monitoring, along with the use of industrial coupons, has been the operational pattern for many years in the centrally planned economy; it is thus well known to the administrative cadres and government departments at all levels. As a result, the organisation of the programme has been quite smooth. However, the process has also had the disadvantage of taking place in a planned economy. For instance, restrictions placed by authorities at higher levels on where investments are directed have made it difficult for the county and township governments to utilise resources flexibly according to local needs. As village communities were excluded from the decision-making process, the programmes approved at higher levels were sometimes not the projects most needed by the local governments and the poor.

10.2 Regional and household-level assessment

10.2.1 Sources of data and information

Interviews with officials of the central and provincial governments in 1990, and two case studies conducted in Guizhou and Sichuan Provinces, form the basis for information at the macro level. Micro-level findings are based on data derived from sample surveys in Sichuan, Shandong, and Ningxia undertaken in May and June 1992. The sample surveys were designed as follows:

1   One poor county was selected from each of three different categories of provinces – developed, partly developed, and less developed – in order to compare differences among various poor regions (see Appendix Table A).
2   Twelve administrative villages were selected from each of the three counties studied. They were divided into three groups of four villages each. The first group consisted of villages participating in road projects, the second villages participating in drinking water supply projects, and the third villages that were not participating in any Yigong-daizhen projects. Questionnaires were designed to identify the natural, economic, and social conditions of the village communities. These were used in interviews with leading members of the villager committees.
3   Household surveys: 10 households from each of the sample villages, selected by random sampling, were interviewed with structured questionnaires. Data collected related mainly to conditions in 1991.

Probit models were used to estimate the probability of participation in the projects for villages, households, and individuals, respectively. Three conclusions can be drawn from the village-level model (Table 10.3).

Table 10.3 Estimation of the probability of participation in Yigong-daizhen projects by village, Probit Model 1

Variable	Coefficient	t-Ratio
Population	0.31068^{-2}*	1.838
Distance from village to township	−0.13630	−1.396
Distance from village to county seat	0.25353^{-1}*	1.860
System of obligatory labour contribution	−0.94305	−0.622
Irrigation index of farmland	4.4919	1.404
Per capita farmland of a village	−1.3306*	−1.836
Constant	0.45017	0.177

N = 34, * significant at .10 level

Table 10.4 Estimation of the probability of participation in Yigong-daizhen projects by household, Probit Model 2

Variable	Coefficient	t-Ratio
Per capita farmland of household	−0.17*	−3.30
Irrigation index of farmland	1.71*	4.80
Labour index of household (labour force/household size)	0.44	1.30
Per capita assets	$−0.45^{-4}$	−1.05
Number of households in a village	0.21^{-2}*	3.10

Constant = −0.80, N = 358, cases correctly predicted = 68.4%, * significant at .01 level

1 The larger the population of a village, the more likely it is to be involved in projects.
2 Villages with favourable environmental conditions are more likely to obtain projects. The role of the irrigation index in the model, which indicates conditions for agricultural production in village communities, seems to testify to this point, but it is not statistically significant at the villager level.
3 Villages with more farmland per capita are less likely to get projects, which means that those with more (surplus) labour are supported more.

Within counties, the more remote areas get preferential treatment.

In the household-level model (Table 10.4), the results indicated that households that are relatively rich in labour resources, poor in land, and low in per capita assets participate more in the projects. While this may be these households' free choice, it can also be interpreted as a result of the regulated access to participation.

Probit Model 3 was derived by estimating the probability of individual participation in the projects (Table 10.5). Data for the estimation are based on the records of individual participants and non-participants between 15 and 65 years of age – a

Table 10.5 Estimation of the probability of individual participation in Yigong-daizhen projects, Probit Model 3

Variable	Coefficient	t-Ratio
Age	$0.19^{-1}**$	4.94
Sex (1 = male, 0 = female)	$0.47**$	4.92
Years of education	$0.32^{-1}*$	1.89
Per capita farmland of household	$-0.21**$	-6.37

Constant = -1.41, N = 1,145, cases correctly predicted = 78.6%, * significant at .05 level, ** significant at .01 level

total of 1,145 people. Several conclusions can be drawn from Model 3 to supplement those drawn from Models 1 and 2.

- Workers from households with less land tend to participate more in the projects. This may be because they have lower opportunity costs in agriculture.
- Male workers show a higher probability of involvement than females. The reasons for this may be twofold. First, the payments for moving earth and stones are according to task rates that may favour males (due to their physical strength). Hence, the active participation of the male workers can be seen as an efficiency decision by the household. Second, the conventional division of labour between males and females in farmers' families assigns household chores, livestock production, and field work to women, thus limiting the extent of their participation in projects.
- Workers with a higher educational level and older workers are more inclined to participate.

The analysis suggests that, even within poor areas, the criterion for government approval for starting new projects is efficiency – the success of the projects and the effectiveness of the investments. This also explains why township governments usually choose villages with better conditions to be the sites of new projects.

In contrast to this practice, village communities have practised the principle of equality in the recruitment of the labour force for projects, which means that rural households and individuals enjoy equal opportunities in project participation. However, the analysis shows that households with a lower land and asset base in fact mm out to be more involved in projects compared with relatively well-to-do people.

10.2.2 Impact of projects on rural household income

As noted above, village communities covered by the projects are mostly those with comparatively favourable economic conditions, and non-poor households in the village communities are not excluded from participating. Thus, it might well be assumed that the distribution of project incomes among households will intensify the inequality of total disposable incomes. This possibility has been investigated by calculating the Gini coefficients. The results of the calculations as listed in Appendix Table B indicate that farming constitutes the main source of income for the sample households. Since access to farmland is distributed on an equal basis to all households, income from farming does not vary widely among households. In contrast, there are higher degrees of disparities in non-farm incomes. The Gini coefficient of income from projects enlarges the overall Gini coefficient. It is only because of its small share that the impact on income distribution is limited.

Opportunity costs and net effects

The above discussion of rural household income from projects has not taken directly into account the farmers' opportunity costs for their involvement. To obtain information on this, the survey included some relevant direct questions to farmers.

Table 10.6 reports the responses to these questions in interviews with households. Several conclusions can be drawn. First, for most of the workers (78.1%), their participation in the projects resulted in a decrease in their leisure time. Because Yigong-daizhen projects were usually carried out during the slack season in farming, the opportunity cost of their participation in the projects was almost zero (the 'leisure time' in this season was not the choice of the farmers themselves but a manifestation of the idleness of the labour force). This fact constitutes the rationale for the low payment and the mobilisation of compulsory labour commonly practised in the construction works.

Table 10.6 Impact of participation in Yigong-daizhen projects on household work time and children's dislocation (%)

Question					
Reaction from interviewees	*Stopped some other work*	*Women work more*	*Children work more*	*Child at workplace (women)*	*Child at workplace (men)*
	(1)[a]	(2)[b]	(3)[c]	(4)[d]	(5)[e]
Yes	21.9	45.8	6.5	6.5	2.0
No	78.1	54.2	93.5	93.5	98.0

[a] Is there any worker in your family who has stopped other production work to take part in the project?
[b] Have the female members of your family increased their working time in farming because of the participation of male workers in the projects?
[c] Have the children under 16 years of age in your family increased their time spent in domestic work because of the participation of their parents in the projects?
[d] Do the female members of your family bring children under 16 years of age with them when engaging in project work?
[e] Do male workers in your family bring children under 16 years of age with them when engaging in project work?

Note: A total of 201 households (56% of the total sample) answered these questions. 40 other households have possibly participated in the projects, but, due to their failure to answer questions concerning the number of days of their participation and their earnings from the projects, they were not included.

Second, in almost half the households, the working hours of women were increased; in other words, their leisure time was reduced in order to meet the requirements of agricultural production while male workers participated in the projects. Rural households made labour inputs by adjusting the deployment of the family work force. In 54.2% of rural households, participation in projects did not affect the amount of time worked by female workers, perhaps because these households had more working members or because the timing of the construction work coincided with the slack season in farming.

Thirdly, it was probably because of the abundant labour supply that the impact of farmer participation on children's work (question 3) and children's dislocation from home (questions 4 and 5) was small.

The implementation of Yigong-daizhen projects has increased the immediate employment and incomes of the participants, both of which represent short-term effects of the projects on rural household income, or first-round impacts. Part of the increased income may be used by farmers for new investments in fixed assets or for the purchase of additional input materials, possibly leading to a further increase in incomes.

Infrastructure effects

The execution of projects also improves the infrastructure and social services in the villages, thus creating the conditions for future increases in rural household income. This is a long-term effect of the projects, which will be assessed in the context of other income-determining factors. Village infrastructure was assessed on the basis of six factors: accessibility of the village by road (conditioned by being accessible by truck); the existence of supply centres for input materials (improved varieties of crops, chemical fertilisers, and other farm chemicals); and the availability of electricity, medical services, drinking water supply centres, and primary schools. To obtain an aggregate impression, each factor was assigned one point. Project villages in the sample generally got more than four points each, while villages in the reference groups got around 2.5 points each, on average. There are, of course, correlations among these infrastructural conditions (Ahmed and Hossain, 1990).

The multiple regression analysis below has included indicators representing the above-mentioned factors including household per capita area of cultivated land, ratio of area under improved varieties to total cultivated land, irrigation index, household per capita fixed assets, family labour resource index (labour force/ household size), and educational level of the household head, as independent variables; the dependent variable is household per capita disposable income. The results show the significance of per capita assets of rural households, infrastructural conditions of village communities, chemical fertilisers applied per mu,[65] and the counties with which sample households are affiliated (as dummy variables) to capture other regional influences. The regression model is as follows:

$$I = 121.23 + 0.11 \text{ PCASSET} + 50.59 \text{ PCLAND} + 0.79 \text{ PMFERTI}$$
$$(-0.885) (7.848)^{**} (2.191)^{*} (3.191)^{**}$$

+ 49.14 INFRA + 162.11 COUNTY1 + 350.54 COUNTY3
(2.253)* (1.573) (3.416)**
+ 47.59 IMR
(1.244)

$R^2 = 0.365$, F (7,350) $- 28.777$, $N = 358$. Numbers in parentheses indicate t-ratios. The signs ** and * indicate significance at the 99% and 95% confidence levels, respectively.

Variables are:

I = household per capita disposable income
PCASSET = per capita assets (excluding land)
PCLAND = per capita cultivated land
PMFERTI = chemical fertiliser applied per mu
INFRA = points for infrastructural conditions of village communities in which the sample households live
COUNTY 1 = Linqu County of Shandong Province
COUNTY 3 = Wangcang County of Sichuan Province
IMR = inverse mills ratio for correcting sample selection bias (Dolton and Makepeace, 1987).

In the income regression equation, several independent variables (excluding two dummy variables) that are significant demonstrate – from different angles – that capital is the most important income determinant. These variables are 'village infrastructure', which results from public investment; 'assets'; and 'fertiliser application', which represents not only a material input in agriculture but also the amount of circulating capital available to rural households. Funds allocated for fertiliser procurement often make up the largest share of circulating capital in farm households. In view of the fact that indicators representing asset value all have a positive correlation with income, it is likely that increases in the capital possessed by rural households will promote income growth.

Yigong-daizhen projects have helped participating households to increase their incomes and enhance their welfare in the same year, while also widening income differences among rural households. Income gaps among rural households are determined, first of all, by regional differences. However, the infrastructural conditions in village communities as well as the material and human capital of rural households, and the modem agricultural inputs applied are also decisive factors in determining rural household incomes. In so far as Yigong-daizhen projects enhance these factors, they can create the conditions for long-term increases in the incomes of rural households.

10.2.3 Food consumption and nutrition in sample households

Among the various Yigong-daizhen projects, the construction of terraced fields clearly has the most direct impact on strengthening the food security of the poor.

The road building and drinking water projects are not designed to solve food shortages directly, but to improve the infrastructure and social services. However, they do have an impact on rural household expenditures, including those for food consumption, through increases in farmers' incomes. This section attempts to explore the determinants of the consumption expenditures of the sample households; it also analyses the food consumption and nutritional status of the sample population and provides insights relevant to policy in this area.

The food consumption of rural families is still strongly tied to subsistence production on the farm; the share of own-produced foods in the total food expenditures of sample households in the three counties was 69.5, 87.6, and 90.4%, respectively. Rural household in-cash consumption expenditures appear to be mainly for non-food consumer goods and service payments (Table 10.7).

Since 1988, farmers participating in the Yigong-daizhen projects have been paid in 'industrial product coupons', redeemable only for commodities purchased in appointed state-owned shops. Multiple-choice questionnaires on how participating households dispose of income earned from the projects showed that 3.8% spent most of this income on farm machinery, farming tools, and transportation equipment; less than 1% invested in building residential houses; 21% bought other productive articles; 58.1% bought daily consumer goods, and the remaining 16.1% used the project income for other purposes. Thus, project income has obviously increased the consumption expenditures of rural households.

Table 10.7 Structure of annual per capita consumption expenses for sample households,[a] China, 1991

Items of expenses		Linqu County			Xiji County			Wangcang County		
		Poor	Medium	Well-to-do	Poor	Medium	Well-to-do	Poor	Medium	Well-to-do
Food of which:	(yuan)	224	286	339	195	259	320	374	596	678
	(%)	66.2	66.4	66.2	68.0	67.9	60.5	70.0	70.7	62.9
Self-provision	(yuan)	138	216	235	165	225	287	350	565	576
Food = 100%		61.6	75.5	69.3	84.6	86.9	89.7	93.6	94.8	85.0
Medical care	(yuan)	20	29	24	42	51	71	58	27	42
	(%)	6.1	6.8	4.6	14.7	13.5	13.5	10.8	3.3	3.9
Cigarettes, wine, and presents	(yuan)	28	34	39	15	19	65	48	83	157
	(%)	8.4	7.9	7.7	5.2	4.9	12.2	9.0	9.9	14.6
Other	(yuan)	65	82	110	35	52	73	54	136	200
	(%)	19.3	18.9	21.5	12.1	13.7	13.8	10.2	16.1	18.6
Total	(yuan)	337	431	512	287	381	529	534	842	1,077
	(%)	100.0	100.0	100.0	100.0	100.0	100.0	100.0	100.0	100.0

[a] Sample households are divided into three groups according to household per capita assets.

Earnings from projects, although they reinforced the purchasing power of the participating rural households, have not necessarily played a decisive role in determining the nutritional status of rural families. This is because most farm households do not rely on purchases for food consumption. So, although Table 10.8 indicates that the nutritional status of households participating in the projects is better than that of those not participating, this difference may not be due to their different decisions on participation. Moreover, the survey was carried out in the middle of the fanning season in Linqu and Wangcang Counties, when the diet of farmers was of better quality than average, and in Xiji County during the off-season, when the level of food consumption was comparatively low. These seasonal conditions led to an overestimation of the indices for Linqu and Wangcang Counties and an underestimation of indices for Xiji County.

Table 10.8 Nutritional situation of participating and non-participating households (sample households), China

	Linqu/Shandong		*Xiji/Ningxia*		*Wangcang/Sichuan*	
	Participating Households	*Non-participating households*	*Participating households*	*Non-participating households*	*Participating households*	*Non-participating households*
	N = 58	*N = 62*	*N = 39*	*N = 81*	*N = 64*	*N = 54*
Calorie intake[b] per person	2,423	2,358	1,708	1,469 (2,600)	3,490 (2,212)	3,223
Supplied by fat (%)	22.2	21.7	14.9	14.6 (15.3)	22.1	20.1
			(13.3)			
Supplied by protein (%)	14.3	13.3	11.7 (10.8)	11.3 (11.5)	10.3	9.6
Protein intake (g)	86.7	78.3	49.9 (70.5)	41.4 (63.4)	90.1	77.1
Diet quality points[c]	87.8	84.8	67.0	66.8	82.5	77.2[a]

[a] Method of calculation: see The Institute of Nutrition of the Chinese Academy of Preventative Medical Science, The Table of Food Components, People's Health Publishing House, Beijing.
[b] Data in parentheses have been calculated according to sample household per capita amount of yearly food consumption, while the others are from three-day recalls on food consumption amounts in the survey season.
[c] The 'diet quality points' can also be termed as 'points of desired diet pattern'. Regarding methods of calculation, see Chen Chunming (1992).

Compared with calorie, fat, and protein intake, diet quality points are a more comprehensive index of the nutritional situation. This method of scoring overcomes the problem of simplification that occurs when the nutritional situation is estimated on the basis of single components. Diet quality points are therefore used as variables in the regression analysis. This identified the following explanatory variables: household per capita predicted income (PREDINC), predicted income squared (PREDINC2), and – representing, to some extent, dietary diversity – an abundant farming product, namely, the number of poultry kept by the household (POULTRY):

$$\text{NUTRIT} = 62.817 + 0.16\text{E-01 PREDINC} - 0.31\text{E-05 PREDINC2}$$
$$(20.731)\ (3.890)^{**}\ (-1.987)^{**}$$
$$- 0.30\ \text{EDUCW} + 0.44\ \text{POULTRY-}\ 0.36\ \text{FNUMHH}$$
$$(1.112)\ (4.545)^{**}\ (-0.740)\ (2)$$
$$R^2 = 0.174,\ F\ (5,352) = 14.884,\ N = 358$$

Factors affecting the nutritional situation of the population are quite complicated. The regression analysis here has identified only some of the significant variables – higher per capita income and, comparatively, abundant farming products. In addition, predicted income squared appeared to be negatively linked to a family's nutritional status, implying that the diet quality scores would no longer rise when income reached a certain level. The number of years spent by women in school (EDUCW) and household size (FNUMHH) did not seem to be significant factors in determining nutritional levels in the sample. However, the educational level of rural women does relate closely to the success of the livestock business, and is of key importance in rationalising family food consumption and nutrient intakes.

The research reported here provides some insights relevant to policy-making:

* General malnutrition persists in the poor counties (such as Xiji County) of the less developed provinces, indicating that food security has not yet been achieved for the inhabitants in these areas. The nutritional intake of the population in 'poor' counties of the more developed provinces (Linqu and Wangcang Counties) has reached the average national level (Chen Chunming, 1992). The problem of food shortages in these areas has been solved.
* Farmers' earnings from Yigong-daizhen projects may not play a direct role in improving the food consumption and nutritional situation of rural families, but the projects themselves have an indirect impact on them. The regression analysis of the nutritional situation shows that rural household per capita income is an important determinant. Project earnings influence the nutritional situation through a chain of indirect effects: (a) Rural household per capita income is determined to a considerable extent by village infrastructure conditions. Improvement of the infrastructure was a major objective of the Yigong-daizhen projects prior to 1991. (b) Starting in 1991, investments for the projects have concentrated on capital construction for farmland and water conservation to increase crop yields and, hence, strengthen food security through improved food availability and income.

Village committees and local governments are best qualified to set project priorities since they are well informed about the situation of village food security and know whether villages would be better served with projects focused on infrastructure or land and water resources or a mix of the two.

10.3 Conclusions

The introduction of freer markets in China during the economic reforms of the 1980s has improved the efficiency of resource allocation and thereby promoted economic growth. However, historical experiences at home and abroad have shown that markets can fail and that economic growth does not necessarily lead to social development. Poverty alleviation and the enhancement of living standards for the whole nation still call for government interventions through income redistribution and public investment. During the 30 years prior to the reforms, when incomes were low, government interventions had provided improved social services universally throughout the rural areas – an achievement that has been seen as an example of support-led security (Drèze and Sen, 1989). The anti-poverty measures since the mid-1980s can be considered an extension of this tradition of public support.

However, in contrast to the past practice of providing only relief to the poor, the poverty reduction policy introduced by the reforms of 1979 laid particular emphasis on tapping existing potentials. The results of the preceding analysis suggest that the Yigong-daizhen projects' utilisation of labour-intensive techniques mobilised the abundant labour resources in poor regions, helped improve the regional infrastructure and social services, and increased job opportunities and incomes. Because of differences between poor and extremely poor regions, the impacts of the projects also differed in particular aspects. Where food shortages are no longer a serious threat, the Yigong-daizhen projects directed to the construction of infrastructure have given impetus to economic growth.

In the implementation of the projects, about one-half of the labour inputs consisted of compulsory workdays contributed by the farmers. This practice is based on two preconditions: first, that farmers recognise their obligation to participate in public investment through labour contributions, and second, that farmers already possess an income that meets their basic subsistence needs. In extremely poor regions, farmers' income from the projects functions as relief. In the absence of projects in these regions, the civil affairs authorities of the state would have to continue to provide relief to the poor. In all project areas, any improvement in the social services signifies development. So it can be argued that the policy of Yigong-daizhen has combined relief, economic growth, and social development.

Yet, our research shows that the policy guiding the implementation of Yigong-daizhen projects also has limitations. For example, it has created only one of the many essential conditions for poverty reduction. The poor need help in all aspects of culture, education, health, and production. Only by taking long-term, comprehensive investment measures can poverty be permanently reduced.

A distinguishing feature of the Yigong-daizhen experience in China is the nature of its targeting mechanism. Some researchers have recommended self-targeting, where wages in public works are fixed at a low level in order to ensure that those coming to work for the projects are the real poor (Ravallion, 1990; von Braun et al., 1991). In the implementation of the Yigong-daizhen projects, this kind of serf-targeting mechanism has not been adopted. The Chinese Government selects the beneficiaries of the projects through its selection of project sites and the direction of its investments. Some features of the targeting mechanism of the Yigong-daizhen projects differ from the targeting mechanisms of public works in other developing countries:

1   The Yigong-daizhen programme in China has been designed for the alleviation of regional rural poverty, hence, the projects are targeted at specific regions. However, the programme does not target the poorest population. The primary purpose of the projects is to improve the infrastructure and social services in poor regions and to create the conditions for regional economic growth. In other words, long-term goals of economic growth take precedence over increases in short-term job opportunities and the supplementary income of the poor. Efficiency has been the guiding principle throughout the establishment and construction of the projects, with the goal being a maximum rate of success in project investment. This priority does not necessarily lead to the extremely poor villages and the poorest populations benefiting first or most.
2   Within the framework of poor regions, the project aims at village communities, that is, village administration, and not at rural households or individuals. During the implementation of the projects, the village communities are responsible for mobilising the labour force. Completed projects represent an improvement in infrastructure (roads, for example) or supply services to village properties (water supply installations), or add value to farmers' resources (for example, by terraced fields and improved soils). Thus, it is obviously impossible to prevent the non-poor of the village from benefiting from such projects.

This distinguishing feature of the targeting mechanism of Yigong-daizhen projects has been determined by the organization and institutional arrangements of rural society in contemporary China. During the present period of transition from a centrally planned economy to a market economy, the village community is evolving into a self-governing body in rural society, while its administrative organ, the villagers' committee, acts as a bridge between rural households and the government in addition to managing public affairs in the village. Since a large number of rural households are drawn into project work, the Yigong-daizhen projects are obviously difficult to operate smoothly without the mediation of village communities. Furthermore, due to the principle of equity practised in village communities and the fact that most of the rural households in the villages of poor regions are poor, the village communities are more useful than any other kind of intermediary in enabling projects to target the poor. If individual brokers were relied upon to enroll the labour force, those who would benefit most would probably be the brokers themselves, the most mobile, and the non-poor. Workers with the highest mobility are currently not the poor, who generally limit their activities to their own village or township, because of their inability to meet the costs of travel.

Operation of the projects combines a regional targeting mechanism with mobilisation of a village community's labour force. This approach achieves both 'efficiency' and 'equity', and thus enables the poor to be the dominant beneficiaries.

This approach to targeting leads to a problem: how can extremely poor villages partake of the benefits of the projects? To solve this problem, project rules stipulate that a certain proportion of the labour force must come from extremely poor villages; this promotes movement of labour, and can gradually eliminate the barriers between village communities and improve the labour resource of extremely poor villages through their 'participation'. The problem can also be addressed if the areas covered by the projects expand to include extremely poor villages. The plan of upgrading farmland since 1991 has emphasised the high and cold rocky mountain areas and the deep mountain valleys. Yigong-daizhen projects might also aim to recruit labour from among the poorest populations.

Finally, it should be stressed that, currently, poverty is mainly a regional characteristic in rural China. However, the new course of market orientation and its related reforms may lead to the evolution of new poverty groups, characterised as follows: (1) urban poverty (depending on the outcomes of enterprise, employment, and wage system reforms); (2) class-based poverty, originating from inequalities in property distribution (since private ownership of property now exists and capital returns increasingly influence the distribution of personal income). The poverty problem may not therefore be limited to the rural sector during the transition period. Future anti-poverty programmes in China should include projects aimed at the urban sector. Yigong-daizhen programmes may also be an appropriate measure to alleviate urban unemployment and to assist the urban poor in increasing their income.

Note

1 The amount of the chemical fertiliser applied per mu may be partly influenced by the infrastructure, but it also depends to a great extent on the financial resources of farmers, on prices, and on the type of fertiliser supplied. Since the use of chemical fertiliser affects farmers' income through its impact on crop production, it is kept here in the income regression model.

References

Ahmed, R., and Hossain, M. (1990) *Developmental Impact of Rural Infrastructure in Bangladesh*. Research Report 83. Washington, DC: International Food Policy Research Institute.

Braun, J. von, Teklu, T., and Webb, R. (1991) *Labour-Intensive Public Works for Food Security Experience in Africa*. Working Papers on Food Subsidies 6. Washington, DC: International Food Policy Research Institute.

Chen Chunming (1992) *The Food Consumpfon and Nutrition Conditions of Farmers in the Six Provinces and a Municipality*. Research Paper. Beijing: Chinese Academy of Preventive Medical Science.

Dolton, R. J., and Makepeace, G. H. (1987) *Interpreting Sample Selection Effects*. Economics Letters 24. Amsterdam: Elsevier Science Publisher BV and North-Holland.

Drèze, J., and Sen, A. (1989) *Hunger and Public Action*. Oxford: Clarendon Press.

Fields, G. (1980) *Poverty, Inequality, and Development*. Cambridge: Cambridge University Press.

Ranis, G., and Kuo, S. (1978) 'Growth and the Family Distribution of Income by Factor Components', *Quarterly Journal of Economics*, February.

Ravallion, M. (1990) *Reaching the Poor through Rural Public Employment*. World Bank Discussion Paper 94. Washington, DC: World Bank.

Tong Zhong, Rozelle, S., Stone, B., Jiang Dehua, Chen Jiyuan, and Xu Zhikang (1994) 'China's Experience with Market Reform for Commercialization of Agriculture in Poor Areas' in J. von Braun and E. Kennedy (eds.) *Agricultural Commercialization, Economic Development, and Nutrition*. Baltimore, MD: Johns Hopkins University Press.

World Bank (1992) *China Strategies for Reducing Poverty in the 1990s*. Washington, DC: World Bank.

Zhu Ling, and Jiang Zhongyi (1990) *Impacts of Yigong-Daizhen on Poor Areas of China*. Washington, DC: International Food Policy Research Institute (mimeo).

Zhu Ling, and Jiang Zhongyi (1994) *Public Works and Poverty Alleviation*. Shanghai: SAN LIAN Bookstore and Shanghai People's Publishing House.

Appendix Table 10.A Selected socio-economic indicators of the areas studied, 1990

	Population (m.)	Area ('000 km²)	Per capita GNP[a] (yuan)	Rural poverty incidence (%)	Adult illiteracy rate (%)	Farm size (mu)[b]	Per capita income of farmers' households (yuan)
China	1,143.33	9,600	3,323.3	11.4	15.9	6.5	629.8
Shandong Province	84.93	156.7	3,825.5	6.8	16.9	5.6	644.7
Linqu County	0.88	1.8	2,389.1	8.0	19.3	3.6	565.0
Ningxia Province	4.66	51.8	2,502.4	18.9	22.1	15.8	534.2
Xiji County	0.39	3.2	332.0	43.5	37.0	16.8	212.0
Sichuan Province	108.13	570.0	2,090.2	11.2	16.2	4.2	505.2
Wangcang County	0.43	3.0	997.6	10.0	26.1	3.5	558.0
Survey data[c]							
Villages in Linqu	–	–	–	–	11.2	4.0	565.4
Villages in Xiji	–	–	–	–	57.7	20.7	350.8
Villages in Wangcang	–	–	–	–	23.2	4.9	914.4

Sources: World Bank (1992).

[a] Data used are gross output value of agriculture, industry, construction, transportation, and commerce, termed as 'gross social products' in Chinese statistical sources; [b] 15 mu = 1 hectare; [c] survey data refer to 1991.

Appendix Table 10.B Income inequality among sample households in three counties, China, 1991

Source of per capita income	Linqu County (Shandong)			Xiji County (Ningxia)			Wangcang County (Sichuan)		
	Share of income	Gini coefficient[b]	Contribution to overall Gini	Share of income	Gini coefficient[b]	Contribution to overall Gini	Share of income	Gini coefficient[b]	Contribution to overall Gini
	(%)			(%)			(%)		
Farming incomes	67.4	0.264	47.0	74.2	0.270	51.7	51.1	0.268	21.1
Family non-farming incomes	6.9	0.961	16.4	3.2	0.947	6.6	19.4	0.930	39.8
Wages	15.1	0.767	25.3	9.2	0.836	14.8	16.4	0.776	20.6
Gathering earnings	0.8	0.960	1.0	0.2	0.981	0.6	1.8	0.929	1.6
Net public transfers	3.6	0.876	2.6	0.8	0.967	0.9	1.9	0.929	1.6
Private transfers	0.7	0.927	0.3	7.2	0.904	16.0	3.1	0.788	2.1
Rental from productive assets	2.1	0.974	4.3	0.1	0.992	0.3	1.4	0.986	2.7
Interest and others	2.7	0.825	1.4	0.8	0.986	1.8	1.5	0.925	1.8
Earnings from public works	1.3	0.803	1.6	5.6	0.837	7.3	4.2	0.974	8.9
Total disposable income	100.0[c]	0.304	100.0	100.0[c]	0.331	100.0	100.0[c]	0.437	100.0

[a] For the method of calculation, see Ranis and Kuo (1978) and Fields (1980); for details of calculations, see Zhu Ling and Jiang Zhongyi (1994).

[b] Gini coefficient of each income component as well as that of the total disposable income.

[c] When the component income of a sample household appeared to have a negative value, it was replaced by zero. Thus, taking the total of sample households as a whole, the overall disposable income would be less than the sum of all the component incomes, while the sum of the shares of the nine income components would be a little more than 100.0.

11 Old age security for the landless farmers

During the course of urbanization and industrialization, a growing number of farmers have become landless as local governments have bought out their land for non-agricultural uses.

Even in the localities where the industrialization process absorbs a vast majority of rural labor, the questions of how to compensate for the economic shock on the rural landless and how to alleviate and eliminate mental suffering as a result of losing land have always been a challenge to government capacity in social stabilization and a yardstick to measure social justice in local communities. In the administration areas of Suzhou City in Jiangsu Province, governments at all levels have successfully coped with this challenge. By means of "swapping land for old-age support" and income redistribution, Suzhou municipality has not only met the demand on land for urbanization and industrialization while maintaining social stability, but also laid a foundation for establishing an integrated pension system for both urban and rural residents. Such a system has changed the tradition of farmers' households relying on land to deal with economic risk and of the aged depending on their sons for livelihood support in rural society.

11.1 Introduction

A traditional pattern of old age support in the rural society of China can be characterized as that of a family taking full responsibility in caring for its elderly. During the 1950s, a "Five Guarantee System" was established in the People's Communes for protecting those who have no kin and cannot support themselves, with the guarantee of food, clothing, housing, medical treatment and burial expenses. Moreover, in the cases where poor villages could not meet the basic needs of the aged covered by the Five Guarantee System, the state provides them with social relief. Such arrangements have encountered growing challenges as a result of rapid socioeconomic transition in the recent two decades.

First of all, as a result of the implementation of the family planning policy and the increase in average life expectancy, China has become an aging society.

(Originally published in *China and World Economy*, No. 1, 2006 with the title "Old Age Security: A Case from Rural Suzhou".)

Those 65 years and over made up 4.91 percent of the population in 1982, increasing to 7.30 and 7.50 percent, respectively, in 2002 and 2003. The size of this age group grew from 83.75 million people in 1998 to 96.92 million in 2003 when the dependent ratio referring to old age support was calculated as 11.96 percent. In contrast to the expansion in the size of the aging group, the average family size was reduced from 4.51 down to 3.60 members during the period 1982–2002; this was considered an outcome of the decrease in extended families (Institute of Population and Labor Economics, Chinese Academy of Social Sciences, 2005). Under such a trend of population dynamics, the individual families have gradually become incapable of undertaking the full responsibilities of old age support.

Second, approximately 100 million young and middle aged rural laborers commute yearly between their home villages and the cities or towns where they are employed. This implies that these temporary migrants would inevitably confront greater economic risk than what they face by working at home as farmers. However, the urban social protection programs do not yet cover most of them because of the urban–rural divide inherited from the system of the planned economy. Therefore, both the migrated and non-migrated rural laborers have to rely on the farmland as basic economic security for themselves and their families. Rural–urban labor migration is linked to the newly-emerged social problem of a lack of daily care for both the aged and the children remaining in the villages. Moreover, average living expenses have escalated because of increasing consumption demand and rising prices of goods and services as a result of the marketization process.

Comparatively, the gross profit generated from land-related agricultural production has grown at a much slower pace. In present China, an average farmer's household with four members owns only the usufruct rights on 0.37 ha of farmland. Without nonagricultural earnings, rural people would face poor living standards and the aged would be in a vulnerable position. This can be evidently seen from the difficulties brought about to the Five Guarantee System since the abolition of the People's Communes. In the past, the operation of the system substantially relied on the income generated by the collective economy and the mutual assistance among the collective members. By the time the agricultural household contract system was implemented, those covered by the Five Guarantee System also received land plots. Since then, the villagers' committee of their home villages has taken the responsibility to arrange labor from other households in rotation to cultivate these plots and provide the five guarantee households the daily care they badly needed. In the market-oriented economic environment, the gap between the land produce and the resources necessary to maintain the subsistence of the elderly becomes wider, which should result in a growing fiscal burden to the state.

Third, farmland area has radically reduced in the accelerated process of industrialization and urbanization. According to the national land survey, a total of 1.134 million ha of farmland was turned over for construction use during the period 1998–2003 (Zhou, 2005). Furthermore, it is estimated that approximately 5 million farmers have had land taken in the period 1987–2001 (Mu, 2004).

Table 11.1 A few examples of current deals of Arable Land

Location	Compensation for hud acquisition	The amount that farmers received	The sales the municipalities obtained
Municipality A in southern China	10–30 yuan/m²	–	150–300 yuan/m²
Municipality B in central China	30000 yuan/mu (15mu = 1ha)	10000 yuan/mu	100–300000 yuan/mu
A municipality	–	30000 yuan/mu	1.35 million yuan/mu

Source: Zhang (2005).

Note: "–" Data not available.

Because the constitution and the law on land management stipulate that the ownership of farmland belongs to the collective entities and only the government representing the state power is authorized to acquire it, the individual farmers have no rights to sell or purchase land freely. The state monopoly on the primary land market has directly led to serious market distortions and apparent social injustices. It was regulated that the local governments must pay the farmers a compensation for the land acquisition equal to approximately 20 times the average agricultural gross production value annually generated per unit area during the 3 years prior to the land-takings (Du, 2005). However, the government possesses strong incentives to acquire more plots by purchasing from farmers because they are able to sell them back at much higher prices for commercial use and to transfer the profits out of the land deals to local revenue (Zhang, 2005). In many cases the actual compensation amount that farmers received was less than what was stipulated (see Table 11.1); findings from a sample survey on 3000 villages, organized by the World Bank and the State Statistics Bureau of China, were similar (Li, 2005). It is commonly known that land deals are one of the biggest causes of social conflict occurring in the recent decade between the land losers and the local government together with the entrepreneurs who buy for land development.

In response to the above illustrated socioeconomic challenges, several rural social protection programs have been added to existing social relief since the 1990s, although further reforms are necessary for tackling the problems emerging with the current regulations on land rights and land markets. Up to the end of 2003, coverage of rural cooperative medical insurance accounted for 14.2 percent of the relevant population, whereas the pension insurance coverage reached only 5.8 percent (Institute of Rural Development, Chinese Academy of Social Sciences and Rural Socioeconomic Survey Team, SSB, 2005). Pension recipients amounted to 1.98 million farmers (News Office of the State Council, 2004). Successful experiences are mostly concentrated in the well-developed coastal areas in eastern China. The rural Suzhou in Jiangsu Province is considered one of those areas. It is in rural Suzhou where the barefoot doctor system originated in the late 1960s and developed into a type of cooperative medical insurance covering 96 percent of the villages and 86.9 percent of the rural residents in 2003. The network of health services and health insurance has provided residents with easy access to low cost health services in villages, from which the aged, women, and children have benefited the most. Suzhou has been subject to increasing rural industrialization because of the rise in village and township enterprises in the 1980s. Vigorous urbanization has been going on with the intensive adoption of direct foreign investment since the 1990s. Therefore, the rapid reduction of highly fertile arable land has affected the livelihood and economic safety of the farmers to a broader extent in rural Suzhou than in less industrialized and less urbanized regions. In aiming to solve these socioeconomic problems, Suzhou municipality took the measure of "swapping land for old-age support" and promoted the founding of a pension insurance system besides the basic living standard guarantee programs for rural residents. In this way, the municipality not only met the growing demand for land use in urbanization and industrialization that already absorbed numerous rural labors, but also realized the goal of maintaining social stability.

This report was a byproduct of household interviews that the author conducted during April of 2005 with an initial purpose of collecting information about rural health care and health relief. A sample survey was undertaken in 24 villages selected from the three counties that were under the administration of Suzhou Municipality: Wujiang, Changshu and Zhangjiagang.[1] Following the introduction section, the report will briefly discuss the institutional innovations in the old-age support system in rural Suzhou. Then, with the information acquired from the household interviews, the complementary functions of the pension system with community services and family care will be discussed. Finally, the policy implication of the Suzhou case is summarized.

11.2 Pension programs for land losers

In the rural areas of Suzhou, the residents name the long-term compensation related to land requisition by purchase To Bao and the rural pension insurance Nong Bao. As it is stated in the reading materials supplied to the farmers in Wujiang County, a pension insurance system was established for those whose land was purchased in 1992. According to the latest regulations, based on the approval date for the land requisition by purchase, those affected by land deals are classified into three age groups. The land administrative authorities are responsible for making different compensations to each group: the age group below 16 years is paid a lump sum of 6000 yuan; the age group between 16 and 60 years (55 years for women) is covered by either the rural or the urban basic pension insurance system; and the men above 60 years and the women above 55 years are entitled to receive 80 yuan monthly from the basic pension fund, beginning with the year of land requisition by purchase. Moreover, for those included in the age groups above 16 years, the land administrative authorities are obligated to transfer an average of 20,000 yuan per person, all at once, as pension funds to the social security office. The staff members from the Social Security Office of Qidu Town in Wujiang County have made the compensation paid for land acquisition through pension funds actually higher than the stipulated amount in several towns with sound financial strength.

Mr. Xuebao Ye, a health worker in the clinic of Wanghu Village (the former Randianbang Village) in Qidu Town, revealed that the town government applies "the old measures to the aged and the new measures to the young" in the course of adopting the rural pension programs. Mr. Ye and Ms. Ming'e Yu, his daughter-in-law, explained the system by taking their own family as an example. They called the compensation method of "swapping land for old-age support" as Tu Bao with the rural basic pension as "old-age subsidy" (Nong Bao). The family Ye consists of four generations with six family members under one roof. Except for a school boy (11 years old), all of the other five members have been included in the pension insurance system in Qidu Town. Mr. Ye (64 years) and his elderly mother (85 years old) each receive 880 annually of Tu Bao from the town government, in addition to 80 yuan of the old-age subsidy per month per person. The younger couple in the family, Ms. Yu and her husband, now aged 34 years, each pay 480 yuan per year to the Social Security Office of Qidu Town as a pension insurance premium. When Yu turns 55 and her husband 60, each of them is entitled to receive a monthly pension of 200 yuan.

The family Ye consumes approximately 1000 kg of rice a year, which costs less than 3000 yuan. Therefore, Mr. Ye considers the amount of cash obtained from Tu Bao plus the old-age subsidy more than sufficient to offset the loss incurred from giving up the land holding. Both Mr. Ye and his daughter-in-law manage and work in the village clinic, where each of them earns over 8000 yuan annually. The husband of Ms. Yu (son of Mr. Ye) worked for his brother-in-law as a salesman in an electrolytic copper plant prior to 2004, where he got an annual salary of more than 50,000 yuan. In 2004, he set up a wooden door manufacturing plant jointly with two other households. The three households run this enterprise with more than 20 hired workers. Apparently, the family Ye is no longer dependent on land for its livelihood.

11.3 Community services and old age security

Now a large number of laborers do not engage in agriculture in rural Suzhou. The average annual income per capita of the rural households reached 7600 yuan (more than two times the national average) in 2004. Even under these circumstances, the pension insurance system is vitally important for social stability. In the villages where the author visited, the aged above 60 years old account for approximately 20 percent of the total population. The pension programs not only provide financial security to the elderly but also enable them to live in dignity.

Mr. Xiao and Ms. Chen, a couple of pension recipients in Hanshan Village administrated by Tangqiao Town in Zhang jiagang, said with confidence that although they live with their son's family, they don't need money from the son because the subsidies from the village and town are sufficient to feed the whole extended family. Mr. Xiao (60 years old) had served as a production team leader of the village from 1973, and even now he still acts as the head of a villagers' group. Currently, he is paid an annual salary of 3000 yuan from the village account. Ms. Chen (57 years old) was born in the countryside of Xuzhou. She and her sister went to Shanghai to work as housemaids in 1967, where she got to know a chef who turned out to be a fellow villager of Xiao. With the help of the chef and her own sister, she started dating Xiao. At that time, Xiao earned less than 1 yuan for a workday, but a train ticket to Shanghai was 2.71 yuan. For the sake of saving money, they got married after dating a few times in Shanghai and then went to live in Xiao's village in 1968. Now all farmland of the family Xiao has been acquired and according to the village rules, anyone 55 years old or above, whether man or woman, is entitled to receive a pension. Besides the 80 yuan per person per month that the old couple receives, the five-member family is further entitled to 7000 yuan of land compensation, because each person is paid 1400 yuan a year according to the rules made in Tangqiao Town.

Financial independence is just a basis for the happy life of the couple Xiao. The rich community activities and social contacts have added to their happiness. The community center of Hanshan Village, close to the residential quarters, accommodates the village committee office, clinic, recreational facilities and a restaurant. Ms. Chen participates in fitness exercises there every day. She also revealed that the village clinic provides women with free physical examinations 2–3 times a year, and each time the village committee pays 5 yuan to the participants to encourage women to have such physical examinations. Ms. Chen is particularly interested in the singing and fitness exercises organized by the village. She said she attends such activities even without the motivation of cash grants from the village.

Hanshan is one of the villages in Suzhou with a relatively high level of industrialization. Every year the village committee obtains 1–2 million yuan of revenue through leasing factory workshops and collecting power fees from enterprises. Therefore, it is financially capable of providing the villagers with entertainment facilities and health services. In the villages with a larger agricultural share of the economy, villagers also have easy access to organized community activities. When a field visit was made on a weekend in Jiulihu Village administrated by Tongli Town in Wujiang, the author observed many villagers gathering at the community center. Youngsters played table tennis or basketball while the elderly chatted or played cards. Such a cheerful scene is rare in either metropolises or underdeveloped rural areas, but in rural Suzhou, where industrialization is under way, it is an indication of the improved quality of life and enhanced sense of community belonging.

11.4 Social support and family care

Pension insurance and community services can be regarded as newly established social mechanisms meeting the basic material needs of aged people and providing them with mental satisfaction in rural Suzhou. It is noteworthy that the family still maintains the function of caring for the elderly, and such a function effectively complements modern mechanisms of care. Family planning has long been in practice in rural Suzhou. Most families that the author interviewed consisted of three or four generations with a family size no larger than five to seven members. Those of age 50–60 years old usually have two children, whereas most younger couples gave birth only once. According to the local customs older generations still tend to live with a son. With changes in demographic structure, however, this family mode is giving way to new practices. The family structure of Mr. Shigen Qin in Beigang Village administrated by Dongbang Town in Changshu is a good demonstration of such changes.

Mr. Qin (81 years old) and his wife (78 years old) brought up three daughters and one son. Their son and daughter-in-law (53 years) have an only daughter who is 28 years old. The granddaughter is married but the young couple still lives with the Qins. Now the young couple has their own son (1 year old). The family Qin turns is a large one with four generations under one roof. At the end of the 1980s, the son of Mr. Qin and three other villagers jointly set up a chemical fiber factory. In 1995, he spent over 500,000 yuan (his dividends accumulated over the years) on building a big house with an estimated floor area of 300 square meters on the family's homestead. The granddaughter and her husband currently run a weaving plant in partnership with others in the neighboring Meili Town. Thanks to convenient transportation, the young couple is able to take pleasure in living in the extended family. The young lady explained that her father takes charge of the big family's daily expenses, and instead of charging the young couple for living in the house, he often gives allowances to them. Of course, she and her husband are not short of money and they would readily contribute whenever her parents are in need.

As a matter of fact, in an extensive family with several generations under one roof, even those in very old age are not necessarily in need of the care of other family members. In most cases, the labor division among all family members leads to mutual care between different generations and efficient utilization of human resources. In response to the current demographic structure, the government of Dongbang Town has set specific standards for providing pensions to the elderly in different age groups. Anyone in the age group 60–70 years old is entitled to receive a pension amount of 800 yuan a year, whereas those in the age group above 70 years old receive 1000 yuan annually, because the older people get, the harder it is to make money and the higher their medical expenses become. However, the old couple Qin so far has had no bulk spending on medical care because of their good health. When the author went to their home from the community center by motorcycle, Mr. Qin led the way by riding his bicycle. His wife, who had been preparing a meal in the kitchen, greeted the visitors at the gate.

On ordinary days, a main activity of the elderly couple is to grow vegetables in a 4-mu field (15mu = 1 ha.). They do not apply mechanic tools in their farming and in fact use spades to turn up the soil. At harvest, they carefully select the vegetables, then wash and tie them neatly before Mr. Qin sells them in the market. The village committee pays for irrigation water and the old couple takes on the costs of seeds, fertilizer and pesticides. The couple Qin annually attain approximately 10,000 yuan in gross profit from growing vegetables, approximately five times the sum of their yearly pensions. In fact, the old couple could have retired at home because their son is fully capable of supporting them. To the question of why they still do farm work in such advanced age, because they have to or because they love to, Mr. Qin simply answered, "Because we are used to it." The behavior of the couple Qin shows that as long as labor is not forced and within one's capability, a habit of working is not only beneficial to the physical and mental health of aged people, but also prolongs their working period, adding to the aggregate human resources in society.

Thanks to continuous economic growth and abundant job opportunities, the elderly in Suzhou, especially those below age 70, have choices in adjusting the variety and intensity of their economic activities. Mr. Baosheng Shi (62 years old), another villager of Beigang Village, had been a worker in a construction team. In May 2004, he had a stroke caused by high blood pressure. After his recovery, he started to grow vegetables with his wife in the village. A bit different from the Qins, the couple Shi cultivates 6 mu of vegetable field and vendors come to their field to purchase the vegetables. Shi and his wife make a gross profit of 15,000–16,000 yuan a year from growing vegetables. Although they receive less pension than the Qins (800 yuan a year per person) from the town government, Mr. Shi, after he turned 60 in 2004, receives additionally 1500 yuan a year from the county bureau of civil affairs. This is because he made a lump-sum payment of 12,400 yuan to a pension fund operated by the bureau of civil affairs in 1996. Shi is entitled to keep receiving an annual pension of 1500 yuan until his death. Therefore, the annual per capita net income for Shi and his wife amounts to more than 9000 yuan, much higher than the average income level in rural China. The couple Shi realized the importance of insurance earlier than most other farmers. Beginning from 1979, the couple participated in a cooperative medical care system. Now, they not only buy insurance for themselves, but also for their son, daughter-in-law and granddaughter (50 yuan per person a year). Shi explained: "This money is spent against serious diseases; it would be best if we get no reimbursement, which means we are free of any serious disease." He must be speaking with his own experience in mind because he was hospitalized twice last year as a result of the stroke. It cost 12,000 yuan total, including 9428 yuan in hospital expenses, of which 2431 yuan was reimbursed by the cooperative medical insurance fund.

11.5 Summary on policy implications

11.5.1 Responsibility of the governments in old age support

In present China, the usufruct right over land is a vital source of income for farmers and a subsistence guarantee for most rural people. The farmland trade in the form of land acquisition often puts the two trading parties at unequal positions. The farmers as the selling party can hardly bargain with the much more powerful buying party, the government. Usually the amount of money received by farmers from land acquisition is insufficient to give them a long-term subsistence guarantee as farmland would have. The government assumes the responsibility of providing such a guarantee to all its citizens. In the industrialization process in rural Suzhou, governments at all levels have fulfilled their responsibilities when they propel the establishment of the rural pension insurance system by means of swapping land for old-age support. Although farmland is owned collectively in name, the state in practice shares part of the ownership when it exercises the land acquisition right. In this sense, the practices of local governments in Suzhou can be regarded as using the state right over land or state assets to expedite the rural pension insurance system. This is parallel to the government's fiscal transfer into urban pension funds, only the mainstream opinion is that compensating the employees of the state-owned enterprises in urban areas with state assets is fine but that rural residents' should not have the same right to state assets.

11.5.2 Justice in institutional designs

The regular pension payment of the local governments in Suzhou to those who have never paid insurance premiums has demonstrated governmental credit to the groups not yet eligible for receiving pensions. This has increasingly urged the rural residents to buy insurance. The operational track of the rural pension system shows that elderly people benefit more from the deal of "land for old-age support" than those younger. However, from the perspective of the human development chain, one generation has not only supported the former generation but also provided material accumulation to the latter generation. Viewed from the theory of intergenerational justice (Rawls, 1971), the transitional system at the initial stage of rural pension insurance in Suzhou is considered a political solution that displays social justice.

11.5.3 Development of the aging people

Over the past two decades, the average life expectancy in rural China has greatly increased. This is a symbol of social progress, but also indicates an expansion of the aged group in need of support. In several developed countries, the retirement age has been postponed in response to a similar trend of demographic change. Accordingly, measures have been adopted to promote the development of aged human resources through lifelong education and health services. The case in rural Suzhou demonstrates that under the prerequisite of a subsistence guarantee by pension, together with a full range of community services and a pleasant family environment, the aged can productively work much longer than the usual retirement age in China. This provides a practical solution for the reduction in young labor within an aging society.

11.5.4 Adjusting measures for old age security to local conditions

The establishment of the rural pension insurance system is preceded by industrialization or the development of non-farming sectors. Logically, it is hard to establish such a system in areas lacking this condition. In any case, as the features of population aging become prevalent even in underdeveloped rural areas, it is necessary that the government adopt measures to ensure the subsistence of the elderly. No doubt, the institutional arrangements for old-age support must adapt to local social, economic and cultural conditions. In recent years, the authorities of civil affairs have provided the rural poor with increasing subsidies. Currently, the poorest aging people are the major beneficiaries of this policy, whereas the aged who are less poor and who live on the margin of the poverty line are not covered. Therefore, whether it is to widen the coverage of the subsidies or to increase the amount of the subsidies, there needs to be an expression of social value for guaranteeing the basic needs of the aged, to be met through the concerted efforts of society. Meanwhile, it will enhance the public knowledge, social security and social identification that forms a solid foundation in public consensus to develop the social pension insurance system.

Note

1 The 3 counties have respectively an administrative city status.

References

Du, Runsheng, 2005, *Notes about the Important Decision-Makings on Rural Institutional Reforms in China* (*Zhongguo Nongcun Tizhi Biange Zhongda Juece Jishi*), Beijing: People's Publishing House.

Institute of Population and Labor Economics, Chinese Academy of Social Sciences, 2005, *Almanac of China's Population* (*Zhongguo Renkou Nianjian*), Beijing: Almanac of China's Population Press.

Institute of Rural Development, Chinese Academy of Social Sciences and Rural Socio-economic Survey Team, SSB, 2005, *Analysis and Forecast on China's Rural Economy* (*Zhongguo Jingji Xingshi Fenxi Yu Yuce*), Beijing: Social Sciences Academic Press.

Li, Guo, 2005, "The Rural Safety Net." An Outline Presented at the China Poverty Assessment Workshop, 3 November 2005, Beijing.

Mu, Jia, 2004, "The existing institutional arrangements are not appropriate for protecting arable land," *The Chinese Commercial and Industrial News*, 3 March.

News Office of the State Council, 2004, Status and Policies of the Social Security in China (Zhongguo Shehui Baozhang Zhuangkuang He Zhengce), White Book issued in Beijing. Available from: www.chinapop.gov.cn/rkzh/zgrk/zywx/t20040907_15598.htm, website of China Population, issued on 20 June 2005, cited on 22 December 2005.

Rawls, J., 1971. *A Theory of Justice* (Chinese translation by H. He et al.), Beijing: China Social Sciences Press.

Zhang, Gensheng, 2005, "Investigation on land management," *Xinhua Digest* (*Xinhua Wenzhai*), 21, pp. 23–5.

Zhou, Jianchun, 2005, "Discussions about protection of farmers' land rights through observations on the reduction in farmland," *Xinhua Digest* (*Xinhua Wenzhai*), 21, pp. 21–3.

12 Pension program for the rural migrant workers

Providing "one size fits all" old-age insurance schemes for rural migrant workers and the employees with urban-Hukou (urban permanent registered residence) alike will lead to inequitable results under the existence of a huge discrepancy in their socio-economic conditions. Firstly, the characteristics of urban social old-age insurance anchored at a certain locality hinder the labor mobility and hurt the interests of the employers and employees that both make pension contributions. Secondly, the excessive old-age insurance premium rates weaken the incentive of the enterprises to create more jobs. The wages of most migrant workers are lower than the floor level of the contribution base but they have actually paid higher premium rates. The contributions made to the old-age insurance have a more severe impact on the disposable income of female workers, as their earnings are even lower than that of the male workers. Thirdly, migrant workers quit formal employment at an age younger than the statutory retirement age but their pension entitlements are lower than the average level. As a result, they are more likely to fall into poverty as they enter old age. Fourthly, female workers have shorter employment tenure and at the same contribution wage level, their pensions are simulated to be only 55%-57% of those for males. While formulating the national old-age insurance policy for migrant workers, factors such as promotion of employment, alleviation of old-age poverty and reduction in gender inequality in pension income distribution shall therefore be taken into account.

12.1 Introduction

As early as in the 1950s, the workers of state-owned enterprises and urban collective enterprises were entitled to receive old-age security under the labor insurance system in China.[1] When the economic reform began at the end of the 1970s, this system was substantively transformed into corporate (enterprise-based) labor insurance. In the marketization process, the corporate pension system that could hardly operate due to funding difficulties was eventually replaced by the social old-age insurance system for urban employees. In most rural areas, however, the agricultural population, except the households without income source but entitled to the "five guaranteed benefits (food, cloth, medical care, housing and bury)", has never been covered by the old-age security system. By the end of 2008, the number of rural migrant workers totaled 225.42 million, including 140.41 million migrants working off their home counties (36% of them were female), but the number of participants in basic old-age insurance was only 24.16 million.[2] By taking the number of the migrants off their home counties as the base, the old-age insurance coverage rate was about 17.3%, the medical insurance coverage rate was nearly 30.4% (with 42.66 million participants), the work injury insurance coverage rate was 35.2% (with 49.42 participants) and the unemployment insurance coverage rate was 11% (with 15.49 million participants). By taking the total number of rural migrant workers as the base, the above insurance coverage rates should have been one-third less.

While rural migrant workers have been included in the industrialization process, they have not received adequate social protection associated with the industrial society to cope with the risks of living and working in cities. If the "rural migrant workers" in the early 1990s were viewed as the first-generation rural migrant laborers,[3] those who were then above 30 years of age are now at or near the retirement age of industrial enterprises. In cities, they worked long hours under poor working environments and earned low wages for high-intensity jobs. Migrant workers were frequently exposed to occupational diseases and work injury accidents.[4] In consequence, the vast majority of migrant workers had to leave the urban labor market before statutory retirement age. Meanwhile, the agricultural land resources are dwindling as farm land is converted to urban uses. It was a long time ago that the agricultural population was no longer able to rely solely on land to meet demand for daily necessities. In addition, the family planning policy poses severe challenges to people who wish to rely on children for old-age security. The fact that over 100 million migrant workers are now uncovered by social old-age insurance indicates that the current urbanization policy and old-age insurance system lack social inclusion and the old-age poverty may become severer in the future.

Actually, the central government has enacted a series of policies with respect to the social security issue of rural migrant workers since 2003. As a result, the old-age insurance program for migrant workers has been experimented in several cities. As pension funds belong to the cities where the pension schemes are located, the rural migrant workers cannot transfer their pension accounts when they move from one city to another. This undermines sustainability of the pension scheme and hampers labor mobility.[5] Under the principle of "low premium rate, broad coverage, easy transferability and interconnectivity with the existing old-age insurance system", the Ministry of Human Resources and Social Security (MoHRSS) drafted *Regulations on the Participation of Peasant Workers in Basic Old-age Insurance* (hereinafter referred to as the "Regulations") and solicited public comments in February 2009.[6] The basic idea of the Regulations is to include rural migrant workers in the urban employees' basic old-age insurance system. However, migrant workers are characterized by low income, weak contribution ability, strong mobility and uncertain future destinations, making it more difficult to manage the implementation of the Regulations. Worse yet, the employers are unwilling to participate in the scheme amid the global financial crisis.

Furthermore, the Regulations are also applicable to the rural migrant workers who work in urban areas and establish labor relations with employers. This implies that the provisions of the Regulations are designed to target formal employees. Among the migrant workers in formal employment, female workers earn less and work for a shorter period. They are more likely to leave formal employment for child care and other family responsibilities and instead pursue informal employment. Under the current retirement system, women usually exit the labor market earlier but have a longer remaining life expectancy. Therefore, women rely on old-age insurance for a longer period of time than men. A combination of these factors will lead to lower pension levels for women. By ILO definition, the informal sector consists of units engaged in the production of goods or services with the primary objective of generating jobs and income to the people employed. These units typically operate on a very small scale. The forms of employment in these units are mainly self-employed, part-time and temporary jobs and the labor relations lack adequate legal protection.[7] In China, they are very close to the so-called "flexible employment". Based on the scope of applicability of the Regulations, informal workers are defined in this report to be employees who work in urban areas but have not established labor relations with their employers. Informal workers also include the self-employed. In China, informal employment is closely related to low coverage of social insurance. In particular, women are more likely to fall into poverty when they enter old age in a social security system without an efficient means of interconnection between old-age insurance for the formal sector and old-age security for the informal sector and without any gender-based contribution arrangements and retirement income redistribution.[7]

This report attempts to examine the institutional arrangements of the existing old-age insurance programs for migrant workers and assess the impacts of the programs on the current and future livelihood of rural migrant workers,[9] with an emphasis on answering the following questions: Can migrant workers (particularly female workers) benefit from participation in old-age insurance? What are the key factors restricting their pension entitlement? Which action do they take to respond to these restrictions? Which obstacles do the Regulations help them remove? Which obstacles still remain untouched? How to solve the residual problems with a perspective of reducing poverty and promoting gender equality? The following institutional analysis will focus on contribution arrangements, as the vast majority of the migrant workers participating in the old-age insurance schemes have not reached retirement age for receiving annuities.

Information used to answer the above questions comes from the fieldwork by a research team of the Institute of Economics, Chinese Academy of Social Sciences (CASS). From 2006 till 2008, the team conducted a study on medical insurance for rural migrant workers and collected sample survey data of 2398 migrant workers (52% of them are female) in Shanghai, Wuhan, Chongqing, Shenzhen and Dalian.[10] In addition, the supplementary information is obtained from the sub-sample data set of the urban and rural household survey conducted by the National Bureau of Statistics in 2006.[11] During March-April 2009, the research team conducted field studies in 7 cities that had set up old-age insurance programs for migrant workers, including Guangzhou, Dongguan and Shenzhen in the Pearl River Delta, Shanghai and Suzhou in the Yangtze River Delta, Dalian in the Liaodong Peninsula and Chongqing – an industrial city in southwestern

China. The key institutions and individuals were interviewed as follows: ① the staff at the local social insurance centers in charge of old-age insurance schemes for migrant workers; ② managers in division of human resource of enterprises; ③ rural migrant laborers in formal employment and informal employment or still in search of jobs. In addition, the team designed a questionnaire and conducted a sample survey on rural migrant workers in Suzhou, Dalian and Shenzhen. The sampling procedures were: first selecting 4–5 female-dominated manufacturing and service enterprises operating in different sizes in each city; then selecting from each enterprise 40–50 rural-Hukou laborers who came from outside of the administrated areas of the city. The research team handed out 780 questionnaires and received 702 valid ones. Moreover, women accounted for 67.4% of the sample.

The rest of this report is organized as follows: Section 2 describes the characteristics of the ongoing old-age insurance schemes for migrant workers in relation with the existing urbanization policy. Section 3 elaborates on the behavior of employers in labor use and its impact on employment of migrant labor under the old-age insurance schemes. Section 4 examines the effects of employees' contribution to old-age insurance on the current disposable income of migrant workers as well as the pension entitlements of female and male participants at different wage levels. Section 5 briefly discusses the old-age security issues concerning informal workers. The concluding section summarizes the findings and policy recommendations of this study.

12.2 The old-age insurance program and urbanization policy

The social old-age insurance system enacted into law determines the rights and obligations of the stakeholders. At present, the old-age insurance program for migrant employees is operated by each municipality in accordance with the policy documents issued by local governments. These local policies shape up the institutional environment concerning the old-age insurance scheme to which the enterprises and migrant employees are related. Below the socio-economic indicators and the key elements of the old-age insurance schemes for migrant labor in 5 studied cities are summarized in the same table, in order to facilitate the description of factors affecting policy formation in different socio-economic environments.

Table 12.1 shows that the old-age insurance programs covering migrant employees can be divided into two categories: (1) An independent program set up for migrant labor only; (2) The urban employees' pension program extended to the migrant labor. Moreover, contribution rates and entitlements relating to the programs vary among cities. First of all, the variation in local policies arises due to the fact that the massive migration of rural labor is a new phenomenon that emerged in the midst of economic reform. The social insurance system for migrant labor has gradually been developed by local governments in an institutional innovation process. Secondly, these variations are also closely related to the differences between the municipalities in local socio-economic conditions and the governments' political will as well as their administrative capabilities in dealing with social affairs. Shanghai and Chongqing are two metropolitan areas densely populated and directly under the administration of the central government. To alleviate population pressure, both municipalities have set high thresholds to prevent migrants other than professional elites from

Table 12.1 Selected socio-economic indicators in 2008 and the local policies on old-age insurance schemes for the migrant labor in a few studied cities

	Shanghai	Chongqing	Dalian	Suzhou	Shenzhen
Population (thousand person)	18,885	28,390	6130	(6298)	8768
Including migrants inhabit over half a year (thous. person)	5174	600	293	4000	6488
Local fiscal revenue (million yuan)	238,234	57,724	33,910	66,891	80,036
Average wage of urban employees (yuan/month/person)	3292	2249	2859	2986	3621
Model of the old-age insurance scheme for migrant employees	Comprehensive insurance program for work injury, health and old-age of migrant workers	Old-age insurance program for migrant workers only	The migrants covered by urban workers insurance in development zone only	Migrant workers covered by insurance for urban-Hukou workers in the city	
Contribution rate to wages	7% contributed by employers (12.5% in total for comprehensive insurance).	5% by employees; 10% by employers. 14% into personal accounts; 1% as mutual funds.	8% contributed by employees into personal accounts; 20% contributed by employers as pooled (mutual aid) funds.	8% by employees into personal accounts; 10% by employers as mutual funds.	
Retirement entitlement	For one full year of contribution, a voucher equal to 7% from the 60% of the average wage of all employees in the city for the preceding year.	Cumulative funds in personal account/ number of months stipulated.	Basic pension + personal account pension. Basic pension = (average monthly wage of local employees in prior year + individual indexed average monthly wage at contribution(α)) ÷ 2 × years of contribution made (N) × 1%. $\alpha = (X1/C1 + X2/C2 + \ldots + Xn/Cn)/N$, where X indicates the wage of a participant at the year when he/she makes contribution; C stands for the average wage of all employees in the city.		

(Continued)

	Shanghai	Chongqing	Dalian	Suzhou	Shenzhen
Retirement age	60 for men and 50 for women	55 for men and women	60 for men and 50 for women (55 for those working at managerial position).		
Minimum years for making contribution			15		

Note:

1. Information about population size and local fiscal revenue in the table is derived from "Statistical Bulletin on the Economy and Social Development in 2008", in the studied cities, which is issued in China Statistical Information Website (May 2009).

   Shanghai: www.tjcn.org/shanghai/9549_6.html,

   Chongqing: www.tjcn.org/chongqing/10166_3.html,

   Suzhou: www.tjcn.org/suzhou/tjgb/9468_4.html,

   Shenzhen: www.tjcn.org/shenzhen/9912_4.html.

   Dalian data were downloaded from the website of the National Bureau of Statistics of China (on June 2, 2009): www.stats.dl.gov.cn/gongbao.asp?STYLETYPE=6&ID=17277.

2. There are 32,353 people with the local-Hukou in Chongqing. The number of the migrants only refers to those who are now living in the city. The figure in parentheses in the column for Suzhou only refers to the residents with local-Hukou in 2007.

3. Information on old-age insurance policy for migrant labor and the average wage for current employees was collected by the research team through interviews with local social insurance agencies and from the documents released by these agencies.

   Shanghai: news.xinhuanet.com/employment/2005–04/05/content_2786907.htm);

   Chongqing: www.cqldbz.gov.cn/common/content.jsp?id=000000000396490&flag=2;

   Dalian: www.ln.lss.gov.cn/infopub25/PubTemplet/%7B538116AD-AF2A-4978-B786–5A2A1621E91C%67D .asp?infoid=10802&Style={538116AD-AF2A-4978-B786–5A2A1621E91C};

   Suzhou: www.js.lss.gov.cn/zcfg/ldzjfg/200810/t20081021_21008.htm;

   Shenzhen: www.szsi.gov.cn//sbjxxgk/zcfggfxwj/zctw/200810/t20081009_755.htm.

   These documents were downloaded on June 10, 2009.

obtaining local permanent residential status. Then, both established separate old-age insurance programs for migrant workers and selected contribution rates lower than the insurance premium rates for urban employees. This helps alleviate resistance from employers and migrant workers in the policy implementation process. Nevertheless, it also rules out the possibility of redistributing pension income between the employees with different residential statuses.

Nearly all social insurance programs for migrant workers started with manufacturing industry. In Dalian, the emerging manufacturing industry is concentrated in the development zone and the manufacturing enterprises are mostly foreign-funded ones with better operating conditions than those located outside the zone. In addition, only the migrants working in the development zone are covered by the old-age insurance for urban employees. Suzhou and Shenzhen are cities renowned for their developed manufacturing industry and both of them are economically stronger than Dalian. Both municipalities have adopted the same old-age insurance policy for migrant labor employed in the formal sector as for employees with local residence status. This practice helps avoid institutional fragmentation, reduce identity discrimination against the rural migrants and attain economies of scale in management.

Furthermore, the insurance model in Suzhou and Shenzhen is also related to the local population structure. In Shenzhen, people with the local-Hukou account for only 26% of the resident population. In Suzhou, this ratio is 62.5%. The proportion of migrants in Suzhou and Dalian is higher than that in Shanghai, Chongqing and Dalian. The vast majority of migrant workers are entitled to receive annuities only after continuously making contributions for many years because of their young ages at present. For an old city like Suzhou, the funds accumulated in the name of this group can be used to fill the gap of pension funds left over by the state-owned enterprises in the old-age security reforms as well as to alleviate the difficulties in funds accumulation resulting from the aging of the residents with local-Hukou. For a new city like Shenzhen, the massive participation of migrant workers in old-age insurance can help lower the contribution rates and make it possible for the pension recipients with the local-Hukou to enjoy greater benefits. In 2008, the average pension benefits of the local-Hukou retirees in Shenzhen reached RMB 3504, which was 96.8% of the local average wage level.

It is also worth noting that the same insurance schemes may lead to different results for the participants with different permanent residential status. To date, the household registration system has not been substantively reformed. In respect of urban public service and welfare provision, social exclusion to rural migrants is still in existence. In the occasion of failing to find jobs or losing jobs, those with urban-Hukou are entitled to employment assistance from the municipalities. However, the rural migrants have no alternative but to try their luck on the market. Whether they can settle down in a city and how long they can stay there is to a large extent dependent on the demand in the urban labor market.[12] It is found in a survey on labor use of enterprises in 2007 that the age requirement for 60% of jobs was in a range of 18–25 years and the age limit for nearly 30% of jobs was 26–35 years. In addition, most jobs require candidates with entry-level occupational training. In respect of gender requirements, the demand on female labor is higher than the male.[13] Under the circumstances that the education backgrounds of the entire rural labor force are poorer than that of the urban, only those young and strong with basic education are most likely to find jobs in the formal sector. In other words, what urban employers need are the most productive rural labor in the prime phase of their life cycle. After passing this phase of life, they are likely to lose jobs in the urban formal sector and in consequence lose their entitlements to the old-age insurance associated with formal employment.

It is indicated by statistics based on the sub-sample data derived from the nation-wide households survey conducted by the National Bureau of Statistics in 2006 that the male and female migrant labor at the age below 30 years accounted for 62.3% and 78.4% of the respective gender groups in the urban formal labor market. This dovetails neatly with the age requirements for employees of the enterprises stated above. In the age group above 40 years, male and female migrant workers only made up 12.1% and 4.3% of the respective gender groups. However, in the same age-gender group, the male and female employees with urban-Hukou accounted for 63.7% and 51.1% respectively (see Figure 12.1). It is stipulated in the old-age

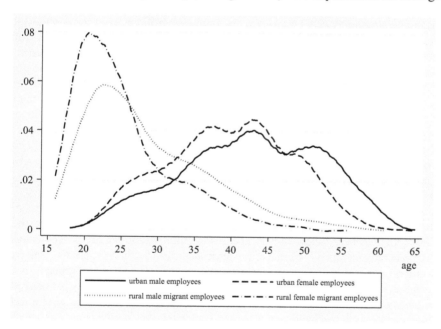

Figure 12.1 Distribution (sample kernel density) of formal employees aged 16–65 in the urban labor market in 2006, by gender and identity of permanent residential registration

Note: The data processed for the diagram are derived from the sub-sample of the urban and rural household survey conducted by the National Bureau of Statistics in 2006. The sub-sample consists of 18,071 households and 65,281 residents, including 10,751 rural households and 43,776 rural residents; 7320 urban households and 21,505 urban residents. The rural migrant workers who have signed labor contracts with urban employers are defined as the formal employees and they totaled 1842 (person). The umber of the urban formal employees is 10,469 (person).

insurance schemes that the longer period the participants work and make contributions, the higher the benefits they are entitled to obtain. Under the same system, the differences in the working period alone without taking into account wage difference will make it difficult for the vast majority of rural migrant workers to acquire equal pension benefits with urban-Hukou workers and for women to get equal pension entitlements with men.[14] Among urban-Hukou formal employees, women have shorter years of service than men due to the statutory retirement age difference between men and women. For female rural migrant workers, the key factor affecting the length of their working period is the lack of child care service suitable for the low-income group in the urban areas. In some cities, the migrant workers have not yet been covered by maternity insurance. As a result, young female workers have no alternative but to exit the urban formal labor market during the child bearing and breeding period. Therefore, the female migrant workers are more likely to lose their pension entitlements compared with the male counterparts.

In fact, the lack of equal opportunity for migrant workers to share equal welfare with urban-Hukou employees is one of the reasons why the migrants tend to move frequently between urban and rural areas and across different cities. According to the local policies in the cities (except Shanghai), rural migrant workers cannot transfer their old-age insurance accounts between pooling areas but they can withdraw their accounts. However, to cancel pension accounts, the migrant participants can only get back the proportion of the funds that they directly contributed. The share of the funds that the employers contributed for the migrant employees will be withheld in the local social insurance pools. This practice is tantamount to encroaching upon the interests of both the migrant participants and the employers as well as to undermining the sustainability of the old-age insurance schemes. If the old-age insurance system is designed without taking into account the special characters of the migrant workers in the urban labor market and proceeding from a gender perspective, the migrants (particularly the females) will not necessarily be able to benefit from participation in the insurance schemes.

It is learnt from the interviews that the "first-generation" rural migrant workers still have farming skills. When they leave the urban labor market, they will return to their native villages because the living expenses are higher in urban areas. By contrast, the "second-generation" migrants (the descendants of the "first generation" migrant workers), particularly those with secondary and tertiary education backgrounds, have long been accustomed to urban lifestyles and as a result they wish to stay permanently in cities or settle down at least in towns. The urban old-age insurance system shall therefore be designed with options reserved for migrant participants. Among the existing old-age insurance programs for migrant workers, only the "Shanghai model" has partially responded to such demand. Under the Shanghai model, when a participant reaches retirement age, he or she can cash out his/her old-age subsidy vouchers in lump sum at any local branch of the designated insurance company. Nevertheless, the excessively small amount of the subsidies has in fact ruled out the possibility for recipients to stay in cities after retirement (see Table 12.5 and Table 12.6).

To address the foregoing issues, the MoHRSS has provided the following solutions in the Regulations. Firstly, migrant workers will be covered by the old-age insurance for urban employees. Secondly, the pension entitlement of the migrant participants will become portable. The migrant participants are allowed to transfer their accounts in the pension funds when they change jobs between different pool areas and this will ensure the continuity of their benefits accumulation. In the event of quitting formal employment and terminating contribution, they can have their old-age insurance records and personal accounts temporarily sealed and kept in custody. Thirdly, when they return to their home villages prior to the retirement age, they can also transfer their records on the pension entitlement from the urban insurance schemes into the old-age insurance system for rural residents to be established in the near future. In addition, this institutional arrangement makes it also possible for them to transfer their pension accounts into the future old-age insurance system for urban residents. Fourthly, in the occasion of moving between different old-age insurance systems and across pool areas, the migrant participants will be permitted to bring the full pension benefits with them, including the amount of funds accumulated in their personal accounts and the amount of contribution matched by employers. More importantly, these regulations will be conducive to the formation of the national urban old-age insurance system and provide a necessary condition for the establishment of a fair and equitable competition environment in the labor market.

12.3 Fringe benefits and job creation

Affected by the global financial crisis and economic downturn, the enterprises in the studied cities began to suffer operational difficulties in the third quarter of 2008. A number of manufacturing enterprises have not received any orders this year. To prevent machine rust and skilled workers turnover, some enterprises have to operate without making any money. An underwear producer operated 3 factories and employed over 900 workers (two-thirds of them are female workers) before the financial crisis broke out. Now the company has consolidated the three factories into two factories and retained only 400 workers. "The number of enterprises entering into contracts with our company reached 600 in 2007 but fell to 300 by the end of March in 2009," said a division manager of a labor dispatch company located in Dalian. The research team was originally scheduled to visit a labor dispatch company in Suzhou. In the first half of 2008, the company managed over 10 thousand migrant workers. In the first quarter of 2009, the company found its business volume shrinking rapidly as a large number of workers was laid off. Unfortunately, the company suspended its business shortly before the arrival of the research team. It is also noticed in the field studies that small and medium-sized enterprises have to date failed to receive strong support with loans from the banks but they have to assume a heavy tax burden as large enterprises do. In early 2009, local governments rushed to take rescue measures and reduce contribution rates to social insurance programs except for old-age insurance schemes. However, the overall contribution rate undertaken by enterprises is still higher than that in the developed countries, and this has severely affected business recovery and job creation. The most frequent complaint that the research team heard by the visits to studied enterprises is that their social insurance burden is too heavy.

When computing the spending on social insurance programs, an employer also takes into account employees' direct contribution to the programs and treats the payments by both the enterprise and employees as costs of fringe benefits to wages or as a part of labor costs. According to the theory on behavior of firms, the excessively higher labor costs will cause enterprises to reduce labor use by raising capital intensities, thereby resulting in a decrease in employment opportunities in the society. Employability is of paramount importance both to the livelihood of workers' families and to social stability. Therefore, the old-age insurance system for migrant workers must be designed to incorporate the following policy trade-offs: the employees' contribution rate shall be designed at a level that enables fund accumulation to meet their basic needs when they retire but does not force them to cut current consumption of daily necessities. The employers' contribution rate shall be designed at a level that meets basic old-age insurance budgets but does not weaken corporate development capability or stifle job creation, while taking into account the overall tax and social insurance burden of enterprises.

According to the human resource manager of a large-sized construction enterprise, the overall social insurance premium rate was 45% of total company payroll in Suzhou in 2008. At the floor level of contribution base, an employer must contribute at least RMB 465 per month for an employee, while the employee must personally contribute at least RMB 150. In response to the financial crisis, the municipal government has reduced the employer contribution rate for medical and work injury insurance by 1% and 0.5% respectively in 2009 (see Table 12.1). However, the reduced total premium rate to social insurance programs is still higher than in the severely "aged" developed countries in Europe.

For example, all social insurance premiums contributed by German employers and employees as a percentage of total wages were 26.5% in 1970 and rose to 41.9% in 2004. High premium rates and high fringe benefits led to rigidity of the labor market. A part of labor would rather remain unemployed than search for or accept low-income jobs; the employers found it difficult to adjust the number of workers as per market demand. The upshot was that the unemployment rate was so high that the German government had to launch labor market reform[15] and promote employment by reducing unemployment benefits and implementing a more rigorous supervision system on social relief provisions. In 2006, the total social insurance premium rate fell below 40% and per capita GDP reached 26,500 euro (about US$ 34,347) in Germany, which was 3.4 times the per capita GDP of Suzhou in 2008. At present, the economic development in most Chinese cities is still behind that of Suzhou but the social insurance premium rates for urban employees in those cities are virtually the same. Based on the relation between the aggregate economic output and social insurance premium rate in Germany, it is considered that the social insurance premium rates are relatively high in Chinese cities. The reasons why these cities have not plunged in a predicament with a rigid labor market and a huge deficit of the pension fund is to a large extent due to the supply of the rural labor with high mobility and to the net contribution that the young and healthy migrant workers have made to the old-age and medical insurance schemes.

Table 12.2 Contribution rates to social insurance programs in the urban areas of Suzhou[1] (January 2009–December 2010)

Insurance	Employer contribution (%)	Employee contribution (%)	Total of contribution rate (%)
Basic old-age insurance[2]	20	8	28
Medical insurance			
Basic scheme	8	2	11
Supplement[3]	1	0	
Unemployment insurance	2	1	3
Work injury insurance	0.5	0	0.5
Maternity insurance	1	0	1
Total	32.5	11	43.5

Source: Social Insurance Fund Management Center, Suzhou City, website at: www.szsbzx.net.cn:9900/web/html/bszn/bsznAction.do?src=/web/html/bszn/bszn_frame.jsp.

[1] The minimum contribution base is 60% of the provincial average wage level of prior year; the maximum contribution base is 300% of the average wage level. When the wage level falls between the upper and floor level, the actual wage is taken as the contribution base. From 2008 till 2010, the minimum contribution base for social insurance programs of urban employees in Jiangsu province is 1369 yuan/person per month.
[2] With regard to the old-age insurance, the contribution rate for individual industrial and commercial households is stipulated as 20% (8% contributed by employees and 12% contributed by employers). The contribution rate for flexible employees with local-Hukou is 20%, which shall be completely contributed by those employees.
[3] Those who are entitled to medical subsidy for public servants shall not participate in local supplementary medical insurance.

Furthermore, the overall old-age insurance premium rate has reached 28% (employer premium rate: 20%; employee premium rate: 8%) in most Chinese cities. By contrast, the old-age insurance premiums contributed by German employers and employees as a percentage to total wages were 17% (equally shared between employers and employees) in 1970 and rose to 19.9% in 2007. The contribution rate of Chinese enterprises is so high mainly because it covers the pension fund shortfall left over as a result of state-owned enterprises restructuring combined with the establishment of the old-age insurance program for urban employees. In fact, it would be more appropriate to cover the fund shortfall with the profits handed over by the large state-owned enterprises and/or with fiscal appropriations either from a perspective of social equity or from a viewpoint of economic efficiency and job creation. To promote employment, the Chinese government shall avoid imposing high premium rates on enterprises, especially the labor-intensive small and medium-sized enterprises incorporated in the past 30 years.

The Regulations on the Participation of Rural migrant workers in Basic Old-age insurance set the employer contribution rate at 12% (employee contribution rate at 4%-8%). The Regulations are naturally supported by business enterprises that were previously subject to higher contribution rates. It is not difficult to imagine that once the Regulations are put into implementation, it will lead employers to prefer hiring rural migrant workers among those with equal skills.

Such implementation would then undermine the employment of the labor with urban-Hukou and cause new social contradictions. A 'lesser of two evils' approach can be used to choose the employer contribution rate set by the Regulations as the upper limit to all schemes of the old-age insurance and reduce the rate of employers' contribution for urban-Hukou employees in order to create a fair competition environment in labor market. The recommended drastic reduction in premium rates will have a substantial impact on the pooled fund size and may affect pension payments for the existing retirees. Moreover, this may be misunderstood by the public as a reduction in social welfare. It is therefore necessary to take the following policy measures associated with premium rate reduction:

- Firstly, China shall set up public pension funds by drawing on experience of the Chilean government in carrying out pension reforms. Public pension funds shall be financed by fiscal resources, including profits turned over by large state-owned enterprises. On the one hand, the public pension fund can be used to cover the fund shortfall left over as a result of state-owned enterprise restructuring. On the other hand, the public pension fund can be used to finance the guaranteed minimum pension system and provide financial aid to retirees whose pension benefits are lower than the poverty line. At present, this can help win broad social support for the reduction measure on the premium rate. In the future, it will help reduce the inequality in retirement income distribution.
- Secondly, for the labor-intensive small and medium-sized enterprises, the Chinese government shall set up a system to link tax concessions with job creation and insurance coverage for rural migrant workers. Among the existing enterprises, the labor-intensive small and medium-sized enterprises are less profitable but they have a strong capability in employing rural migrant workers. In some cities (such as Dalian), the vast majority of enterprises have not yet included rural migrant workers in the old-age insurance system. The managers require putting the Regulations on hold until the economy turns around. Even so, the small and medium-sized enterprises will incur much higher social insurance costs and thus they could be supported with tax reduction measures. According to the information released by Ernst & Young about marginal cooperate tax rates in over 140 countries and regions, China is a high tax rate country. In Korea, enterprises were subject to an income tax rate of 25% for a taxable income of 100 million won or more (about 83,752 dollars) in 2007–2008. The applicable tax rate was 13% for a taxable income of less than 100 million. During the same period, the marginal tax rate for Chinese enterprises was generally 25%; the applicable tax rate for small enterprises and low-profit enterprises was 20%.[16] Therefore, reducing the tax burden for small and medium-sized labor-intensive enterprises will help improve the international competitiveness of these enterprises and motivate them to pay old-age insurance for migrant workers, thereby enhancing the extent of social security for migrant workers and promoting social stability.

12.4 Impact of contribution arrangements on disposable income of migrant participants

In the past 20 years, the rural migrant labor has been significantly diversified. First of all, the migrant labor is divided into formal and informal employment. Secondly, the gap between the skilled and unskilled labor is widening in respect of education, income and occupational characteristics.[17] However, even for migrant laborers who have climbed into management positions, their average wage is also lower than the level of the average wage in the cities where they are working (see Table 12.3 and Table 12.4). This has a decisive impact on the actual needs of migrant workers to participate in old-age insurance or their ability to make contributions to the insurance schemes. The key group that this report focuses on is the low-income migrants (particularly women workers). The main issues to be addressed in this section are: How does the contribution arrangement made for individuals in the urban old-age insurance system affect the disposable income of the migrant participants? What pension benefits will the migrant participants receive under the existing contribution arrangement?

Whether migrant laborers in formal employment participate in old-age insurance is dependent to a large extent on the insurance system designed by municipal

Table 12.3 The socio-economic characteristics of sample migrant workers

	2006			2009		
	Total	Male	Female	Total	Male	Female
Number of Observations (persons)[1]	1247	561	686	702	233	469
Proportion of each group (%)[2]						
Ages 16–30	67.31	61.18	72.30	85.84	83.55	86.85
High school or equivalent	26.08	26.74	25.55	45.49	40.63	47.61
Junior college or above	2.97	2.85	3.07	18.46	26.34	14.78
Management staff	17.36	17.53	17.15	15.13	20.36	12.44
Workers	58.39	56.55	60.65	69.44	69.68	69.35
Average Monthly wage (yuan)						
Management staff	1271	1385	1179	1549	1814	1296
Workers	954	1077	846	1057	1186	986
Total of the sample	975	1076	893	1146	1338	1044
Percentage of those willing to participate in old-age insurance	–[3]	–	–	89.98	91.28	89.39
Percentage of those who actually participated in old-age insurance	21.29	15.16	26.23	56.84	57.27	56.50

[1] The 2009 sample survey was conducted in Shenzhen, Dalian and Suzhou. In consideration of proximate comparison, we only retain the observations in Shenzhen, Dalian and Shanghai in the 2006 sample.
[2] Group size/observation x 100%.
[3] " – " Indicates no data available.

Table 12.4 The floor level of contribution base to the old-age insurance for migrant workers in the sample cities in 2008* (yuan/month/person)

Studied cities	2007 Urban average wage	2008 Contribution base (floor level)	Average wage of male migrant workers[1]	Average wage of female migrant workers
Suzhou	2617	1369	1253	1137
Dalian	2353	1412	1050	891
Shenzhen	3233	Special economic zone: 1000 yuan Non-special economic zone: 900 yuan	1553	1125

* In March-April 2009, the social insurance agencies in the studied cities were still implementing the insurance premium collection regulations issued in 2008. The floor level of the contribution base was generally 60% of the average wage of urban employees in the province or city in 2007.

[1] The average wage of migrant workers is based on the sample survey data collected by the research team in 2009. The sample size in Suzhou: 310 (29.2% male; 70.8% female); the sample size in Dalian: 194 (21.9% male; 79.1% female); the sample size in Shenzhen: 198 (48.5% male; 51.5% female).

governments and the decisions made by employers. Government regulations stipulate that the insurance premium to be paid by employees shall be deducted by their employers from their wages and as a result employees are left with few options.[18] Table 12.3 indicates that about 90% of the sample migrant workers are willing to participate in old-age insurance but the actual participation rate is way below this level. In the 2006 and 2009 samples, the participation rates were 22% and 57%. The facts behind these figures are firstly that some municipalities did not vigorously implement old-age insurance programs for migrant workers. In Dalian, for instance, the old-age insurance program is solely limited to migrant workers in the development zone. Secondly, under the high premium rate policy, employers have tried evasion tactics, for example, by changing employee status from formal into informal through a labor dispatch company registered outside of the development zone. Thirdly, the insurance system design is not appropriate to the employment characteristics of the migrant labor and to the ability of the migrant labor for making contribution to the schemes. In this case, the migrant participants can respond only by withdrawing from the schemes. In 2007, there were 4.40 million migrant workers participating in old-age insurance in Shenzhen but the number of withdrawal cases reached 830,000.[19] In 2008, 877,000 migrant participants withdrew. Around the Spring Festival in 2009, Shenzhen underwent a new wave of withdrawals.[20] Similar things also happened in Suzhou and Dalian.

It is worth noting that setting the contribution rate at a higher level than the migrant worker's ability to pay will have the unintended consequence of forcing low-income groups to save excessively even if the problems in portability pension entitlement are solved. In the absence of special institutional arrangements on contribution and entitlement for the low-income groups, it is very difficult to ensure that they will benefit from old-age insurance in the future. By participating in old-age insurance, migrant workers have to reduce current consumption of themselves and their families. This may even affect their subsistence or jeopardize their normal labor reproduction. In this situation, the participation rate means nothing more than the extent of the insurance coverage. In the studied cities, Suzhou, Dalian and Shenzhen are the cities where the migrant workers are included in the old-age insurance system for urban employees. The municipal government in Shenzhen is the only one that formulates special provisions to address the issue that the average wage of migrant workers is lower than the floor level of the contribution base (see Table 12.4). In Suzhou and the development zone in Dalian, the individual contribution rate is set for 8% of wages. Based on the floor level of the contribution base in Table 12.4, the minimum contribution per worker per month is RMB 109.52 in Suzhou and RMB 112.97 in Dalian. In consideration of the average wage level of the migrant workers in the two cities, the average premium rate is then accounted for 8.7% and 9.6% respectively for male and female migrant participants in Suzhou, while 10.8% and 12.7% for male and female migrant participants respectively in Dalian Development Zone.

The actual contribution rates of the low-income group are apparently higher than the statutory premium rates. The actual contribution rates of women are higher than those of men because women earn lower wages. Although the funds in the personal account will be used to support migrant workers when they enter old age, their saving capability will become extremely limited after paying contributions from their meager wages. An adoption of the urban employee premium rate for migrant workers will lead to a substantial deduction in their disposable income. In other words, such an arrangement will inevitably squeeze the space for subsistence and development of low-income groups. The employee contribution rate is set at 4%-8% in the Regulations for migrant workers, which will certainly offer a wider range of options for the low-income groups.

The crux of the issue is that most migrant workers are at the low end of the urban labor market and they can find jobs only when they are young and strong. Given the labor intensity of their jobs, migrant workers will lose their advantages in age and physical strength beyond the age of 40 for men and 30 for women such that they may even have to exit the formal employment market (see Figure 12.1). As the actual years when the migrant participants work in the urban formal sector and make insurance contributions are less than that of the workers with urban-Hukou who will end their service at the statutory retirement age, even by taking 60% of the social average wage as the contribution base and making a contribution at 8%, the wage replacement ratio (monthly pension benefit/social average wage) will be far below that of urban-Hukou employees entitled to receive pension benefits after statutory retirement age. This point is well illustrated in the simulation scenarios in Table 12.5 and Table 12.6. The figures listed in both tables are the results of rough estimation about the pension benefits of participants at three different wage levels as contribution bases according to the policies enacted by the municipal government in the studied cities with respect to the participation of migrant workers in old-age insurance (see Table 12.1).[21]

Table 12.5 The wage replacement ratio (pension/social average wage) estimated as per local regulations on old-age insurance for migrant workers

Contribution wage/ social average wage* 100%	Gender of Employees	Shanghai (%)	Chongqing (%)	Suzhou and Dalian (%)
60%	Male	10.05	15.09	45.08
60%	Female	5.94	15.09	32.39
100%	Male	16.74	25.16	61.14
100%	Female	9.90	25.16	43.31
300%	Male	50.23	75.47	141.41
300%	Female	29.70	75.47	97.94

Note: The formula for computing the wage replacement ratio is based on the old-age insurance systems designed by the municipal government in the studied cities for the migrant workers. In Suzhou and Dalian, the pension benefit includes the funds accumulated in personal accounts and the base pension from the pension pool. Assumptions in the estimations: (1) the yield of the fund in personal account is 3% (based on the annual interest rate of bank deposits) and the annual growth rate of social average wage is 5%; (2) typical rural male and female labor begin to work in cities at age 18 and participate in old-age insurance schemes. The male workers make consecutive contributions until age 60 (55 in Chongqing) and then exit the urban formal labor market; the female workers make consecutive contributions until age 50 (55 in Chongqing) and then exit the urban labor market.

Table 12.5 simulates the scenarios under which the monthly pension benefits the insurance participants of different gender groups would receive after their retirement at the statutory age: Firstly, at the same contribution rate, the differences in the average wage replacement ratios between the income groups reflect the wage disparity between them. Secondly, under the institutional arrangements in Suzhou and Dalian, the migrant workers participate in the old-age insurance scheme for urban employees. Now that only urban-Hukou employees retire at statutory age, the estimations on pension entitlements or benefits of insurance participants in Suzhou and Dalian have actually simulated only the scenarios referring to the local employees with urban-Hukou. Thirdly, when the contribution rate and wage level are the same for women and men, the women's wage replacement ratio is way below the men's if women have a lower retirement age and fewer years of service and contribution than men. In Suzhou and Dalian models, the women's pension level is equivalent only to 70% of the men's.

In respect of the current age distribution of migrant workers, the scenario simulation in Table 12.6 is much closer to the actual situation. Simulation results indicate that the pension benefits available to the migrant participants in the pension modals of Shanghai and Chongqing are too low if their contribution wage is equivalent to 60% of the social average wage (which is the floor level of the contribution base). Their maximum wage replacement ratio will be less than 9%. In addition, the gender gap in the pension benefit is more pronounced because the gender disparity in actual years of contribution is greater than the gender differences in statutory retirement ages in the existing system. In Suzhou and Dalian models, the pension level of women is estimated as 55%-57% of that of men.

Table 12.6 The wage replacement ratio (pension/social average wage) estimated as per actual service years of migrant workers

Contribution wage/ social average wage* 100%	Gender of Employees	Shanghai (%)	Chongqing (%)	Suzhou and Dalian (%)
60%	Male	4.99	8.98	25.70
60%	Female	2.25	4.68	14.57
100%	Male	8.32	14.97	34.51
100%	Female	3.75	7.80	19.28
300%	Male	24.95	44.92	78.52
300%	Female	11.24	23.41	42.84

Note: Except for the following assumptions, the rest of the assumptions for the estimations are the same as those given in Table 12.5: a typical rural male laborer begins to work in urban areas at age 18 and participate in old-age insurance scheme. He'll make consecutive contributions for 25 years and exit the urban formal labor market at age 43; a typical rural female laborer begins to work in urban areas at age 16 and participate in old-age insurance scheme. She'll make consecutive contributions for 15 years and exit the urban formal labor market at age 31.

Actually, for the needs of marriage and child care, most female workers have to quit their jobs in the formal sector and eventually enter the informal sector before their years of contribution reach 15. This implies that they will lose eligibility for receiving a monthly pension benefit after reaching retirement age. To protect the basic pension rights and interests of female migrant workers, the government shall provide a linkage between the old-age insurance program for urban employees and the future old-age insurance program for rural residents or urban residents in the social pension system. This makes it possible for migrant participants to switch between different pension programs. Furthermore, the considerable gender gap in pension benefit is related to the unfavorable position of women in the labor market. Statutory maternity insurance can partially improve women's employment conditions. This insurance is intended to compensate women for their income losses during the child bearing and breeding period because the time they spend on child bearing and breeding is in essence a contribution to the human resource reproduction for the society. Chilean experiences indicate that providing a guaranteed minimum pension has a noticeable effect of narrowing the gender gap in retirement income because the vast majority of women belong to low-income groups but their life expectancy is longer than men's. Therefore, women stand to benefit the most from this system.

12.5 The old-age security issue for informal workers

Employment experiences indicate that informal workers in the migrant rural labor force can be divided into two categories: (1) migrant workers exiting from the formal labor market; (2) migrant workers engaged in informal employment from the first day of entering into the urban labor market. Common employment identities indicate that one group of the informal workers consists of the self-employed while the other mainly includes those employed by micro-enterprises or urban households. Among the informal workers, most females are engaged in sales, reception, tour guide, housework, hospital nursing, cleaning, hairdressing and sewing services.[22] When there is market demand that cannot be promptly met by the formal sector, there will be informal workers coming up to cover the shortfall with flexible labor supply. Although the flexibility is a tool used by them to cope with unemployment, they may have to earn less than the formal workers and their income is very unstable. A large proportion of informal workers are the "working poor" in cities. Most informal workers are not covered by any insurance. It was found in the interviews of the research team that work injury and medical insurance are the types of social insurance coverage most needed by informal workers. Some interviewees had participated in rural cooperative medical insurance schemes. However, considering that the time and travel costs to return to their native villages for reimbursement of their medical expenses were so high, they were better off withdrawing from the schemes. Apparently, the migrant informal workers need such social protection programs that are tailored to their employment characteristics to help them cope with the risks they face in an industrialized urban society.

As far as the existing social insurance system for the old-age is concerned, it lays numerous "thresholds" for the participants such as the continuity of pension contributions at a fixed interval and a combined premium rate of 15%-28% for employer and employee contribution. The vast majority of informal workers have been excluded by these thresholds.[23] Moreover, the local old-age insurance system for the self-employed and flexible employees is designed to target only those with urban-Hukou (refer to notes to Table 12.2). In the studied cities, Shanghai is the only city where a door is left open for the self-employed migrant labor to participate in comprehensive insurance. However, none of the self-employed migrants have participated in the scheme up to now. This may result from the fact that they cannot afford to accept a premium rate of 12.5% and a fee of 2% for the case of delayed contribution delivery. In the event of handling business with a huge number of individual participants every day, the social insurance agencies will incur hefty administrative costs and therefore lack any incentive to allow the self-employed migrants to participate in the insurance schemes. The agencies treat the self-employed with the local urban-Hukou differently because of the enforcement from the municipal governments.

How to allow low-income informal workers to participate in old-age insurance is a global difficulty.[24] If we take prevention and reduction of old-age poverty as an objective, it is possible to blaze a new trail and find a way of replacing the costly formal sector insurance model. Firstly, by means of the social relief programs, the informal workers can be guaranteed to be "well taken care of when they are old". The old-age assistance provisions shall be set up in the urban and rural minimum living security system to afford financial assistance to the poor and elderly people ineligible for pension benefits. Secondly, it shall be made possible for informal workers to participate in old-age insurance schemes to be established for the rural and urban residents outside of the formal sector in the near future.

A currently viable policy is to extend the coverage of the insurance schemes most needed to the informal migrant workers with a stepwise approach. For the rural migrants employed through labor dispatch companies, housework service firms and construction teams, the insurance for work injury, medical and maternity shall be firstly provided; then a "tailored" old-age insurance scheme shall be designed to target these quasi-informal groups as their wage level increases. For the migrant labor without any linkage even to the loosest labor organization, the municipal government shall take action and extend social assistance and insurance services to such informal workers at their urban residence through the administrative network of neighborhood communities.

12.6 Conclusions

It can be seen as historical progress to include rural migrant labor in the old-age insurance for urban employees. However, providing "one size fits all" old-age insurance schemes for rural migrant workers and the employees with urban-Hukou alike will lead to inequitable results under the existence of a huge discrepancy in their socio-economic conditions.

Firstly, under an urbanization policy without social inclusion, migrant workers can only work in urban areas but cannot live there permanently. What urban employers need are the most productive rural labor in the prime phase of their life cycle. After passing this phase of life, they are likely to lose formal employment positions in urban areas and in consequence lose their old-age insurance entitlements associated with formal employment. In the midst of changing labor market demand, they have no alternative but to move between urban areas to cope with unemployment risks. Under the existing local old-age insurance policy for rural migrant workers, old-age insurance entitlements cannot be transferred. This has not only undermined labor mobility but also hurt the interests of employers and employees making pension contributions.

Secondly, the old-age insurance premium rates paid by employers for their employees are higher than those of some developed countries (well known as "welfare states") in Europe. In addition, the tax burden of Chinese firms is higher than the international average level. This has dampened the incentive for entrepreneurs to increase labor use but bolstered their motivation to evade insurance obligations. As a result, it has hurt the workers' welfare and undermined corporate efforts to create jobs.

Thirdly, the floor level of the contribution base set by some of municipal governments is higher than the average wage of migrant workers and as a result their actual contribution rate is higher than the statutory level. Setting the contribution rate at a higher level than the migrant workers' ability to pay will have the unintended consequence of forcing low-income groups to save excessively. By participating in old-age insurance, migrant workers have to reduce the current consumption for meeting the basic needs of themselves and their families. In other words, this will jeopardize their normal labor reproduction. The actual contribution rate of female workers is higher because they earn lower wages.

In consequence, the obligated contributions to the insurance have more severe impacts on the disposable income of female workers.

As the existing urban social old-age insurance scheme is designed without taking into account the employment characteristics of the migrant workers, therefore, they will not necessarily be able to benefit from "participation in old-age insurance". To address the above issues, the MoHRSS responded constructively by drafting *Regulations on the Participation of Rural Migrant Workers in Basic Old-age Insurance*. On the one hand, the employer and employee contribution rates are reduced. On the other hand, employees are allowed to transfer old-age insurance accounts across different local pools. It is worth noting that when migrant workers transfer pension accounts between urban and rural old-age insurance systems and across different pool areas, the transferable fund includes the cumulative balance of personal accounts and the cumulative amount of contribution made by employers. These principles will help protect the interests of migrant workers and integrate them into the urban society.

However, the cumulative pension fund of low-income workers will be much lower when the contribution rate is reduced. In the absence of any further policy intervention, the Regulations may reduce the current extent of poverty of low-income workers when they are young but will expose them to greater poverty in the future (when they are old). Furthermore, the longer your years of service, the higher your wage level, the greater the amount of pension fund accumulated under the name of yourself, the higher the pension benefits you are entitled to receive after the statutory retirement age. Under the same institutional conditions, two factors: years of service and wage level will make it difficult for the vast majority of rural migrant workers to receive equal pension benefits as urban-Hukou workers. It is more difficult for women to receive equal pension benefits as men. Among the migrant workers, women exit the formal labor market earlier than men because they need to take child care and other family responsibilities. Our simulation results show that at the same contribution wage level the pension level of female migrant workers is only equivalent to 55%-57% of that of male workers due to the difference in years of service between them.

To promote employment and reduce old-age poverty and gender inequality in retirement income distribution, the central government needs to formulate the following policies associated with the Regulations:

* First of all, to set up public pension funds with fiscal resources, set a price index-linked minimum pension and guarantee the aged of low-income groups receive an amount of pension no less than the poverty line.
* Secondly, to issue regulations for entitling migrant workers to maternity insurance and require municipal governments to fund the child care service facilities that target low-income groups.
* Thirdly, the old-age security issues concerning the migrant labor exiting from the formal sector and the informal workers can be settled now only by relying more on social assistance rather than social insurance. The future social old-age insurance system for rural residents and urban residents outside of the formal

sector will hopefully help remove the obstacles standing in the way of the informal workers to participate in old-age insurance schemes.

- Fourthly, to reduce the tax rates on those small and medium-sized enterprises identified to make contributions continuously to the old-age insurance for migrant workers.

Given the strong impact of the global financial crisis and economic downturn on Chinese enterprises (particularly on small and medium-sized enterprises) and a huge number of migrant workers laid off, it is thus recommended to launch the national old-age insurance program for migrant workers until the economic recovery is firmly established.

Notes

1 CASS and Central Archives Bureau (1994), *Selections of Economic Archival Materials on the Economy of the People's Republic of China during 1949–1952 (Labor Wage and Employee Insurance Entitlements Volume)*, Chinese Social Science Publishing House, pp. 631–727.
2 Refer to the "Statistical Bulletin on Labor and Social Security Development in 2008" released by the Ministry of Human Resources and Social Security and the National Bureau of Statistics on May 19, 2009. This document was downloaded from http://news.xinhuanet.com/politics/2009–05/19/content_11400984.htm on July 10, 2009.
3 The rural migrant laborers are prevailingly named "peasant workers" (Nong Min Gong). However, it is a misnomer because it has already been unable to accurately express the socio-economic characteristics of rural migrant laborers: (1) most rural laborers working in cities are no longer "partly peasants and partly workers" and they have completely moved to industries from agriculture; (2) "peasant workers" who were born since the economic reform began never did any farming work and they went to work in urban areas immediately after graduation from school. The most salient identity distinction between rural and urban laborers lies solely in household registration (Hukou) rather than anything else. In this report, the author intends to use the phrases "rural migrant laborer" and "rural migrant worker" to replace "peasant worker" wherever practical. On the one hand, it indicates that this cohort of migrant laborers has different socio-economic characteristics than the migrant laborers with urban residence status. On the other hand, it is also intended to separate rural migrant laborers from the local population that lacks urban residence status.
4 See: Wei Liqun (2006), *Correctly Understand and Pay Utmost Attention to Solving Problems Concerning Peasant Workers*, A Team of Research Office under the State Council, *Report on a Survey of Chinese Peasant Workers*, China Yanshi Press, p. 2.
5 See: China Australia Governance Program, "Report of the Baseline Study on the Social Security Programs for Peasant Workers", Part 2-Theme 3 (January 8, unpublished).
6 See: Ministry of Human Resources and Social Security, Notification of Soliciting Public Comments on "Regulations on the Participation of Peasant Workers in Basic Old-age insurance" and "Provisional Regulations on the Transfer of Basic Old-age insurance Relationship for Urban Enterprise Employees", February 5, 2009, http://www.mohrss. gov.cn/mohrss/Desktop.aspx?path=mohrss/mohrss/InfoView&gid=7575d82c-0764–4b78-b459-c65d64e032b1&tid=Cms_Info, May 1, 2009.
7 Employment Sector and International Labor Office (2002), *Women and Men in the Informal Economy: A Statistical Picture*, pp. 7–13, http://www.ilo.org/public/libdoc/ilo/2002/102B09_139_engl.pdf, June 4, 2009.

8 James, E., A.C. Edwards and R. Wong (2003), "The Gender Impact of Pension Reform", Policy Research Working Paper 3074, The World Bank, Poverty Reduction and Economic Management Network, Gender Division.

9 This research team has another 4 separate reports on i) old-age insurance for peasant workers in formal employment; ii) old-age insurance for peasant workers in informal employment; iii) wage trends of peasant workers; iv) the effects of demographic characteristics of rural migrant workers on pension entitlement.

10 Zhu Ling (2009), "The Working Hours and Occupational Health of Rural Migrant Workers", *China Social Sciences* (Issue No. 1), pp. 133–149.

11 For the detailed explanation of this data set, refer to Zhu Ling and Jin Chengwu (2009), "Income Distribution Pattern and Policy Options in Response to Global Financial Crisis", *Management World* (Issue No. 3), pp. 63–71.

12 Pan Yi and Li Wanwei (2006), *Voices of the Voiceless—Life Stories of Chinese Migrant Women*, Beijing Sanlian Press.

13 Refer to the "Report on an Analysis of the Current Status of Labor Market Supply and Demand" released by the Ministry of Labor and Social Security on June 13, 2007, downloaded from http://www.molss.gov.cn/gb/news/2007–06/ 13/content_182044.htm on July 27, 2009.

14 Yao Yu (2009), "Effects of Demographic Characteristics on the Old-Age Insurance System for Peasant Workers", a research report written by the research team of Institute of Economics at the CASS.

15 Source: Federal Ministry of Economics and Technology, 2007, Annual Economic Report 2007, p. 50, Berlin.

16 Source: Ernst and Young (2008), *The 2008 Worldwide Corporate Tax Guide*, pp. 156 and 502.

17 Deng Quheng (2009), "The Characteristics of Peasant Workers and Their Participation in Old-Age Insurance", one of the forthcoming research reports, the research team of the Institute of Economics, CASS.

18 Similar findings have been reported in the existing studies and especially those on female participants in insurance. Refer to Liu Cheng (2008), An Analysis of the Social Insurance Dilemma for Migrant Women, *Journal of Suzhou Institute of Technology*, 2008 (Issue No. 11), pp. 43–47.

19 Xinhua News: "Deep Thoughts on the Withdrawal of Peasant Workers from Old-Age Insurance in Shenzhen", February 28, 2008, http://news.xinhuanet.com/world/2008–02/28/content_7682948.htm, June 22, 2009.

20 Wu Hongying et al., "The Massive Withdrawals on Old-Age Insurance by Non-Local Peasant Workers in Shenzhen Are Glowing in Spotlight", March 30, 2009, http://www.ahsp.org.cn/2006nwkx/html/200903/%7BAFBEDF69-18F2–4D4F-BF21-A0ABC2E9486A%7D.shtml, June 22, 2009.

21 The wage replacement ratio = social average wage replacement ratio of base pension + social average wage replacement ratio of the pension derived from personal account. The wage replacement ratio of base pension = (social average wage of the year prior to the retirement + wage index for contribution* social average wage of the year prior to the retirement) * years of contribution / (200* social average wage of the year prior to the retirement) = (1 + wage index for contribution)* years of contribution/200. Assume a "typical" migrant worker works only in one city and the pension policy in the city will not be changed for a long time; "a" stands for age that a new laborer begins to work; "k": wage index for contribution; "r": annual rate of investment returns to the funds at personal account (constant); g: annual growth rate of social average wage (constant); c: percentage of contribution into personal account; M: number of months for pension payment; N: age of exiting formal employment; T: years of contribution, then the replacement ratio of the pension derived from personal account can be calculated using the following equation:

$$\frac{12kc}{M(r-g)}\left(\frac{1+r}{1+g}\right)^{N-a}\left[1-\left(\frac{1+g}{1+r}\right)^{T}\right]$$

22 Ye Wenzhen, "A Gender-Based Analysis of the Occupational Development of Migrant Women", March 3, 2006, http://www.china-gad.org/HR_NewsDetail.asp?strDetailId=8737 (downloaded on July 10, 2009).

23 Wang Zhen (2009), "Informal Employment, Gender and the Old Age Security", one of the forthcoming reports by the research team, Institute of Economics, CASS.

24 Hu, Y. and F. Stewart (2009), "Pension Coverage and Informal Sector Workers: International Experiences", OECD Working Papers on Insurance and Private Pensions, No. 31, OECD publishing.

13 Income distribution policy options amid the global financial crisis

This statistics-based study shows that in China the urban-rural income gap is contributing more to general income inequality than regional income gaps are. The regional income disparity sets in an east-west plus central contrast, while the urban-rural gap is most significantly present in the west and central areas between the cities and the countryside. Rural migrant laborers have helped shrink the urban-rural and regional income gaps. However, when the economy is slowed by the global financial crisis to, a number of public actions are crucial and urgent to reduce income inequality and enhance social stability. The actions would include an immediate social bail-out and provisions for social security for rural-based migrants currently working in the cities, employment programs targeting low-income group as well as encouraging entrepreneurship.

Although the effects of the global financial crisis and economic recession on the income of Chinese residents cannot be accurately measured at this point in time, one thing is certain: the crisis has taken a heavy toll on the economic security of families living on the brink of poverty, as they are not covered by the social security net. Meanwhile, the medium high income group has also suffered asset and income losses to varying extents. Income distribution policy can no longer be relegated below any direct economic stimulus initiative. On the one hand, this is because the low income group's propensity to consume is higher than that of the medium-high income group and the income transfer to the low income group will definitely help boost effective demand and stimulate economic growth. On the other hand, it is because sharing the fruits of economic growth is equally important as growing the economy. This is especially true when

This report is adapted from the key research project titled "Harmonious Society and Social Equity Policy Options" conducted by the research team of the Institute of Economics of the Chinese Academy of Social Sciences (CASS). In writing this paper, the authors benefited tremendously from the results of research and discussion by other team members. In particular, HE Wei joined with the data processing for this report. The key contents of this article were presented at the annual academic seminar organized by the Department of Economics of the CASS on February 3, 2009. Prof. CAI Fang and YANG Shengming provided constructive comments and suggestions during the presentation. We wish to acknowledge and extend our sincere thanks to all those who lent their expertise to improving this report.
(Co-author with Chengwu JIN, originally published in *China Economist*, Jul-Aug. 2009.)

economic growth slows because an adverse impact on the economic security of the low income group may affect social stability and economic growth, and severe income inequality will lead to similar consequences. Empirical studies show that severe income inequality causes social and political instability, which in turn reduces investment and adversely affects economic growth. In addition, in a society with severe income inequality, the demand for fiscal redistribution will be extraordinarily high and will lead to a lower economic growth rate (Gerald M. Meier and James E. Rauch, 2004).

Discussing income distribution issues requires gaining a clear understanding of the existing distribution pattern and the status of the bottom income group and taking remedial measures to enhance the economic security of that group, improve the income distribution pattern and create favorable conditions for faster economic growth. In the following sections, we first provide an overview of the status of income distribution in urban and rural areas. Secondly, we decompose the income gap and identify the key factors affecting income inequality. Based on the above statistical analysis, we describe the path by which the financial crisis impacts the income distribution pattern and devise income distribution policy options to respond to the crisis.

13.1 Income inequality trends

The income gap has increasingly widened among Chinese residents over the past 30 years. Among all factors affecting the income distribution pattern, the urban-rural disparity is the largest contributor to income inequality. This point is reflected both in the higher income of urban residents than that of rural residents and in the following analytical result: the urban-rural disparity is also one of the significant factors explaining the income gap between different regions and industries and the inequality of education and healthcare opportunity. Therefore, this paper focuses on presenting changes in the income gap between urban and rural residents.

The original sample household data currently available for use by this research team are the sub-sample dataset of the household surveys conducted by the National Bureau of Statistics in 2002 and 2006. The low income group, which accounted for 50% of the total population, earned only 18.3% of total income, which was 3 percentage points less than the share of income earned by the top 5% of the population (nearly 21.3%) (see Table 13.1). In 2002, the 50% low income population held a 19.2% share of total income, whereas the top 5% high income population had a share of 20.4%. Resident income distribution became more unequal in 2006 over 2002.

Table 13.2 presents the average income gap between the lowest and highest income groups and the population composition of different decile groups. In 2002, the average income of the top 10% was approximately 18.7 times that of the bottom 10%. In 2006, the average income gap between the two groups widened 22.6 times. During this period, the average income of the bottom 10% increased significantly. It is worth noting that the share of the urban population increased 6% in

Table 13.1 Personal income distribution in 2006

Top income group as % of sample population	Annual average income (yuan/person)			Share of income (%)		
	National	Urban	Rural	National	Urban	Rural
1%	52,353.67	62,680.82	21,187.72	6.75	4.99	5.62
5%	32,953.91	41,776.08	12,719.68	21.25	16.57	16.82
10%	26,076.72	33,823.04	10,191.75	33.62	26.69	26.95
25%	18,083.95	24,749.94	7415.09	58.29	48.82	49.02
50%	12,680.61	18,673.54	5611.85	81.74	73.67	74.18

Source: Sub-samples of the household samples collected by the National Bureau of Statistics in 2006. Sample size: 18,071 households and 65,281 residents, including 10,751 rural households and 43,776 rural residents; 7,320 urban households and 21,505 urban residents. Unless otherwise stated, the following tables have the same source.

Table 13.2 Average income and demographic composition within decile groups

Decile group	2002				2006			
	Average income of each group		Urban-rural population ratio in each group (%)		Average income of each group		Urban-rural population ratio in each group (%)	
(Low→high income)	(yuan/person/year)		Urban	Rural	(yuan/person/year)		Urban	Rural
Lowest group	812.09		0.82	99.18	1151.59		3.38	96.62
Group 2	1346.94		2.87	97.13	2060.48		4.50	95.50
Group 3	1776.36		4.32	95.68	2790.97		7.12	92.88
Group 4	2248.50		9.45	90.55	3590.47		15.45	84.55
Group 5	2802.10		19.77	80.23	4575.33		27.11	72.89
Group 6	3541.02		36.06	63.94	5894.85		48.10	51.90
Group 7	4583.29		55.50	44.50	7658.30		69.49	30.51
Group 8	6105.41		77.02	22.98	9997.56		82.81	17.19
Group 9	8312.36		87.73	12.27	13,772.89		92.24	7.76
Highest Group	15174.86		93.51	6.49	26,076.72		96.67	3.33
Total	4670.98		38.71	61.29	7757.39		44.69	55.31

[1] This column of data is calculated based on the 2002 household sub-sample dataset compiled by the National Bureau of Statistics 2002. Sample size: 16,035 households and 58,601 residents, including 9,200 households and 37,969 residents in rural areas and urban 6,835 households and 20,632 residents in urban areas.

2006 over 2002 as a result of urbanization. In the bottom 1–3 low income groups, the rural population accounted for over 90% of each group. In other words, poverty and low income are primarily a rural phenomenon.

This column of data is calculated based on the 2002 household subsample dataset compiled by the National Bureau of Statistics 2002. Sample size: 16,035 households and 58,601 residents, including 9,200 households and 37,969 residents in rural areas and urban 6,835 households and 20,632 residents in urban areas.

13.2 Income gap analysis

First of all, the Theil index decomposition technique is used to examine the resident income gap between urban and rural areas and across regions and its effects on the national resident income gap. Secondly, the Gini coefficient decomposition method is employed to validate the effects of different income components on the total income gap.

The statistical results in Table 13.3 show that in 2006 the per capita income gap between central and western regions was lower than each of their gaps with the eastern region. In western China, income inequality was the highest and the Gini coefficient reached 0.459. In addition, the western region also had the highest urban-rural income gap with an urban/rural income ratio of 3.45. The eastern region had the lowest urban-rural gap with an urban/rural income ratio of 2.98. This indicates that the income level of rural residents in western China was the lowest nationwide.

Table 13.3 A profile of household income per capita in different regions in 2006

	Total	*Urban*	*Rural*
Sample household income per capita (yuan/year)			
Eastern region	10,586.40	15,420.73	5167.52
Central region	5962.41	10,025.70	3157.50
Western region	5043.90	9391.91	2719.93
National	7757.39	12,676.50	3783.21
Percentage			
Eastern region	59.07	62.28	50.40
Central region	26.31	24.74	30.55
Western region	14.62	12.99	19.05
Total	100.0	100.0	100.0
Gini cocllkicni			
Eastern region	0.442	0.354	0.341
Central region	0.420	0.266	0.309
Western region	0.459	0.342	0.304
National	0.468	0.350	0.355

Table 13.4 Urban-rural decomposition of the national personal income gap[1]

Group	As % of population	Per capita income (yuan)	Theil index	Absolute contribution	Relative contribution (%)
2002					
Urban-rural	0.15	0.15	43.0		
Urban	0.39	7792.60	0.18	0.12	34.7
Rural	0.61	2560.41	0.23	0.08	22.3
National	1	4585.77	0.35	0.35	100.0
2006					
Urban-rural	0.16	0.16	42.2		
Urban	0.45	12,340.93	0.21	0.15	41.3
Rural	0.55	3796.90	0.22	0.06	16.5
National	1	7615.00	0.37	0.37	100.0

[1] After removing the number of households with a negative income as required in calculating the Theil index, the final urban sample size (2002) used in calculation is: 6,832 households and 20,645 residents; rural sample size: 9,194 households and 37,947 residents. The final urban sample size (2006) used in calculation is: 7,318 households and 21,499 residents; rural sample size: 10,726 households and 43,687 residents. Therefore, the per capita income figures in this table may be different from those in other tables.

Table 13.5 Regional decomposition of the national personal income gap

Group	Share of sample population	Per capita income (yuan)	Theil index	Absolute contribution	Relative contribution (%)
2002					
Inter-region	0.03			0.03	9.9
Eastern region	0.42	6018.14	0.32	0.18	50.7
Central region	0.35	3683.40	0.27	0.08	21.8
Western region	0.23	3392.37	0.36	0.06	17.6
National	1	4585.77	0.35	0.35	100.0
2006					
Inter-region	0.05			0.05	13.2
Eastern region	0.43	10,325.29	0.33	0.19	52.2
Central region	0.34	5951.70	0.29	0.08	20.6
Western region	0.23	4929.63	0.36	0.05	14.0
National	1	7615.00	0.37	0.37	100.0

The statistical data in Table 13.4 and Table 13.5 are derived by decomposing the national resident income gap in 2002 and 2006 on the urban-rural dimension and regional dimension. First of all, the Theil index of the national resident income increased 0.02 from 2002 to reach 0.37 in 2006, suggesting that the income gap widened between 2002 and 2006. Secondly, the urban-rural

Table 13.6 Decomposition of Gini coefficient (urban sample households, 2006)

	Share of total income (%)	Concentration ratio	Contribution to Gini coefficient (%)
Wage and subsidy income	75.74	0.365	79.05
Pension benefits	18.93	0.296	16.03
Other earnings	1.69	0.219	1.06
Business income	5.68	0.332	5.39
Property income	2.07	0.541	3.20
Other transfer income	5.40	0.366	5.63
Social insurance and income tax	−9.50	0.381	−10.35
Total disposal income	100.0	0.350 (Gini coefficient)	100.0

Table 13.7 Decomposition of Gini coefficient (rural sample households, 2006)

	Share of total income (%)	Concentration ratio	Contribution to Gini coefficient (%)
Wage income	46.02	0.387	50.14
Incl.: Non-business organization	(4.90)	(0.612)	(8.45)
Local labor	(19.01)	(0.424)	(22.73)
Migrant labor	(22.10)	(0.304)	(18.97)
Household business income	46.24	0.307	40.01
Property income	2.41	0.702	4.76
Transfer income	5.65	0.332	5.30
Tax	−0.32	0.238	−0.21
Total net income	100.0	0.355 (Gini coefficient)	100.0

income gap accounted for 42.2% of the national resident income gap, whereas the inter-regional income gap accounted for 13.2% of the national income gap (see Table 13.5). It is fair to say that the inter-regional income gap was attributable more to the income gap between central and western and eastern regions; the urban-rural income gap was attributable more to the urban-rural gap in the central and western regions.

The Gini coefficient decomposition technique is used in this section to validate the effects of different components of resident income on the inequality of total income. The results are summarized in Table 13.6 and Table 13.7. First of all, wage and subsidy income and pension benefits, which accounted for nearly 95% of the disposal income of urban residents, contributed approximately 95.1% of the urban Gini coefficient (0.350). Similarly, wage income and household business income, which accounted for nearly 92.3% of the net income of rural residents, contributed approximately 90.2% of the rural Gini coefficient (0.355). Secondly, the concentration ratio of a particular income component represents the distribution of this specific income item in the income groups at different total income levels. When the concentration ratio of an income item is lower than the Gini coefficient of the total income, it has the effect of reducing the total income inequality. Among the income items or components of urban residents, the pension benefits, other earnings and business income have the effect of reducing the total income inequality. Such a positive effect arises because the level of inequality in pension benefits distribution is low and the bottom income group is mainly engaged in the informal economy. Among the income items that contribute to expanding the urban Gini coefficient, property income distribution is the largest contributor. Thirdly, among the income items of rural residents, the wage income from non-business organizations mainly refers to the wages from government agencies and institutions and the subsidies for village cadres or officials. Like property income, this income is extremely unequally distributed and it is combined with local wage income to expand the rural Gini coefficient. The rural household business income is mainly derived from agricultural production and constitutes a vital source of income for the bottom income group. Since the 1980s the distribution of rural household business income has contributed to reducing the rural Gini coefficient. The migrant labor income distribution has the effect of reducing rural income inequality and boosting rural resident income. Therefore, it helps narrow the urban-rural income disparity and reduce national income inequality.

A recent World Bank estimate shows that one in five rural laborers works in urban areas; one-half of rural households have 1–2 migrant workers per family. At present, rural migrant labor accounts for approximately one-third of the total number of people employed in urban areas (World Bank China Office, 2008). This estimate is consistent with the findings of a sample survey conducted by the Ministry of Agriculture. By using the dataset of the sample survey system in 2007, we calculated migrants' earnings as a percentage of the per capita net cash income and net income of rural households. The statistical data cover 16 provinces, most of which are from central and western China. In 2007, migrants' earnings accounted for 40.1% of the per capita net cash income and 34.1% of the per capita net income of rural households in the 16 provinces. Here we pay special attention to the net cash income of rural residents because it indicates how much cash each rural household has at its disposal to spend for consumption items. In a market economy, consumption items such as education, medical care, transportation, communications and diverse food products other than self-made ones, play an increasingly important role in meeting the demand of rural residents for a minimum standard of living. As shown in Figure 13.1, migrant earnings accounted for approximately 50% of the per capita net cash income of rural households in Henan, Guangxi and Jilin; 55%-59% in Chongqing and Hubei; and 75% in Sichuan, the largest source of migrant labor in China.

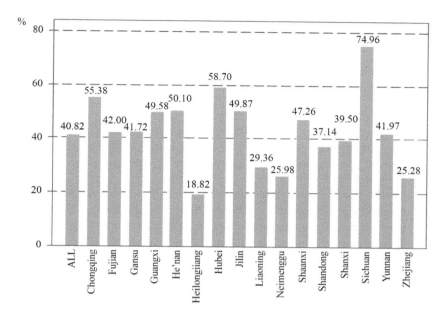

Figure 13.1 Migrants' earnings as a percentage of the per capita net cash income of rural households in 2007

Source: The sample survey conducted by the Ministry of Agriculture through Long-standing Observation Stations in rural areas in 2007; sample size: 18,255 households. The sample size used in calculating in the figure is 11,590 households and 45,504 residents.

13.3 Policy conclusions

The global financial crisis and economic recession affect the income distribution in China through the following path: decrease in overseas orders → enterprise downsizing, shut down and bankruptcy → employment difficulty, especially for rural migrant workers → fewer sources and lower levels of income for rural residents → widened urban-rural and regional income gap → exacerbated national resident income inequality. Although the crisis transmission mechanism must be more complicated than envisaged above and the crisis has a more far-reaching repercussion on China's economy, one thing is certain: the crisis has inflicted the heaviest toll on China's manufacturing industry and other closely related industries. Although business owners and laid-off permanent urban residents also face the threat of income decreases, they are better protected than rural laborers and migrant workers by social security and asset and savings accumulation. Even in the event of decreases in resident income in urban and rural areas, rural residents will face a sharper decline than their urban counterparts will.

At present, the Chinese government has taken measures to deal with the crisis in a very pertinent way. On the one hand, our research can be statistically bent to support the existing measures. On the other hand, we can offer supplementary policy suggestions on income distribution and redistribution based on our analytical results:

1   Strengthen social emergency aid. The basic living allowance system is meant to support urban and rural residents who have long been living in extreme poverty. In times of crisis, those who live on the brink of poverty may find it more difficult to make ends meet. It is therefore imperative to set up a social emergency aid program under which the government offers timely aid to the low income group, particularly women and children, who are struggling for survival. The first aid program can be administered through the civil affairs authorities and local community organizations.

2   Promote reemployment and entrepreneurship. Expanding employment can effectively reduce income inequality (Fang Cai, 2008). Stimulating labor-intensive industry development has the dual effects of transforming the economic growth modes and expanding employment. In addition, the informal sector can effectively absorb jobless urban bottom-income residents and rural migrant laborers. Relaxing administrative control over those who are self-employed, such as peddlers, helps boost the employment rate of the bottom income group. More importantly, in the event of a crisis, it enables the governments at all levels to take effective measures to break down industrial monopoly. Opening up monopolized industries and safeguarding the market order of fair competition is the most efficient entrepreneurship and employment promotion policy that encourages people to start up businesses.

3   Expanding social security coverage. The policy initiative of expanding urban social security coverage to rural migrant workers is now at the trial stage. This is both a crucial means of maintaining social stability in times of crisis and an important strategy of strengthening social inclusion and reducing income inequality over the long-term process of urbanization. As this group is characterized by job instability, strong mobility and informal employment, it is imperative to set up security programs tailored to the special needs of these people. Flexible system design will not only help enhance the willingness of enterprises and migrant laborers to participate in social insurance programs but also help maintain the sustainability of the security system.

4   Add investment in central and western rural infrastructure and agriculture to the national economic stimulus package. This can help not only increase rural income in central and western regions and reduce national income inequality but also improve food safety for local residents living under the poverty line.

The empirical-study part of this report mainly involves analyzing the actual status of income distribution. The policy options put forward in this report are built upon the fundamental principles of "equal opportunity" and "equal conditions." "Equal opportunity" not only emphasizes same entrepreneurship and employment opportunity for different people but also stresses equal social responsibility for different people (Robert William Fogel, 2003). "Equal conditions" recognize that the initial market entry conditions vary from person to person, for example, with regard to parent and household conditions, education opportunity, healthcare opportunity and social relations. The unequal entry conditions require the government to undertake redistribution and public service projects to assure the survival of the bottom income group and mitigate the unfavorable effects of the unfavorable initial conditions for the people to get economic opportunities (Yang Chunxue, 2009). For the transitional Chinese society, however, fundamentally changing the present income distribution pattern also requires drastically changing the production factor allocation system, because the resource allocation pattern determines the initial conditions for income distribution. As for the urban-rural income gap issue, it is possible to reverse the widening urban-rural income disparity trend only by allowing rural residents to making decisions on public resource allocation and repealing the discriminatory permanent household residential registration system.

References

Fang Cai. (2008). *Lewis Turning Point: The New Stage of China's Economic Development*, 177–199. Beijing: Social Sciences Academic Press (China).

Robert William Fogel. (2003). *The Fourth Great Awakening and the Future of Egalitarianism*, 1–18. Beijing: Capital University of Economics & Business Press. (Translated by Wang Zhonghua, and Liu Hong).

Gerald M. Meier, and James E. Rauch (Eds.). (2004). *Leading Issues in Economic Development* (7th ed.), 416–466. Shanghai: Shanghai People's Publishing House. (Translated by Huang Renwei, and Wu Xueming).

The World Bank's Representative Office in China. (2008). *The 11th Five-Year Plan of China – Mid-term Progress Evaluation*, 53–102. siteresources.worldbank.org/EXTEAP CHINAINCHINESE/Resources/China_11th_Five_Year_Plan_main_report_chn.pdf

Yang Chunxue. (2009). The Political Economy Foundation of Harmonious Society. *Economic Research*, 1, 30–41.

14 Addressing extreme poverty and marginality

China's experiences with addressing extreme poverty and marginality are presented and analyzed. The evolution of effective and efficient policies, especially in rural areas, is found closely connected to China's economic growth in the past three decades, as well as to regional inequality. The "Di Bao" (minimum livelihood guarantee system) in different areas is reviewed. In developed regions, the "Di Bao" social assistance program, social insurance and public services have effectively mitigated the difficulties of the extremely poor. In poor areas, however, addressing extreme poverty and marginality remains a challenge. Increasing the effectiveness of poverty reduction efforts in poor areas is, and will continue to be, central to the eradication of extreme poverty in China.

14.1 Introduction

In the past 30 years China has made significant progress in poverty reduction. According to the poverty line set by the World Bank (US$1.25/day per capita consumption or income), China's urban poverty incidence dropped from 44.5% in 1981 to 0.9% in 2008, whereas the incidence of rural poverty dropped from 94.2 to 22.3% during the same period (Chen 2010). According to China's official poverty line, rural poverty was reduced from 250 million people affected in 1978 to 26.88 million people affected in 2010, with the overall incidence of poverty dropping from 30.7 to 2.8%. Though data vary considerably based on different poverty lines, they all reflect a trend of substantial declines in poverty in China.

China's poverty line has remained lower than the international standard. For instance in 2010, the rural poverty line was defined in terms of per capita annual net income at 1,274 yuan (US$193), which was equivalent to 21.5% of the national average rural income of 5,919 yuan (US$896.82) (NBS 2011a). If converted into $US at the year-end exchange rate (US$1.0 = 6.6 yuan), the amount was about US$0.53/day per capita, which is equivalent to 42.3% of the international poverty standard. The comparison shows that those rural residents who still live below

(Originally published in *China Economist*, No. 6, 2011.)

China's poverty line fall within the category of the extremely poor. The previous antipoverty policies in China have always targeted absolute poverty.

During the period of the 12th 5-year national socioeconomic development plan (2011–2015) and over the next decade the Chinese government will continue prioritizing the elimination of absolute poverty in its antipoverty strategies. The extremely poor areas that are adjacent to each other (especially areas inhabited by ethnic minorities, border areas, and ecologically delicate areas) will be the key regions for carrying out China's antipoverty program through increasing poverty relief funds and gradually raising the poverty line (Fan 2011a). However, western China has experienced a slower pace in poverty reduction than eastern China, despite regional targeting antipoverty strategies that have been implemented since the 1980s. Among the current rural poor, nearly two-thirds are scattered across the western areas of the country (Fan 2011b), which indicates that in order to improve the effectiveness of antipoverty efforts the Chinese government should come up with more innovative poverty relief means and targeting mechanisms by taking into consideration the specific hardships faced by the extremely poor in western China.

In this paper, I focus on the following questions. First, in the last 30 years, especially during the period 2000–2010, what measures have been taken to alleviate poverty in rural China? Second, what new policies are being carried out in response to the most imperative living and development needs of extremely poor households and individuals? Third, what other crucial measures should be taken to help the extremely poor escape marginality and poverty? The main primary sources used in this chapter include policy documents from the central and local governments, rural poverty monitoring reports released by the National Bureau of Statistics (NBS) of China, existing research papers, and the results of field work that I conducted personally.

14.2 From poverty reduction programs to social protection system

In its transition from a planned economy to a market economy, China has witnessed an accelerated process of industrialization and urbanization. In addition, due to the strict implementation of family planning (the one-child policy in particular), the problem of an aging population has come to the surface. Meanwhile the government and the public have developed a deepening understanding of the causes of poverty and adopted new ideas about social protection in the era of globalization (García and Gruat 2003). The goal of antipoverty policies has extended from guaranteeing the basic livelihood of the poor to reducing causes of poverty, with an emphasis on helping the underprivileged achieve their potential and take advantage of opportunities for self-advancement. Such changes have not only prompted the adjustment of antipoverty strategies and policies according to socioeconomic development, but also facilitated the establishment of a social security system.

In this period of transition and development, social relief has become the main source of assistance to the poorest households and individuals. Under the planned economy during the period of 1950–1970, rural society was segregated from the urban sphere and lacked a social security system. The major programs responsible for social protection were the "social and disaster relief" and "five-guarantee" policies, the former providing temporary resources for the poor and the latter providing long-term resources and services.

The target groups of the five-guarantee policy include: the elderly, the disabled, and rural residents under 16 years of age who have no ability to work, no income to support their livelihood, and no legal guardians to take care of them. So far the categorization has not changed substantially in amendment of the policy (SCC 2006). The "five guarantees" refer to the provision of food and fuels, clothing and daily necessities, housing, medical care, and burial services for the target groups (the policy also guarantees educational expenses for target group children). The resources of the five-guarantees program, provided by the People's Commune and production teams, could only support the most basic needs of poor households when poverty prevailed in the communes. Since the abolition of the People's Commune in 1985, local governments have become the main administrators of the resources provided through the five-guarantees program, whereas village committees have remained responsible for caring for the households that enjoy program benefits. In 2010 the number of rural residents who received relief from the five-guarantee program reached 5.549 million beneficiaries (NBS 2011a).

The rural economic reform during 1978–1985 strongly promoted agricultural growth and thus enabled a majority of rural households to attain food security. However, in areas with insufficient resources and weak infrastructure, a considerable number of rural households did not benefit fully from economic growth and nearly 102 million people suffered from food shortages. To address this problem the central government initiated a nationwide antipoverty strategy in 1986 and clearly defined the goal of providing food and clothing for the poor through promoting development in poor areas (SCC 1989). By 1994 the goal of food security was virtually achieved. In the subsequent antipoverty schemes, the central goal has been the elimination of income poverty. The key targets have expanded gradually from poor counties to poor towns and villages, and the main antipoverty measures so far have been carrying out socioeconomic and human resource development projects (CDRF 2007). However, these projects are economic growth oriented and those who have priority in acquiring investment opportunities are mostly the residents of predominantly poor areas who are not poor or else belong to the borderline poor. Therefore those who are able to get out of poverty first are usually not the poorest.

For the extremely poor, even those who have the ability to work, it is difficult to be granted the opportunities of the commodity production projects in the antipoverty schemes. For example in 2009, less than 3.0% of the poor households that had members capable of working were granted antipoverty funds (NBS 2011b). Two major reasons have contributed to this inequality. One has to do with the existing social exclusion, in that those who are not poor have a greater voice than the poor in the distribution of antipoverty resources. The other reason has to do with the expectations for the projects of the administrative institutions. Given that the extremely poor are in an unfavorable position with regard to aspects of their living locations, access to information, open mindedness, health conditions, education levels, working skills, and management abilities; even if they were granted market oriented investment projects, they would suffer a much higher risk of failure than other groups. Therefore the limited participation of the extremely poor in antipoverty projects actually reflects their marginalized position.

Though the extremely poor find it hard to benefit directly from antipoverty projects, they have enjoyed an increasing amount of social relief. By 2008 China's social relief system was made up of the following policy tools: "relief of basic living," "special relief," "preferential policies," and "temporary relief." "Relief of basic living" largely supports recipients with food and clothing. "Special relief" solves specific difficulties the recipients encounter in medical care, housing, education, and disasters. "Preferential policies" refer to the provision of public services free of charge or at reduced prices. "Temporary relief" is mainly responsible for hardships resulting from emergencies (MCA 2008). Among them the Minimum Livelihood Guarantee Scheme (Di Bao in Chinese) provides a social safety net for the extremely poor. A pilot program was launched in a few provinces and cities in 1996 and was later extended to rural areas nationwide in 2007. In principle the local governments provide subsidies with local funds for rural resident households whose per capita income is below the minimum living standard (the Di Bao line), in order to ensure that their basic needs are met (SCC 2007). In 2009 the Di Bao program beneficiaries received an average cash benefit of 816 yuan (US$123.64) per person annually (Table 14.1). Since 2011 urban and

Table 14.1 A national statistical profile of the Di Bao program in China during the period 2001–2009 (NBS 2011c)

Year	Total number of rural people (millions)	Poverty line (Yuan/ person/ year)	Population in poverty (millions)	Average Di Bao line (Yuan/ person/ year)	Number of Di Bao participants (millions)	Di Bao participants/ total rural population (%)	Average cash benefits (Yuan/ person/ year)
2001	933.829	869	90.30	–	3.05	0.33	–
2002	935.025	872	86.45	–	4.08	0.44	–
2003	937.506	882	85.17	–	3.67	0.39	–
2004	942.537	924	75.87	–	4.88	0.52	–
2005	949.075	944	64.32	–	8.25	0.87	–
2006	933.913	958	56.98	–	15.93	1.71	–
2007	939.130	1.067	43.20	840.0	35.66	3.80	465.6
2008*	954.048	1.196	40.07	987.6	43.06	4.51	588.0
2009*	946.579	1.196	35.97	1,209.6	47.60	5.03	816.0
2010*	960.000	1.247	26.88	1,316.4	52.28	5.45	–

The total number of rural people refers to those with permanent rural residential registration. The totals in 2008, 2009, and 2010 were estimated based on the incidence of poverty. Data were unavailable for boxes without values.

rural Di Bao standards have been linked to a price index to reduce the impacts of inflation on extremely poor households (CN 2011).

Several major factors have contributed to the enhanced role of social relief. First, the risks of poverty are increasing in an era featuring a market economy, globalization, climate change, and the subsequent food, energy, and financial crises. As a result there has been an increase of newly impoverished residents in areas that have lagged behind in developed areas, even though aggregate poverty rates have exhibited a declining trend over time. Moreover the newly poor households are spatially scattered and it is hard for antipoverty projects to reach all of them. Second, there are increasingly diverse causes of poverty, such as unexpected disasters, severe illnesses, disabilities, and the deaths of household income earners, each of which could drive an entire household into poverty. When there was an absence of a social insurance system or low payment of insurance benefits, social assistance proved to be a timely means of protection to relieve income shock on households.

In fact, the Chinese government has actively promoted the establishment and extension of the "New Type of Rural Cooperative Medical System" and the "New Type of Rural Old-age Security Scheme" initiatives during the 11th 5-year plan period (2006–2010) in order to address the problem of remarkable increases in poverty associated with illness and aging. By 2010 the Rural Cooperative Medical System covered 96.3% of rural residents and in pilot regions (10% of the counties nationwide) of the Rural Old-age Security Scheme the number of insured has reached 102.77 million. Among them, those over 60 years of age receive an allowance of 55 yuan (US$8.3) per month allocated from specific funds. There is no doubt that both policies help to reduce the risks of poverty.

With regard to the vision for 2020, the Chinese government has developed a plan to build a social protection system that would cover both urban and rural residents, with emphasis on the basic pension program, basic medical care, and the Di Bao (CPC 2006, 2007). It can be expected that these three schemes and the ongoing antipoverty policies will provide more opportunities for the poor who currently have jobs, who are unable to work, and other vulnerable groups to escape poverty and marginality.

14.3   Coordination among Di Bao, public services, and social insurance policies: Institutional innovations in developed areas

According to the Di Bao program "Notification on the Establishment of Nationwide Rural Minimum Livelihood Guarantee Scheme" enacted by the State Council in 2007, "the target group of the Di Bao program includes rural residents whose net annual household per capita income is below the local Di Bao line, mainly rural residents who have been in poverty for many years due to illness, handicap, old age, physical weakness, the loss of working ability, and adverse living conditions." This means that people covered by the Di Bao program are likely those living in extreme poverty. Thus it can be deduced that the

Di Bao line should not be higher than the poverty line and that the number of Di Bao participants should be at most equivalent to size of the population living in poverty. However, Table 14.1 presents data that suggest that since 2008 the number of Di Bao participants has been larger than the size of the poor population. Since 2009 the Di Bao line has been higher than the official poverty line. In 2010 the number of Di Bao participants was larger than the population in poverty by 94.5%, and the Di Bao line has been 5.6% higher than the official poverty line. How can this puzzle be explained?

First, the statistics for each group come from different sources. The official poverty line is defined by China's central government. Based on the official poverty line, the NBS estimates the size of the population living in poverty using a national rural survey sample. The Di Bao line is defined by local governments above the county level, with a similar formula to the one used for the calculation of the official poverty line, but that can be adjusted to reflect local circumstances of socioeconomic development. According to the latest guidance from the Ministry of Civil Affairs (MCA), the Di Bao line should include essential food and nonfood spending of rural residents for subsistence purposes for a year (clothing, water, electricity, coal or gas, public transport, daily necessities, etc.) (MCA 2011). Due to significant regional disparities the Di Bao line is considerably higher in developed regions, so that the average level of regional Di Bao lines is leveraged over the national poverty line and the number of the Di Bao participants is larger than that of the poor.

Secondly, the formation of the Di Bao line and the implementation of the Di Bao policy are highly decentralized. Local governments, village committees, and villagers all have a certain level of discretion regarding the identification of recipients. As a result the actual coverage of the Di Bao program may not satisfy both conditions at the same time: family income lower than the Di Bao line and special personal difficulties. For instance, although for some families their income is higher than the national poverty line or the Di Bao line, their family financial status is insolvent due to spending on the costs of childhood education or serious illness. Commonly villagers and village committees decide that Di Bao benefits be granted to this type of family. Statistically, the increase of Di Bao participants outpaced the decrease of the poor.

In the actual implementation of the Di Bao policy, the various localities observe the same procedure defined by the State Council, particularly the requirement for village committees and villagers to take part in decision making. According to the procedure villagers first submit a Di Bao application to a village committee to organize either a villagers' representative meeting or a formal meeting to assess the financial status of the applicant. After assessment the applications are submitted to the local township government. Township civil officers are responsible for verifying the household property, income, work ability, and the actual living conditions of the applicants, and then submit the results to county-level civil affairs bureaus for approval. In order to ensure a fair and transparent decision-making process, village committees, township governments, and county civil affairs bureaus make the application, assessment, review, and approval information public through local media and community notice boards.

This decision-making process leaves room for local governments and village committees to engage in institutional innovation according to local conditions. In developed regions with rapid rates of industrialization and urbanization, local authorities developed an integrated urban and rural Di Bao system. Urban and rural residents must follow the same procedures to apply for and obtain Di Bao benefits, and the only difference lies in the Di Bao line and amount of the allowance. All families eligible for Di Bao benefits are covered by the Di Bao system. However, the Di Bao program targets individuals who are in the greatest difficulty, such as the aged, handicapped, and seriously ill. Recipients at different levels of poverty severity are entitled to different financial benefit amounts. In identifying the level of assistance according to the socioeconomic and demographic features of the beneficiaries, local governments do not have a standardized income threshold for Di Bao. Instead some parameters have been included in a threshold determination. For instance, the provincial government in Jiangsu has issued Di Bao guidance lines for the prefectures within that province with disparate levels of development. The provincial finance provides part of the Di Bao fund to the prefectures below the average level of provincial development. In practice, this adds a regional parameter to the Di Bao line.

In the implementation of assistance at the municipal and county government levels, other parameters related to household size and individual characteristics have been included. For instance, the Zhangjiagang municipal government delivers allowances that are equivalent to 140% of the Di Bao line to the five-guarantee households (or "Wu Bao Hu," the rural poor who are infirm, widowed, childless, orphaned, or have lost the capacity to work). An additional 10% of the full Di Bao allowance will be delivered to the following four target groups: (1) the elderly aged 70 years or older, (2) the ill with malignant tumors, kidney transplants, uremia, and leukemia, (3) the handicapped with a certificate of disability, (4) the single member households. Moreover, an additional 20% of the full Di Bao allowance will be delivered to the two types of target groups other than the five-guarantee households: recipients without any income source, work capacity, legal support, foster parent, or support provider, and the blind and/or seriously handicapped with a certificate of disability (Hong et al. 2006).

Since its inception the Di Bao system has been supported by public service and social insurance policies. Aside from monthly allowances, the target groups can also access related policy preferences. The allowances and other social benefits have been raised along with the increasing local finance revenue and average resident income. In January 2011 I visited a Di Bao recipient in the village of Xibang, in Tongxiang county of the province of Zhejiang. There were four members from three generations in the household. Mr. Jia, the household head, was deaf and his wife was congenitally retarded. Ten years ago Mr. Jia received a monthly allowance of 150 yuan (US$22.72). Since 2009 his monthly allowance had been increased to 630 yuan (US$95.45). Printed on his Di Bao certificate were other preferential treatments offered by the county government. Usually the cash value represented by these assistance policies is far higher than the amount of Di

Bao allowance received by target group recipients. Benefits received by Mr. Jia included:

- A monthly allowance
- Free access to 9-year compulsory education and entitlement to an educational coupon for high school and vocational school
- Free access to a cooperative medical program and exemption of hospital registration fees
- Access to financial assistance for those affected by serious illness
- Free access to vocational training and employment placement services
- Exemption of commercial administrative fees for a family-operated business
- Entitlement to legal assistance.

In order to prevent extreme poverty among households whose income is only slightly higher than the Di Bao line, some local governments have identified a special group of "Di Bao fringe households" (the marginal poor), which includes households with per capita income of up to twice the level of the Di Bao line and that have seriously ill or handicapped family members. These households can also access social protection that combines relief with public services. In January 2010 I visited a Di Bao household in the town of Shajiabang near the city of Changshu in the Jiangsu province. Both daughters of the family were married. The parents had worked in a township enterprise and were both pension recipients. Ms. Xu (58 years old) suffered kidney disease and needed regular dialysis. Due to her serious illness she was identified as belonging to one of the marginal target groups of Di Bao. In 2008 she received a monthly allowance of 116.2 yuan (US$17.61). In 2009 the allowance was increased to 126.2 yuan (US$19.12) per month. According to the medical bills shown by Ms. Xu, her dialysis treatments cost 1,600–2,000 yuan (US$242.42–303.03) per visit. By the end of 2009 her cumulative annual medical bills amounted to 41,981.78 yuan (US$6,360.76), of which 47.7% (20,025.92 yuan or US$3,034.23) were paid by a cooperative medical fund, and 31.2% (13,111.29 yuan or US$1,986.56) were paid by the medical relief fund for those affected by serious illness. These medical relief payments were equivalent to 8.6 times the total of her annual Di Bao allowances (1,514.4 yuan or US$229.45). In 2009 the premium for participating in the cooperative medical care scheme in the city of Changshu amounted to 300 yuan (US$45.45) per capita, of which 80 yuan (US$12.12) comes from individual contributions, while the rest was divided among municipal/township and village finances. Under this funding level the average reimbursement ratio for the hospitalized was 45%, but Ms. Xu's actual reimbursement ratio was almost 80%, reflecting the significant benefits from the social safety net.

Local governments conduct a re-identification of Di Bao recipients once a year. The purpose of this effort is to include newly impoverished households into protection, adjust assistance levels, and exclude those who have escaped poverty, although in reality very few people are excluded from protection. This suggests that the majority of those who are covered by the Di Bao program are chronically poor (Ravallion 2010). At the local level an assistance policy has been practiced to encourage recipients who are of working age and have the ability to work their way out of poverty through increased employment. If a recipient declines a job introduction for public employment in a service institution three times, the amount of their allowance will be reduced and ultimately canceled. For households whose per capita income has stayed above the Di Bao line due to increased employment, a Di Bao allowance of 3–6 months will be retained before withdrawal from the program (Xinhuanet 2008).

At the county level or above, social relief, public service, and social insurance are the responsibilities of different governmental departments. Coordination of multiple programs for recipients is achieved through information sharing among the departments, the extension of financial services to townships and villages, and computer networks. After recipients are approved by the civil affairs bureau, the names and family information will be transmitted to the other civil affairs bureaus for finance, education, health care, employment, and social insurance. Benefits in cash or services that these departments are authorized to deliver will be allocated according to the names listed for each household. All cash transactions are supported by a banking service, permitting allowances to be distributed directly to the recipient's account through monthly bank transfers. This has greatly benefited recipient families and made financial supervision easier.

It should be noted that the above mentioned institutional arrangements in the developed regions only target residents who have local permanent residential registration status (hukou). The nonlocal residents (such as rural migrant workers) and their families have not had the same access to public services and social protection as permanent local residents. This phenomenon of the social exclusion of migratory populations is a pressing problem of urbanization that needs to be resolved.

14.4 Linking Di Bao with nongovernmental assistance and poverty reduction programs: Challenges in poor areas

After having been initially confined to a few developed regions, the rural Di Bao program was expanded throughout China in 2007. So far this program still faces great implementation challenges in poor areas of China's central and western regions. The biggest problems are the large size of the poor population and limited local finances. Despite special financial support from the central government, there is still a considerable part of the poor population that is not covered by the Di Bao program. In addition, Di Bao allowances are low and play a very limited role in improving the well-being and development of extremely poor recipients.

First, local financial capability has become the dominant criterion for initiating the Di Bao target identification process. According to the amount of available finances, provincial governments first identify the proportion of coverable Di Bao target group recipients of the total rural population (Di Bao ratio) and then break down the value of this indicator to different administrative areas. These breakdown quantities are further divided by county and township governments and are finally converted to individual quotas for villages. In this respect Di Bao coverage is largely dependent on local government allocation of financial resources, rather than the actual scope of the population below the Di Bao line. For instance, in 2007 the Qinghai provincial government identified a rural Di Bao ratio equivalent to 6–7% of the population. In the Guoluo prefecture, which is located on a plateau at 4,200 m above sea level, poverty incidence was as high as 12.5%, but the approved Di Bao ratio was only equivalent to 10% of the population (Ding 2010).

Second, with given Di Bao quotas, village committees usually identify the poorest families based on their own ranking of poverty according to family property and labor status. Then they present a public notice with a list of Di Bao candidates' names, including the seriously ill, handicapped, or aged. This practice apparently departs from official protocol, but has been popular among villagers because the official Di Bao line is only based on per capita income at certain points in time. The villagers' perception of poverty is based on the long-term earning capacity of farm households. Moreover, for village committees the costs of conducting an income survey of all individual farm households precludes such an alternative. Taking advantage of societal familiarity and participatory appraisal is undoubtedly an option of socioeconomic rationality. When the number of local poor households exceeds Di Bao recipient quotas, village committees prefer to identify individuals that are the neediest rather than entire households. This actually increases Di Bao coverage at the village level by reducing household allowances. Moreover, evenly sharing resources is a tradition of rural grassroots society and therefore the determination of recipients through village committees is easily recognized and accepted among villagers.

Against this backdrop the assessment of Di Bao targeting accuracy based on the present sample survey statistics could deviate from reality, but this approach helps researchers assess the socioeconomic impacts of the program through understanding the characteristics of Di Bao recipients. The national rural poverty monitoring sample surveys conducted by the NBS are just such an authoritative avenue of procuring information. This long-term annual survey effort has been conducted in 592 key poor counties across central and western China. In 2009 the survey sample consisted of 5,400 villages, 53,270 farm households, and 225,298 people. Survey results indicated that 5.3% of the total sample population had an income level below county level Di Bao lines, while 9.6% received Di Bao allowances that year. It seems that the Di Bao program can cover all qualified candidates, but in reality only 12.2% of the eligible candidates received Di Bao allowances. It should be noted that among sample households that had Di Bao recipients, about 7.5% were households with relatively large businesses or farming operations and 5.9% had family members that were village cadres (Wu 2011), indicating that even within the narrow coverage of Di Bao there was welfare leakage.

As for demographics, most Di Bao recipients are the aged, handicapped, or under-aged. Among Di Bao recipients in the key poor counties, the above-mentioned three groups accounted for a total of 55.6% of the program beneficiaries. According to MCA statistics this ratio was 56.4% for China's rural Di Bao recipients (Figure 14.1).

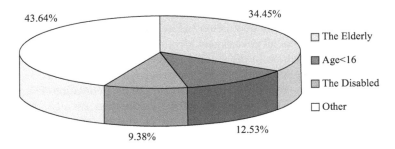

Figure 14.1 Composition of Di Bao recipients in rural China at the end of 2009
(MCA 2010)

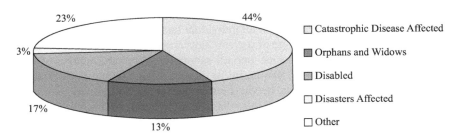

Figure 14.2 Composition of Di Bao recipients in Suichuan County, Jiangxi Province of
China in 2008 (Wu 2011)

In 2011 a Beijing Normal University task force conducted a five-province rural survey in Anhui, Fujian, Jiangxi, Henan, and Shaanxi that found that the disabled accounted for about 43.8% of Di Bao recipients (Zhang 2011). Despite different standards and methods across regions regarding the selection of Di Bao recipients, the results were similar. This means that when village grassroots cadres and villagers made adjustments to the Di Bao poverty line, they focused on the causes of household and individual difficulty. Hence these adjustments are helpful for targeting those that face real need. In fact, when local civil affairs bureaus approve a Di Bao recipient's eligibility, the most common benchmark is justification due to poverty. In Suichuan county in the Jiangxi province (one of the key poor counties) natural disasters are also contributors to transient poverty (Figure 14.2).

In 2009 the average annual net income of rural Chinese households reached 5,153 yuan (US$780.76) per capita. With this reference the statistics presented in Table 14.2 can be explained as follows. First, the per capita net income of rural households in the key poor counties amounted to roughly 2,842 yuan (US$430.61), which is not yet above the poverty line set by the World Bank, but represents 55.2% of the national average income. The per capita income levels of registered poor, Di Bao, and lowest-income households were 50.5, 46.8, and 20.8% of the national average respectively. Second, since 2004 public transfer funds for farmers have increased rapidly. In the calculations for the values presented in Table 14.2, ten types of public transfer funds were included, such as agricultural production subsidies, Di Bao allowance, subsidies for returning farmland to forest, the disaster relief and assistance fund, etc. For farm households in the key poor counties public transfer funds have become their third largest source of income. They account for 11.6–17.6% of the net per capita income of low-income groups. Third, among all types of farm households, Di Bao households get the largest share of public transfer funds. Public transfer funds for Di Bao households were equivalent to 1.77 times the average level of the total sample and 3.44 times the lowest income group. The reason for this is that both agricultural and rural development policies provide preferential treatment to Di Bao households. Di Bao eligibility has already become a symbol that attracts social attention and public support.

Public support for the extremely poor in poor areas is far from sufficient. The statistics presented in Table 14.2 indicate that farm households receive meager amounts of Di Bao funds. Even Di Bao households only receive a per capita

Table 14.2 Composition of per capita annual net income of rural households in the state designated key poor counties in 2009 (aggregate data provided by the NBS rural poverty monitoring sample survey conducted in 2009)

Income source	Total sample		Registered poor households		Di Bao participating households		Bottom decile income group	
	n = 53,270		n = 10,015		n = 5,859		n = 5,327	
	Amount (Yuan)	Share (%)	Amount (Yuan)	Share (%)	Amount (Yuan)	Share (%)	Amount (Yuan)	Share (%)
Per capita annual net income	2,842.1	100	2,600.0	100	2,408.5	100	1,068.7	100
Wages	1,011.2	35.58	833.8	32.07	630.2	26.17	325.0	30.41
Family-run economy	1,522.4	53.57	1,392.2	53.55	1,291.9	53.64	602.0	56.33
Returns to assets	40.4	1.42	38.4	1.48	32.6	1.35	9.1	0.85
Private transfer	29.3	1.03	27.6	1.06	29.8	1.24	9.1	0.86
Reimbursed medical expense	10.5	0.37	11.8	0.45	10.7	0.44	1.5	0.14
Di Bao cash benefits	19.3	0.68	53.4	2.05	162.1	6.73	24.1	2.26
Other public transfer	209.0	7.35	242.8	9.34	251.2	10.43	97.9	9.15

The registered poor households accounted for 18.8% of the total sample. Among the registered poor households, *Di Bao* households made up 58.8%, while the bottom decile income group made up 26.7%. Moreover 8.0% of the households in the bottom decile income group received *Di Bao* allowance. Possibly this group contains many transient poor.

monthly allowance of 13.5 yuan (US$2.05). Private transfer income accounts for around 1.0% of the net income of farm households. The relatives and friends of the poor are usually poor as well, and mutual cash donations and in-kind assistance are both limited, although labor assistance from relatives and neighbors are not included in the statistics. During the field work conducted in the Qinghai-Tibetan plateau in 2007, I observed that most of the Di Bao recipients spent their allowance on food. They relied partly upon medical assistance to resolve difficulties regarding access to health care. Community members took part in assisting disabled Di Bao recipients (including five-guarantee households) to maintain daily activities and social interactions. Assistance from monasteries makes sure that the locally recognized poor not only receive material aid, but psychological comfort as well. Private assistance and social assistance went hand-in-hand for the same target groups; however, this type of private assistance is not an institutionalized and regular activity. Despite contributing to the subsistence of the poor, it cannot eliminate developmental barriers for the recipients and help them escape poverty and marginality.

China's poverty reduction policies have always featured poverty elimination through development. In key poor counties a special poverty reduction fund appropriated by the central government is a major source of income for county governments. Hence in the process of expanding the Di Bao program from the urban to the rural sector, the Chinese government has attempted to link Di Bao with poverty reduction policies. In 2008 and 2010 the State Council clearly identified the target groups of the Di Bao program and poverty reduction policies in the pilot work documents. The target group of the poverty reduction policies was defined as "rural residents whose annual per capita family net income is below the rural poverty line and who have working capacity or the willingness to work, including rural Di Bao recipients" (SCC 2010). The problem is that the combination of the two programs has not been achieved because there were no substantial changes to the regional targeting mechanisms of the poverty reduction program and the government departments in charge of the different programs do not use the same information platform. It does not matter whether beneficiaries are former Di Bao recipients who have the capacity to work or poor households that withdrew from the Di Bao program, neither have received the expected poverty reduction support (Wu 2011).

Drawing upon policy coordination experiences of developed regions, the following approaches can be attempted in poor areas:

- First, treat the extremely poor, general poor, and marginal poor people as an "axis" of connection among the various public support programs.
- Second, establish an information sharing system. In developed provinces the databases of poor households and individuals in the civil affairs bureaus system provide an information platform for all government departments and public service institutions. Using this platform various agencies exchange data and share information. This system certainly saves organizational costs and enhances poverty reduction intensity. In poor areas the existing database of registered poor households could be used as a foundation to further build an adequate information platform.

- Third, expand existing poverty reduction programs to individual households. For the extremely poor households and individuals, access to socioeconomic development is deprived due to difficulties with access to road networks, electrical power, telecommunications, drinking water, housing, sanitary equipment, education, medical care, technological extension, and financial and information services. There used to be poverty reduction projects in all of these sectors, but they often targeted service providers rather than households and individuals. Even for programs that target households, most investment avenues require matching funds from the households. The extremely poor cannot provide matching funds and therefore they are usually excluded (Cao et al. 2011). These problems are not addressed in the implementation of the Di Bao program. Hence the key to improving the social benefits of poverty reduction programs and linking poverty reduction programs with the Di Bao system lies with changing the targeting mechanisms and investment approaches of poverty reduction programs.
- Fourth, expand the intervention areas of poverty reduction policies. The Di Bao program only provides subsistence guarantees to the extremely poor. The food security objective of poverty reduction policy emphasizes freeing the poor from hunger. In order to prevent the intergenerational transmission of poverty it is important to start with nutritional interventions for women during pregnancy and nursing infants, as well as for children. Some nongovernmental organizations have already achieved successful outcomes with childhood nutritional interventions (CDRF 2011). The government needs to establish long-term intervention programs in order to extend these experiences to all poor regions.
- Fifth, increase project management funding. China's central government has launched a series of new long-term programs for social relief, social insurance, public service, and poverty reduction. Project funds have also been allocated to key poor counties, however, these special transfer funds generally do not include any support for program management. The local budgets of all of the key poor counties run on deficits. In order to maintain project operations, the managerial agencies either appropriate funds from other sources or charge the recipients for assistance rather than providing it for free. In addition, it is common to see inadequate project management because better management would cost more (Zhu 2006). Successful experiences in developed regions show that intensive management is needed for projects in order to target the specific difficulties of extremely poor households and individuals. In order to improve the efficiency of social assistance it is imperative for the central and provincial governments to allocate increased project management funds to the poor counties.

14.5 Summary

China has developed its rural social protection system during a process of socioeconomic transformation. Relevant policies stress the following key points. First, they intend to ensure the subsistence of the poor. Second, they intend to mitigate poverty-inducing risks. Third, they intend to help poor households develop their own labor potential, take advantage of development opportunities, and get their families out of poverty. In developed regions the Di Bao social assistance program, social insurance, and public services appear to have effectively mitigated the difficulties of the extremely poor. In relation to this, children from poor and marginal poor families have been guaranteed access to education and health care. Family members with the capacity to work receive free vocational training and employment support. These comprehensive policy interventions and intensive social investment programs tend to help recipient families escape poverty traps and prevent intergenerational poverty transmission. Sound targeting mechanisms and delicate project management are prerequisites for the interventions to achieve significant effects. It should be noted that rural migrant workers and their families have failed to receive the same policy treatment as local permanent residents.

In poor areas there are significant difficulties in fighting extreme poverty and marginality. First, the size of the extremely poor population is large, but locally available financial resources are very limited, and as a result the intensity is inadequate despite the implementation of comprehensive poverty interventions. Second, the issue of linkage building between the Di Bao program and other poverty reduction programs has been put on the agenda, but this policy objective has not yet been achieved. The reason for this is the lack of coordination between program administration institutions, different targeting mechanisms, and different information platforms. Third, insufficient coverage and welfare leakage exist in both programs.

Increasing the effectiveness of poverty reduction efforts in poor areas is and will continue to be the key to the eradication of extreme poverty in China, but will require a number of changes. First, increasing the transfer of the Di Bao fund from the central government to local governments in poor areas would help provide subsistence security to all extremely poor households and individuals. Second, while implementing comprehensive interventions on economic risks encountered by the extremely poor, the government and public should also take actions to eliminate social exclusion. This may not bring any significant changes in poverty incidence in the short-term, but is an essential step to eradicate poverty and promote inclusive development over the long term. For this reason it is necessary to make adjustments to the indicators used to assess local government efforts. A shift should be made from over-attention on changes in the incidence of poverty to an increasing consideration of how much the poor are benefited from multi-dimensional intervention policies.

References

Cao, H., Wang, X. et al. (2011) *Multi-dimensional poverty measurement and intervention for special types of poor areas: Case studies on Aba Tibetan and Qiang autonomous prefecture in Sichuan Province.* Agricultural Press of China, Beijing.

CDRF (2007) *China development report 2007: Eliminating poverty through development.* China Development Publishing House, Beijing.

CDRF (2011) Boarding primary school nutrition improvement plan. China Development Research Foundation, Beijing. 211.144.32.61/project/project.php?cid=18&subcid=869 &aid=2299. Accessed 12 June 2011.

Chen, S. (2010) Monitoring China's progress against poverty and evaluating its anti-poverty policies. Paper presented at the CASS Forum, Social Protection and Human Development in the Era of Post-Financial Crisis, Beijing, 22–24 October 2010.

China News (2011) China established dynamic urban and rural minimum livelihood guarantee scheme linked to price index. www.chinanews.com/gn/2011/05–18/3049913. shtml. Accessed 12 May 2011.

CPC (2006) Communiqué of the Sixth Plenum of the 16th CPC Central Committee. news. xinhuanet.com/politics/2006–10/11/content_5190605.htm. Accessed 12 May 2010.

CPC (2007) Report to the seventeenth National Congress of the Communist Party of China. news.xinhuanet.com/newscenter/2007–10/24/content_6938568_7.htm. Accessed May 2010.

Ding, S. (2010) Social relief and non-governmental assistance in rural Tibetan inhabited areas. In: Wang, L., and Zhu, L. (eds.) *How to get out of the poverty trap*. Economic Management Press, Beijing.

Fan, X. (2011a) China strives to eliminate absolute poverty in ten years. Hong Kong Commercial Daily. www.cpad.gov.cn/data/2011/0121/article_343820.htm. Accessed 13 April 2011.

Fan, X. (2011b) Make contiguous extremely poor areas the main battlefield of anti-poverty efforts. www.cpad.gov.cn/data/2011/0307/article_343991.htm. Accessed 13 April 2011.

García, A.B., and Gruat, J.V. (2003) Social protection: A life cycle continuum investment for social justice, poverty reduction and development. Social Protection Sector, International Labour Organization, Geneva. www.ilo.org/public/english/protection/download/ lifecycl/lifecycle.pdf. Accessed 10 November 2009.

Hong, D., Wang, H., Li, M., and Wan, H. (2006) *Guidance and establishment of rural Dibao program compatible with economic development level: Report on rural Di Bao survey in Jiangsu Province*. Minimum Livelihood Security Department, Ministry of Civil Affairs, Asia Development Bank, Beijing.

MCA (2008) *General research report of social relief system*. Department of Social Relief, Ministry of Civil Affairs, Beijing.

MCA (2010) The composition of Di Bao participants in rural China in December 2009. Ministry of Civil Affairs, Beijing. files.mca.gov.cn/cws/201001/20100128094132409. htm. Accessed 10 May 2011.

MCA (2011) Notification on further regulation of urban and rural minimum livelihood standards, MCA issue 80. Ministry of Civil Affairs, Beijing. www.mca.gov.cn/article/ zwgk/fvfg/zdshbz/201105/20110500154356.shtml. Accessed May 2011.

NBS (2011a) Statistical Communiqué of the People's Republic of China on the 2010 national economic and social development. National Bureau of Statistics, Beijing. www. stats.gov.cn/tjgb/ndtjgb/qgndtjgb/t20110228_402705692.htm. Accessed 10 May 2011.

NBS (2011b) *The poverty monitoring report of rural China 2010: NBS division of rural socioeconomic survey*. China Statistics Press, Beijing.

NBS (2011c) Unpublished data provided at a meeting about the poverty dynamics organized by the Poverty Reduction Office under the State Council, Beijing, 26 November 2010.

Ravallion, M. (2010) A guaranteed minimum income? Theory and evidence on China's Di Bao program. Paper presented at the CASS Forum, Social Protection and Human Development in the Era of Post-Financial Crisis, Beijing, 22–24 October 2010.

SCC (1989) *Poverty reduction office under the state council: A compilation of documents on economic development in rural areas.* State Council of China, Beijing.

SCC (2006) The regulations for rural five-guarantee work, order 456 of the State Council of the People's Republic of China. State Council of China, Beijing. www.gov.cn/zwgk/2006–01/26/content_172438.htm. Accessed 10 May 2011.

SCC (2007) Notification on the establishment of nationwide rural minimum livelihood guarantee scheme. State Council of China, Beijing. www.gov.cn/zwgk/2007–08/14/content_716621.htm. Accessed 10 May 2011.

SCC (2010) Notification on scaling-up the experiment on linking rural Di Bao program with poverty reduction developmental policies. State Council General Office issue 31, State Council of China, Beijing. www.gov.cn/zwgk/2010–05/11/content_1603979.htm. Accessed 10 May 2011.

Wu, G. (2011) A study on the linkage between rural Di Bao program and developmental poverty reduction policies: A research paper submitted for the State Council Poverty Reduction Office. State Council of China, Beijing (unpublished).

Xinhuanet (2008) Xinhuanet.com Jiangsu channel: Suzhou's social relief expansion picks up speed, cancellation of assistance to those no longer in need. www.js.xinhuanet.com/suzhou/2008–04/17/content_13000765.htm. Accessed 12 June 2011.

Zhang, X. (2011) Strengthening the antipoverty effects of social assistance in China. Presentation prepared for Asian Development Bank (unpublished).

Zhu, L. (2006) Management cost and efficiency of Rural Medical Assistance Program. *Chinese Journal of Population Science* 4: 16–27.

Index

For Product Safety Concerns and Information please contact our EU
representative GPSR@taylorandfrancis.com
Taylor & Francis Verlag GmbH, Kaufingerstraße 24, 80331 München, Germany